MAN
IN THE
PLACE
OF THE
GODS

What Cities Mean

PRAISE FOR *THE AGE OF RAND* ...

Creative, thought-provoking ... beautifully written ... superb analysis of the true nature of altruism ... fascinating synthesis of the minarchist and anarchist positions ...
– a former law review editor, Rochester, NY

Refreshing, insightful ... Treats the subject with even-handedness, optimism, good-natured humor ...
– GMB, Washington

Enjoyable light read ... I enjoyed the historical blurbs, particularly regarding New York City history and comments about George Washington. I happen to read a lot about both Washington and Rand and was pleasantly surprised to find both featured in the same book.
- John Christmas, author of Democracy Society

I enjoyed your take on Gandhi – non-co-operation with evil ...
– MP, musicologist

There are so many parts that must be read several times for the intellectual pleasure.
- MS, Vienna

I loved your "Age of Rand" and still refer to it often for historical reference and psychological insight.
- MH, Kansas

THE AGE OF RAND:
IMAGINING AN OBJECTIVIST FUTURE WORLD
BY
FREDERICK COOKINHAM
iUniverse, 2005

MAN
IN THE
PLACE
OF THE
GODS
What Cities Mean

Frederick Cookinham

MAN IN THE PLACE OF THE GODS
WHAT CITIES MEAN

iUniverse books may be ordered through booksellers or by contacting:

iUniverse
1663 Liberty Drive
Bloomington, IN 47403
www.iuniverse.com
1-800-Authors (1-800-288-4677)

Because of the dynamic nature of the Internet, any web addresses or links contained in this book may have changed since publication and may no longer be valid. The views expressed in this work are solely those of the author and do not necessarily reflect the views of the publisher, and the publisher hereby disclaims any responsibility for them.

Any people depicted in stock imagery provided by Thinkstock are models, and such images are being used for illustrative purposes only. Certain stock imagery © Thinkstock.

ISBN: 978-1-4917-9405-0 (sc)
ISBN: 978-1-4917-9406-7 (e)

Library of Congress Control Number: 2016905611

Print information available on the last page.

iUniverse rev. date: 04/15/2016

CONTENTS

PRECÍS

This book (a bit of "light extemporanea" as Ben Franklin would say) shows how the city, and New York City in particular, embodies Ayn Rand's Hellenistic man-worship, in architecture, public art, advertising, the media, and the whole Twenty-first Century way of life.

I start by comparing cities to temples. I describe what a temple is and the role it plays in our moral and psychological lives. Then I show how Man and the city take the place, in our time, of gods and temples.

I focus on the New York Stock Exchange, on Grand Central Terminal, on Rockefeller Center, on Battery Park, and on other New York City institutions that have demonstrated an ability to grip the imagination of the general public, and especially the tourist and the immigrant. I show how movies do a great part of this transformation of (literal) concrete to abstraction, to legend, to symbol, and to inspiration.

In *The Age of Rand*, I used the expression "a new and deeper meaning" over twenty times. I continue that theme here. In *Man in the Place of the Gods*, landfills become magic mountains, parks become the scene of nature giving meaning to cities and vice versa, and rivers become narratives of the births of cities and of Man's creative genius.

I let the reader into three private mental/moral closets of my own that relate to cities: a blue place, a bridge, and a tower.

I discuss musical impressions of cities.

And all this is sprinkled with enough Rand quotes to show who is the prophetess in this temple. As you can see, this is really a book of poetry. It's prose, but it sings with imagery.

Later in the book, I zero in on Rand herself, clarifying the waters made muddy by the industrious Rand-smearers.

After *Man in the Place of the Gods* proper come three of my Atlasphere columns. Then I finish with some short essays that have not appeared on The Atlasphere or anywhere else, including THE BOTTOM LINE, which is the talk I gave at Freedom Fest 2012.

INTRODUCTION

I very deliberately chose a book title with a double meaning.

"THE PLACE OF THE GODS" is a reference to a story by Stephen Vincent Benet. It was called "By the Waters of Babylon," and it was published in the *Saturday Evening Post* in the summer of 1937. In the story, a primitive tribesman has been warned that travel down the local river is forbidden because it leads to the feared and fancied Place of the Gods. He defies the tribal law and paddles his canoe down the river to a mighty ruined city on an island. We realize that it is New York, after a war. We know that Ayn Rand read the *Saturday Evening Post* – I suspect it was one of her ways of learning English – and we find that she wrote her novelette *Anthem* within two weeks of the appearance of the Benet story. More on this below in the chapter FEDERAL HALL.

By *Man in the Place of the Gods* I also mean "how Man sees himself as revealed by the public art and architecture of New York City," and I mean that to imply "Man worship." On that point I will refer you to Leonard Peikoff's fascinating lecture "Why Ancient Greece is my Favorite Civilization." Modern Man puts Man in the old place of the gods.

Here, in a nutshell, are some of Peikoff's points. The ancient Greeks had no religious faith at all. They seem to have assumed that the gods were real; were facts, but they later started to question even that. They assumed that the gods were a part of nature and had to obey her rules. They scorned belief without proof, and they scorned the notion of letting nature's mysteries remain mysteries. They hated uncertainty and ambiguity and any notion of the infinite or the unknowable. They worshiped excellence in Man. They would scorn today's over-specialized athletes, because they honored the well-rounded man – what we today call the Renaissance Man.

Those points give some idea of what Objectivist culture might look like if today's tiny subculture of Objectivism grows into an Age of Rand.

When I told someone that I was writing about "secular spirituality," she went "Ooh!" And others have expressed interest in the concept. So I gather there is a market for explorations of that as-yet-unexplored aspect of Objectivism. On the inside cover of *Atlas Shrugged*, Rand poses the question "What moves the world?" My question to you is: "What moves *you*?"

The germ of this book lay in a line I thought I remembered from Ayn Rand: "The city was the birthplace of capitalism and has always been its stronghold," or something like that. I can't find it now. Odd, because that line was one of the most influential Rand lines, on me anyway. I had never thought of it that way before. I had thought of Jefferson's yeoman farmer as the repository of free enterprise and all the virtues that go with it. It is the conservatives who think in terms of the corrupting influence of the Sinful City. This line made me appreciate cities, and it also showed me that Rand, contrary to the smears, was not a conservative. That got me thinking about the city as the expression of Man's nature and of the meaning – the moral meaning – of free enterprise. This really came home to me on my first trip to New York City in 1972. I had seen rows of shops in my hometown of Syracuse, but in New York I saw street after street of shops. Hundreds. Then thousands. Each one a brave gamble by a small entrepreneur. And so many clever and inventive different kinds of shops. There used to be a chess shop right next to Teddy Roosevelt's birth house on E. 20th Street. They sold chess sets – that's all. Chess clubs met in the back room. And I visited Laissez Faire Books for the first time on that trip.

A whole bookstore just for the small, highly specialized libertarian and Objectivist markets. Here was the meaning of the abstraction of free market economics, made concrete. Concrete and brick and mortar. And above all, glass – the symbol of free Man's need to show the public his goods. Architectural nudism. Nothing to hide. Governments need secrecy. Economic Man needs its opposite: transparency. Every time you look in a shop window you are seeing economics and architecture reveal their underlying *moral* lesson.

A book about Ayn Rand *has to* be about cities. Rand's and Aristotle's whole project was about the question "What is Man? What is the nature of the human animal? What does he require, by his nature, for his survival and well-being?" He requires freedom of choice. Being human is all about observing facts, forming plans of action, choosing one, and carrying it out. Rand's ethical system, Egoism, is all about choice. Cities are where humans congregate, so as to expand their range of choices. Cities are for shopping and competition, and that means choice. That's *why* cities were the birthplace and stronghold of capitalism. Cities are a built landscape; an artificial world, and artifice means the chosen. Cities are where you go to be more human.

A city serves the same purpose as an office. There is you, sitting in your seat. At hand in front of you are your writing and reading surface, you computer keyboard, screen and mouse, and your phone. Around those is your Reference Zone: the things you need to be able to reach sitting down, because you use those things most often, like your coffee cup and your whiffle ball. Around that zone is your Stand Up and Take One to Ten Steps Zone, for things you use once an hour or once a day. Around that zone are the offices of your co-workers, the conference rooms and the bathroom. Still farther away are the elevators and the lobby. An office building lobby, however ornate visually, is a machine for getting the worker from the street to the elevator. Around that is your neighborhood: your sources of breakfast, lunch, and Kleenex, and your subway entrance or parking lot. Around that you see the same set up, but on a scale of miles and hours instead of feet and seconds:

the CBD (Central Business District), then the Middle City, with its apartment buildings and neighborhood stores, then the industrial belt, then the suburbs, exurbs, farm belt and vacationland. After that, you travel inward from zone to inner zone of the next city, because Aristotle said that, for you, the city is the area in which you can do your business and get home without having to take an overnight trip.

The colorful libertarian writer Karl Hess compared his view of the world to Gandhi's. "Gandhi believed that the world is really made up of towns; villages. That's where everyone *lives*. That's where your citizenship *rests*. And there should be no national borders to separate the interests of one village from those of another."

I have not put any maps or illustrations in this book about cities because I am thinking that you, the reader, are probably much more computer-adroit than I am, and if you don't know who Karl Hess was, you can google his name and see a picture of him and read all about his very interesting life. And you can also google a picture of any city and any building in any city, if it is famous. Try Panama city, Panama. Wall-to-wall skyscrapers! Some sleepy Spanish colonial town!

In this book I will expand on my first book, *The Age of Rand*, especially the chapters DUSTING OFF THE GOD and THE ART DECO PHILOSOPHER.

A building or other place in Manhattan or elsewhere serves, in this book, as the key to a story. The city serves as the raw material for periodic spiritual refreshments, shall we say, for the secular person looking for meaning and hope.

That is how this book will take you into the sanctuary of the secular temple, namely, the city. Why should the religious folks have a monopoly on the word "spirit"? For the secular reader, "spirit" means what Aristotle meant: "consciousness."

Gandhi, in his autobiography, writes that in his youth he crossed the dry desert of atheism. Alvin Toffler, in his *Playboy* interview of Ayn Rand, asks whether a rational way of life wouldn't become "juiceless and joyless." Both men were making the "Mr. Spock" mistake: fearing that reason and emotion are conflicted; in a zero-sum competition: one must lose as much as the other one wins. It's not like that at all. Nathaniel Branden said "Feel deeply in order to think clearly." Rand would have said the opposite, and both are right. Evading thought and facts and reality can lead to only one emotion: anxiety. There used to be a TV commercial for Miller beer showing workers, after quittin' time, adjourning to a bar, grinning, hoisting tankards, and proclaiming "It's Miller Time!" Doing the thinking you need to do, to put food on the table, by the light blue sunlight of day, leaves you free to knock off and have fun during Miller Time – the dark blue sky hours of the evening – the time to enjoy the rewards of your thinking and working. That's when you take in music and painting and theater and other arts and entertainment – and therein lies your juice: your fun, and diversion and relaxation, that can be had only as a reward for rationality. And what message do you seek in that art? That very thing – the meaning of your rational life on this secular Earth. The religious folks seek that spiritual meaning after death. You, however, can get it here and now. They have to die first. You can get your reward while you are still here to enjoy it.

I was tempted to capitalize the word PURPOSE every time I used it in this book. This may seem strange, but it would have served a PURPOSE. It was to remind you, and me, of this all-important term. That word is a temple all by itself – one of those portable little temples I wish to give you.

A mighty temple it must have been, for the roof was painted like the sky at night with its stars.

They had turned night to day for their pleasure – they did not sleep with the sun.

Restless, restless were the gods and always in motion! They burrowed tunnels under rivers – they flew in the air.

And always, as they labored and rested, as they feasted and made love, there was a drum in their ears – the pulse of the giant city, beating and beating like a man's heart.

--Stephen Vincent Benet, "By the Waters of Babylon," *Saturday Evening Post*, published two weeks before Ayn Rand wrote *Anthem*, in 1937.

Big thanks to Jon Carriel, Don Hauptman, and always, Belen

CHAPTER 1
WHAT IS A TEMPLE?

You have been told that your body is a temple. Your doctor, or your gym teacher, meant that your body is sacred and deserves to be kept in tip-top shape. In *Anthem*, Ayn Rand writes "For in the temple of his spirit, each man is alone. Let each man keep his temple untouched and undefiled."

The word "temple" comes from the Latin "templum," which comes from the Greek "temenos," which comes from "temnein," meaning to cut. The ancient high priest would cut a furrow with a plow around in a circle or square, to mark out a sacred enclosure. That acre or ten acres or however big it was would be the place cut apart from the rest of the tribe's land, and into which the tribe would bring its statues of gods. In the sacred enclosure they would build buildings to house and protect their gods, and there observe the auguries. Around that sacred enclosure a city would grow, beginning with the market.

The "temple" you have between your eyes and ears also comes from Latin, but it may not go back beyond Latin to Greek. Webster is silent on its origin. But perhaps it too comes from the Greek temnein, since it is a space marked out by your eye, your ear, your crown, and your cheekbone.

"Contemplate" means "with templum." Since a temple was a "space marked out for the observance of auguries," to contemplate must have meant to gather with others in the temple to contemplate the auguries

1

together, or perhaps it meant to gather with others to focus on a common object, with everyone sitting with their index fingers pressed to their temples.

A temple is the most important building in your life. Whatever, to you, is a temple, is in effect a temple to you.

In ancient times, a temple was a building where a statue of a god was kept, protected from the weather and thieves and invaders, and to that god in his temple you would bring offerings. These offerings got to be called "sacrifices," but as Ayn Rand would point out, a "sacrifice" means the giving up of a greater value in exchange for a lesser value or a non-value, and that is decidedly not what your ancestors had in mind when they brought a bushel of wheat to the god. It was not a sacrifice; it was a straightforward business transaction. You offered wheat or olive oil or some other commodity to the god in exchange for something you wanted. Good weather and a bountiful harvest would be at the top of the list, along with victory in battle, or recovery from disease or injury, for yourself or a loved one. Gods have magical favors to give out, but you have to pay for them. That is why your ancestors came to the temple and offered offerings and prayed. "Pray" means "ask."

But today we no longer believe in propitiating supernatural powers with burnt offerings. We do, however, go places to look at things. Not to look at them and appraise them for buying, and not to learn from those things for college credit, but we look at these things for some kind of intangible reason. If the place is called an art museum, we are looking at the paintings and sculpture in order to be uplifted. It's still a transaction, of sorts – we pay admission to the building hoping to get something out of the visit. But what we get is an inward experience. We don't call it worship. We call it art.

A market is a place where people gather to buy and sell. So if a temple is a place to buy favors from the gods, then a temple and a market are at base the same thing. Jennifer Burns wrote truer than she knew when she titled her book *Goddess of the Market: Ayn Rand and the American Right*.

We can also use a whole city as an art museum, and gain inward uplift from what we see in the cityscape. We can get that for free.

We can feel proud of our ability to see more in the scene than others can, just as the novice is proud to be chosen to be the acolyte assigned to extinguish the candles at the end of the worship service. We feel proud to be in an exclusive group. But the spirit of today's increasingly Objectivist world (we'll come back to that point in Chapter 2) is *non-exclusivity*. Bigger fortunes are made by the Henry Fords with their millions of inexpensive Model Ts than by the Mercedes's with a few luxury cars. We in the 21st Century now understand that we all benefit from the uplift of all. Let me therefore charge a dollar or two for a book designed to help readers new to Ayn Rand become just as adept an acolyte of the worship of Man and his cities as you are.

Jealous? Of new acolytes? Grow up! The fact of others becoming adept at Man worship does not threaten your reputation for adeptitude. It's not a zero-sum game. On the contrary, the later adepts will honor you as a pathbreaker for them. Learn to take pleasure, not alarm, at the sight of the success of others. They might be friends, whose joy is your joy. And if they are strangers, their success will earn them money that they might someday invest in you. And, since this is not a business book, but an inner-experience book, we are talking about spiritual experiences, and those are always fun to share. In fact, more than just fun – it is thrilling to describe your emotional reaction to an art work, or anything else, and hear the person you are talking to say "Yes! I feel the same thing – and for the same reasons!" Any time you share an emotional reaction with someone who clicks with you like that, you are doing what people go to church to do: public worship, or its secular analog.

See how religious terms and experiences *have* secular analogs? Ayn Rand was a religious soul trapped in an atheist's body, you might say, and she fixed that dilemma by finding the sense of awe in secular things that others find in religion. Every man creates his own god in his own image – and Rand made a god out of Man.

"Man," with a capital M, is an abstraction. It means anything that any Homo Sapiens has ever done or been, or ever will or might.

She wasn't the only one, either: the French revolutionaries outlawed Catholicism and re-consecrated churches as Temples of Reason. But they staged worship services in those churches, parodying Christianity. That means that they had not thought outside the box of religion. They only *thought* they had. And they never thought to ask whether the nation-state had any right to outlaw some people's private beliefs. So much for the socialist claim that the French Revolution was more radical than the American.

All the Greco-Roman architecture, all the classical references in American culture, such as the Roman figure on Virginia's flag beheading a king and saying "Sic Semper Tyrannis!," and the female figures on New York State's flag symbolizing Justice and Liberty, all the quotes from Addison's play "Cato" in the revolutionary literature (see below and *The Age of Rand*), all the 18th Century essays signed with classical pseudonyms, such as "Publius," who wrote *The Federalist Papers* – all these things and many more show Revolutionary, Enlightenment America as the birthplace of a new secular age. Even a Catholic church, New York's St. Peter's, was designed to look like the Parthenon – the temple of a Greek, pagan goddess – in 1836. (It is on Barclay Street at Church Street, in Tribeca.)

Buffalo, New York is worth a visit just for the architecture. The Buffalo Savings Bank (1901) is now the M & T Center. It sports a huge dome covered with real gold. Inside, under the dome, is a mural of Roman buildings and a quote from Confucius: VIRTUE IS THE ROOT, WEALTH THE FLOWER. (See *The Age of Rand* chapter THE SELFISHNESS OF VIRTUE.) Other artworks on the walls represent Buffalo's strengths: Commerce, Industry, Power, and The Arts. (See "Motive Power" in Chapter 10 below.) Also, the nearby Niagara Mohawk Building (1912) is modeled on the Alexandria Pharos, or lighthouse. The theme is light – just as Rand rhapsodizes about light in *Anthem* and Atlas. Buffalo and the whole Niagara Frontier have made themselves the temple of the Power and Light made possible when George Westinghouse and his chief engineer, Nicola Tesla, harnessed the energy of Niagara Falls.

I urge the reader to pay particular attention to words that someone chose and paid money to have cut in stone or otherwise presented to the public on a building or monument meant to last for lifetimes – precisely because I don't think many people do. Carvings are not meant just for carving-buffs. They are someone's idea of eternal truths. Maybe you don't agree with all such sentiments, but if the ones you violently disagree with are being cut in stone, you should be alarmed, and do some cutting of *your* favorite words. The only way to fight an idea is with another idea.

Go to the New York Public Library's branch in the old B. Altman Department Store, Fifth Avenue to Madison, between 34th and 35th Streets. Ayn and Frank did their shopping there. Now it is the Science, Business and Industry Branch of NYPL. Walk into the lobby. You are greeted by words painted high on the wall in front of you. You can't miss them. There is a quote from Einstein about science, and there are others about business and industry. This is a particularly fascinating collection of quotes, because of the Altruist world's conflicted feelings about business. This is New York, after all, the capital of capitalism, and this is the library branch specializing therein, so they have to put on the lobby wall quotes that might glorify business, and we can't have that in a culture that believes that it is easier for a camel to pass through the eye of a needle than for a rich man to enter the kingdom of Heaven.

Here are some examples of the many ways people use the term "temple" and related concepts:

Ivor Novello, in his 1935 song "Shanty Town," refers to "the temples of the west." He wants to evoke temple-like rock formations, like canyons and natural bridges and buttes that look like cathedrals, as well as the quiet spaces suffused with leaf-filtered sunlight found in Redwood groves. In what way is such a place like a temple? It is quiet. It is in a quiet place that the visitor is left undistracted, face to face with his own musings. That's why the Divina Commedia tells us

> Oft have I seen at some cathedral door,
> A laborer, pausing in the dust and heat,
> Lay down his burden, and with reverent feet
> Enter, and cross himself, and on the floor
> Kneel to repeat his paternoster o'er;
> Far off the noises of the world retreat;
> The loud vociferations of the street
> Become an indistinguishable roar.
> So, as I enter here from day to day,
> And leave my burden at this minster gate,
> Kneeling in prayer, and not ashamed to pray,
> The tumult of the time disconsolate
> To inarticulate murmurs dies away,
> While the eternal ages watch and wait.

Here, a temple becomes a quiet place: being cut apart from the noisy world, it provides a place to focus on the great questions.

Mind you, the religious folks tell you that a place of big natural formations leaves you undistracted and face to face with big natural formations, and that is supposed to force upon you the conviction that there must be a Creator to explain Creation. But Man's scientific advances are making that argument unnecessary, as well as a non sequitur. You don't need a Sky Fella (that's Pidgin for God) to explain things that have been explained by science, and besides, Sky Fella does not explain anything. The Sky Fella image merely puts an imagined human face on natural processes, like evolution and wind erosion.

Take out the mystical Creation myth, and the bargaining with the god for victory in battle and harvest, and what is left in that image of the temple is ... you, in communion with your own thoughts. But the mere fact of a quiet moment encourages you to think about the eternal ages, which you had no time to think about out on the tumultuous and disconsolate street.

"The East, with all its magic" is the other half of that Novello line. "East" usually means New York City, and only the skyscraper and theater districts at that. There's your secular temple, and your secular magic.

Funny how people who live in someone else's temple forget that they live in a temple. New Yorkers are notorious for not ever going to the top of the Empire State Building or to the Statue of Liberty – even before the National Parks Service made you take off your shoes and belt before they even let you on the boat. In 1792, a model of the city of Jerusalem toured the United States. People paid money to look at a model. It was an object of reverence. But some people *live* in the city of Jerusalem. To them, their city is just a place to live.

On Marketfield Street, in colonial New York, stood the tiny Huguenot church, which was named Le Temple du Saint Esprit: Temple of the Holy Spirit. These were French Protestants – Catholics would never call a church a temple. The Knights Templar were organized to guard the site of Solomon's Temple in Jerusalem during the Crusades.

Wikipedia calls itself a temple.

Anything can become a temple, in someone's mind. John Keats tells us

A thing of beauty is a joy forever ...
Such the sun, the moon, trees old and young ...
And such are daffodils, and such too ...
Are all the lovely tales we have heard or read ...

7

Even as the trees
That whisper round a temple become soon
Dear as the temple's self, so does the moon
The passion poesy, glories infinite,
Haunt us till they become a cheering light
Unto our souls, and bound to us so fast
That, whether there be shine, or gloom o'ercast,
They always must be with us, or we die.
(from Endymion)

And now, in a world where people are stepping into manholes because they cannot tear themselves away from their eyepods and earpods for one second, all the things – music, photos, emails, tweets – that we cherish can be with us at the touch of a button … to cheer us even in the manhole.

Gloria Swanson tells us that the huge Roxy Theater, Seventh Ave at 50th St., was the "cathedral of the motion picture." "Cathedral" is short for "cathedral church" – throne church – the headquarters of a bishop. A throne church would be bigger than a mere parish church; likewise, the Roxy was big. But it was also a place where people sat in rows idolizing Rudolph Valentino instead of sitting in rows worshiping Christ. But sitting in rows in any case. In the 19th Century, preachers were always complaining that churches were being turned into sinful theaters. They were, but sometimes it went the other way – theaters have also become churches. It makes sense – both kinds of buildings have naves – rows of seats, like rowers in a naval ship, hence the word "nave," all facing the altar, where they focus on their object of worship.

The Roxy Theater has now been replaced by one of the Rockefeller Center buildings. You can see a cutaway model of it in the Museum of the Moving Image in Astoria, Queens. It is described in Anthony Bianco's *Ghosts of 42nd Street* as having been a "temple of the motion picture."

Brooks Atkinson, in his book *Broadway*, reports that Kurt Weill's score, and Langston Hughes's lyrics, for the 1946 show "Street Scene" was a "musical microcosm of Manhattan, conveying the violence, the misery, the sociability, the cautious hope, the blighted romance, and the immense vitality of Cosmopolis." Hughes "knew the city intimately and loved it with humor and forgiveness." That's what people tend to do with the big cities of their dreams and their reality: they find in cities a heightened experience of ... everything! – of all of life, and so they forgive the city when the heightened things include the bad things with the good.

When Alexander Hamilton led to victory New York State's ratification of the Constitution, he was so lionized that there was talk of re-naming the city "Hamiltoniana." "Cosmopolis" might have been a better choice.

Atkinson also tells us that Irving Berlin's "There's No Business Like Show Business" became "the theme song and *devotional* of the Broadway theater." See how people always come back to religious imagery whenever anything is important to anyone?

Bill Bryson, in his book *In a Sunburned Country*, says that when you are at the hotel at Ayer's Rock, or Uluru, in central Australia, your eyes keep coming back to the rock. You can't take your eyes off it. Why? It's just a big rock, isn't it? The second biggest exposed monolith in the world, but still just a rock. What keeps your eyes returning again and again is the fact that the desert all around is dead flat and featureless. Nothing else competes with the rock for your attention. You can't help but study the moods of the rock, as lighting conditions change through the day with the rise and fall of the sun. So the site is a natural temple: nature has done for Uluru what the builders of temples do for Athena of the Parthenon or Diana of Ephesus: the building takes away all visual and aural distractions, so the worshiper can concentrate on the goddess.

President William McKinley was assassinated while shaking hands in the Temple of Music at the Pan American Exposition in Buffalo.

The building looked like a domed Roman temple. Anyone who was present that day, expecting to concentrate on music, was distracted by politics. "Music" comes from the Greek *mousike*: any art presided over by the Muses. They were the nine sister goddesses of Greek mythology presiding over the arts and sciences. Mine is Cleo – the Muse of History. To study those arts and sciences, you go to a museum. But the verb "muse" does not come from the Muses. It comes from the Latin *musus* – the mouth of an animal. It means to be sunk so deep in thought that your mouth hangs open like a panting dog's. To amuse means to occupy the attention of, so as to deceive, and to bemuse means to bewilder, so those words don't come from the muses. They come from dogs.

The chronicler of Evacuation Day (the day the Redcoats evacuated New York City) calls the ragged American troops returning to New York "virtuous citizens who had sacrificed opulence and ease at the shrine of liberty." A shrine originally meant a box in which are kept the bones of a saint or other holy relics. Over time, that definition has been expanded to mean a niche for a saint, a sanctuary, a tomb, and finally just a place or object hallowed by its associations.

The Margaret Herrick Library of the Academy of Motion Picture Arts and Sciences calls itself the "temple of films."

The 1983 French movie "Life is a Bed of Roses" deals with someone who organizes a "Temple of Happiness," and with "the danger from those who impose their ideas of perfection on the world." (the *Leonard Maltin Movie Guide, 2012*) On the whole world? How can anyone do that? You can suggest, but you can't impose, unless you are the State.

If you visit St. Paul's church in London, and ask about its architect, Sir Christopher Wren, you will be advised "*Si monumentum requiris, circumspice!*" "If you seek his monument, look around you." Photographer Stefan Lorent concludes his book *Sieg Heil!* – his photo history of Germany from Bismarck to Hitler – with shots of Germany's bombed-out cities of 1945, and an ironic echo of that line. "If you seek his monument, look around you." A monument, like a shrine or a god's statue, is something you preserve in a temple and venerate, and show to your children so that they will carry the veneration on to their children. A church in Berlin, a building at Hiroshima's Ground Zero, and other pieces of broken masonry have been preserved from World War II as monuments, not of aspiration, but of warning. The German word for monument is *Denkmal* – *denken* means to think, and *Mal* means time. A time to think. Apparently the word for the activity, thinking, has become the word for the object that occasions that thinking.

There is Frank Lloyd Wright's Unity Temple in Oak Park, Illinois. This must have been Rand's inspiration for the "Stoddard Temple of the Human Spirit" story in *The Fountainhead*.

If I were to design a big tomb for Ayn Rand, it would be a Stonehenge-like ring – not of stones, but of mirrors. Standing inside the ring, the visitor would see only reflections of himself.

How many times have you heard someone promise you that a certain experience, such as volunteering or climbing a mountain, will "lift you out of yourself"? If someone kicks an alcohol or drug addiction, how many times have you heard his story described as "a victory he won over himself"? Nathaniel Branden liked to quote Carl Gustav Jung's saying that "the self is a crowd." Your "self" subsumes maybe a dozen "ego-states." By doing something out of your ordinary routine, you are not lifting yourself out of your *self*, you are merely stepping out of one compartment of your *self* and spending some time in a different compartment of your *self*. By kicking an addiction, you are not winning a victory over yourself; one compartment of yourself – Jung and Branden call it your Higher Self – is winning over another compartment, or "ego-state," or call it what you will. The Altruists have kept you in a life-long habit of making the word "self" always the bad guy. There is a different name on each of those Stonehenge mirrors. My Child Self, my Mother Self, my Father Self, my Other Sex Self … and my Higher Self. And my Conscious, Reasoning Self mediating among them.

In Nashville, Tennessee, there is a full-sized reproduction of the Parthenon. Unless there are worshipers of Athena in Nashville, this must have been intended to honor the magnificence of one of the great architectural achievements of all time, and one of the most influential. A temple ... to a temple. All it needs is a plaque with the whole Fountainhead Dean Scene on it, especially the line where Roark tells the Dean "I stand at the end of no tradition. I may, perhaps, stand at the beginning of one." Roark shocks the Dean by saying that the Parthenon is not great architecture.

That scene sets the stage for the whole novel. The plot – the newspaper headline – of *The Fountainhead* is: Genius tries to establish himself in a profession, against the resistance of those who feel threatened by his "creative destruction."

There is no greater name in New York City architectural history than Stanford White. One tradition that he started is designing banks to look like Greek and Roman temples. You can see the results at the Bowery and Grand Street, Manhattan (the Bowery Savings Bank, called the "temple of savings"). But you can see another much like it in downtown Brooklyn, at DeKalb and Fleet Streets (Albee Square). The one in Buffalo we already mentioned, and there is one in downtown Utica, and we could go on. White started a tradition.

Prospero, in Shakespeare's The Tempest, speaks of "solemn temples." "Solemn" started out as the Latin word *sollemnis*, meaning "regularly appointed," that is, appointed according to strict rules and with all official pomp and ceremony. It has come to mean grave and serious. Rand said you should be serious when discussing ideas. You don't want to confuse your audience and leave them wondering whether you really mean what you are saying or are just kidding. Since a temple is a means of blocking out the sounds and sights of everyday life, so as to focus on more important thoughts, the appropriate demeanor in a temple is a serious one, as long as serious does not get overdone and start to look like anger or meanness or robotic mien. I went to a Lutheran Easter

Sunday service once, and the pastor gave very clear instructions on when and where and how to come down to the rail to take communion, because, he very sensibly said, "I don't want anyone not participating because they don't know what to do." That's what might come of too strict an insistence on punctilio; excessive solemnity.

Air Force General Curtis Lemay used to give his staff what he called "blackout briefings." He would have no lights on in the room except lights on himself and whatever maps or other displays he was showing, to cut distractions down to zero. Perhaps he got the idea at the movies. British General Montgomery used to forbid coughing at briefings – and this was when everyone used to smoke!

In Atlas, Lillian asks Hank, with a sneer:

> "What are they, your mills – a holy temple of some kind?"
> "Why, yes," he said softly, astonished at the thought.
> (page 209)

Truman Capote, in the very first paragraph of *In Cold Blood*, describes the lonely, flat landscape of western Kansas, with "…a white cluster of grain elevators rising as gracefully as Greek temples." Since grain elevators are often round, these probably reminded Capote not of a whole temple, but just of a row of columns. That image is never far from at least the Western subconscious. Just look at the covers of scholarly books. Often the book jacket designer will use an image of a column, or just the capital of a column, or just a simplified, schematic suggestion of a column and capital. That is the university press's way of saying "You had better take this newly-written book as seriously and reverently as you do a book written by the ancient Greeks!" Apparently, if "The Greeks" said something, it must be true, like the belief that matter is composed of the Four Elements.

I asked Iris Bell, who designed the cover of *The Objectivist* Magazine to Rand's specifications, whether the three white stripes down the left side of the field of blue-green on the cover was meant to represent a Greek column, perhaps stripped down, in the Art Deco style, to a mere abstract suggestion. Mrs. Bell did not know. I also asked her whether it might represent the Fifth Avenue face, or edge, really, of the RCA Building in Rockefeller Center, or the vertical stripes on the Center employees' uniforms, themselves clearly meant to suggest the RCA Building's verticality. Mrs. Bell was sure it did not. What else could those three vertical stripes have meant to Rand? Anything literal? Just a balance on the left side for the table of contents on the right? Just the suggestion of the soaring vertical lines of an Art Deco skyscraper – whether RCA or not? That's probably it – skyscrapers got deep into Rand's head during the writing of *The Fountainhead*. Thirty-six years after publication, while describing novel writing to Tom Snyder, on NBC's "Tomorrow" show (in the RCA Building's NBC studios), Rand said "It is much more complicated than [designing] a building. It's killingly difficult. But wonderful when you've succeeded."

If "holy" means "other; set apart from the rest," then Hank Rearden, in *Atlas*, means that he thinks of his mills as embodying a meaning beyond the utilitarian. He may be the only one who sees them that way, but that's okay: they are his mills. He is astonished at the thought because he has not yet put his feelings into words, being a Type-A Personality: a restless, hyper-vigilant businessman. He is not a professor or author. And his values are not yet perfectly formed and smelted out of raw ore and cleansed of contradictions and confusion. Your professors told you that Rand had no such conflicted heroes in her novels, but they were mistaken.

(Wynand remains conflicted at the end of his story. Rearden and Dominique land on the good side, and Dr. Stadler the bad.)

On page 272, Mr. Mowen, another businessman of divided loyalties, who ends up on the dark side, has one solemn moment. He feels "reassured by the thought of New York in its ring of sacred fires, the ring of smokestacks, gas tanks, cranes and high-tension lines." "Sacred fires"! Rand sounds positively pagan here. Or Hindu. And the image of a ring! Rand *is* a pagan, by the gods! A temple is a sacred enclosure.

On page 376 there is a remarkable passage that takes us inside Hank's mind – his subconscious mind – and shows Hank going back and forth from analysis to emotion, from symbol and inspiration to decision and action, from the lights of New York out the window to the figure of Dagny pacing and talking, from the thought of what those lights and that skyline represent to the thought of the men who had invented both, to the thought of the man who had invented the motor that he and Dagny had found. He feels a "life-restoring shot of admiration." Even if the inventor had since died, he had lived once. He was possible. "It's a pleasant thought, isn't it?"

Rand said "I can bear to look around me levelly. I can't bear to look down. I want to look up."

Taking a moment now and then to appreciate all the things you take for granted the rest of the time: it's all over *Atlas Shrugged,* and it makes Rand sound spiritual and even Japanese! The Tea Ceremony – the *chanoyu* – is all about concentrating on a simple act like making and drinking tea, and reminding yourself of the ideals represented by this simplicity: Harmony, Respect, Purity, and Tranquility. Part of the ceremony is stopping to concentrate on your host's flower arrangement as you enter his house. Find the connection between a city's ring of smokestacks and a floral display, and you've got it.

Grand Central Terminal and the original Pennsylvania Station have often been called cathedrals of light. A cathedral implies not just a church or temple, but a really BIG church or temple, with high windows letting sunlight stream in.

Stanford White's Knickerbocker Bank, 1903, was compared to a temple by the *New York Times* real estate section in 2009. It had Corinthian columns, after all. The image of the Greek temple for any building that aspires to importance still has meaning to the building-admiring public. The AT&T Building, 1923, at Broadway and Fulton, has more columns than the Parthenon. Cass Gilbert's Woolworth Building, 1913, is often called a "cathedral of commerce," but Gilbert's inspiration was actually a medieval guildhall.

A favorite theme architects used for skyscrapers just before the Art Deco era was that of a "temple on a mountaintop." Stand at Fulton and Gold Streets downtown, or Broadway at 29th Street, and look around. *Circumspice!*

Henry Villard, Civil War ace reporter and future railroad tycoon, married Fanny, the daughter of abolitionist leader William Lloyd Garrison. Neither Villard nor his prospective in-laws ever went to church or belonged to any denomination, but they were Victorian, if nominal, Christians, and Villard had a way with words. He wrote to Fanny during their engagement: "This shall be our Sunday service: worship in the temple of pure love, comparison of our doings in each week to our standard of right and duty, and vows of improvement in case we find that we did not fully attain it." Tell that to those who have always unquestioningly assumed that ethics is always and only a department, and a monopoly, of religion.

The *Times* calls skyscrapers "totemic." A totem is a "revered symbol." It is an Ojibway term for a clan emblem. The "Turtle Clan" will identify itself with a picture of a turtle. The same *Times* article, by Michael Frank in 1997, says of New York's skyscrapers: "They are our temples, after all, our Parthenon and our Pantheon; only the god worshipped in them is Mammon." Mammon comes from the Aramaic (late Hebrew; the language Jesus would have spoken) *mamona*: riches. Webster calls Mammon "material wealth or possessions, especially as having a debasing influence." Matthew says "You cannot serve God and Mammon." Mr. Frank, and every other writer in history except for Rand, snidely accuses his reader of debasement – a debasement that Church and State will be happy to relieve you of.

O. Henry was a favorite writer of Rand's, but he was one with Michael Frank and the rest: "...down in the part of town where they worship the golden calf."

The Roman Mercury – the Greek Hermes – is the god of commerce. In fact, "commerce," "market," "mercenary," and "merchant" all come from the god Mercury. In Roman Britain there was a market three miles south of Camulodunum (modern Colchester), the capital of the Trinovantes nation. Over it presided a statue of Mercury. The market building included a temple and a theater. Three miles out of town and including a theater? Sounds much like a modern suburban mall. The presence of Mercury meant that tribal fighting was forbidden there. Trading, worship, and entertainment were not to be disturbed by fighting. I. A. Richmond, in *Roman Britain*, writes: "...in Britain, as throughout the ancient world, many [fairs and markets] were specifically associated with ancient sanctuaries whose deity hallowed the transaction and gave to the market or fairground a sacred peace which folk no less superstitious than quarrelsome would not violate by quarrels and brawls."

The blood-soaked State claims we need it for protection from Mammon, who needs and enjoins peace and quiet for trade.

A woman I know married an athletic Greek fellow. I asked her whether he was a member of the Greek Orthodox Church. "No," she said, "he does his worshiping on the soccer field." Fitting that he was a Greek, because I will show you in this book how to make a soccer field, or any field of human endeavor, a place of worship – your own portable temple.

CHAPTER 2
EFFUSION REACTOR

A book that I read in college, and I suspect Rand read too, was *The Ancient City*, by Numa Denis Fustel de Coulange. I discuss this book in *The Age of Rand*. The book is not really about cities, but about the fact that every aspect of Greek and Roman life was determined by religion. You worshiped your ancestors, and later the gods of the Roman pantheon, and still later the One God Jupiter. The Christians just changed the One God Jupiter to the One God Jesus. An army fought only if the omens were favorable. You captured the statues of an enemy city's gods and carried them to your city to add to your pantheon. The more gods you captured, the more gods you would have fighting on your side in the next war. You burned your offerings because smoke rises – it carries your requests and the smell of the valuable food or other sacrifices you have burned for favors up to heaven, or Mount Olympus.

Rand has a remarkable paragraph in *Anthem*: "At first, Man was enslaved by the gods." I suspect she read Fustel. When a numerically superior army runs from a smaller foe just because the omens predicted defeat, that is where superstition interferes seriously with your rational decision making.

"Then he was enslaved by the kings." Rand was born under one of the last royal absolutists.

"He was enslaved by his birth, by his kin, by his race. But he broke their chains." An awful lot of history is summed up in those three short

18

lines. Elsewhere, Rand wrote of the need a dictator has of burdening his taxpayers with the expense of building statues, pyramids, and other monuments to his august self. Those same politicians tell us that only they can save us from the dreaded advertising we all complain about under Capitalism. Rand contrasted the palaces of the potentates with the austere republican simplicity of Independence Hall in Philadelphia. And she called some editorial writer's comparison of the Vietcong with the Minutemen of Lexington and Concord "blasphemy." Again, for issues this important, only the old religious formulas will do. But in Rand's hands, as in Nietzsche's, they are old religious formulas given a new and deeper meaning. (See Rand's Introduction to the 25ᵗʰ Anniversary Edition of *The Fountainhead*.)

Rand called art "emotional fuel." "A soul, too, needs fuel. It can run dry." So when we look at the art in a museum, or when we look at a city skyline or other sources of inspiration, or read a novel or see a play or movie, we are replenishing our emotional fuel, or rather our moral or spiritual or motivational fuel.

The trick is to distinguish between "spiritual," as in the spiritual uplift we get from art, and literal belief in spirits, as in: "There is a god, a Great Spirit, who will strike you with lightning unless you do as I say. Being a spirit, he is invisible, which gets me off the hook of actually producing proof of his existence while I threaten you with his wrath." "For those who believe, no explanation is necessary. For those who do not, none is possible." This last sophism comes from *The Song of Bernadette*, by Franz Werfel. Rand and Branden used to love to quote that line "For those who believe ..." derisively.

As to my use of the expression "public worship": Have you ever found yourself sharing an intense moment with strangers? I remember one: the 1986 World Series. I was walking down a Manhattan street and saw a car parked at the curb. The driver had his door open and his radio playing full blast. About ten people had gathered around and were listening to the game. The next day I heard Dan Rather on TV

19

remarking on similar scenes around the city. This was the spontaneous sharing with strangers of an experience they all got a charge out of – and that is what is meant by a spiritual experience. In this case it was sports and cheering the home team on. It was not work. It was not something we were being paid to do. It was therefore spiritual. And since it was shared with others, it was, so to speak, public worship, and all the more thrilling because it was a spontaneous experience shared with strangers. We might never meet again, but we had had a moment of shared exultation. The seeker after secular public worship has to get experiences like that wherever he can find them. In her article "Apollo and Dionysus," in *The New Left: The Anti-industrial Revolution*, Rand describes strangers smiling and excited and talking to each other – after the Apollo 11 astronauts' tickertape parade had passed by. "*This* is the essence of a genuine feeling of human brotherhood: the brotherhood of *values*. This is the only authentic form of unity among men – and only values can achieve it."

When people use the term "temple," they usually mean a place of solemnity. If the subject is important, then the feelings it generates are the kind you are supposed to experience on your knees. Here is Lewis Mumford, architecture critic for the *New Yorker* magazine, on Cass Gilbert's Federal Court Building on Foley Square (and a sample of Ellsworth Toohey's sarcasm in *The Fountainhead*: Mumford was one of Rand's models for Toohey). "As for the court building proper, you can tell in an instant that it is a temple devoted to august matters – either a bank, an insurance company, or a hall of justice. You can tell because it is fronted with a Macedonian phalanx of preposterous – and also preposterously expensive – classic columns." The word "temple" goes with the word "august," as "important" is always paired with "solemn" and even "somber."

On the other hand, Noel Coward, responding to critics who dismissed his comedies as unimportant theater, said "Who says laughter is unimportant?" *Puck* was a humor and satire magazine in the late 19th Century. It was apparently important enough, in its publisher's mind, to rate a whole building, and a big, prominent one, at Houston and Lafayette Streets on New York's Lower East Side. Go look at the sculpture of Shakespeare's Puck character, from "A Midsummer Night's Dream" on the building's corner. You can spot him a block away, saying "Lord, what fools these mortals be!" He is the Parthenon's Athena, the Diana of Ephesus, of humor.

Is ours an increasingly Objectivist world? Yes – just because of advancing technology, with or without Ayn Rand's own influence helping Man to improve his life. Improving his life forces Man to ask himself the questions asked by Rand and by Aristotle: What is Man? What is the nature of the human animal? What are his needs? Aristotle defined Man as the animal that thinks. What kind of life is the life proper to the animal that thinks? You did not have to ponder and choose your values back when you were struggling just to stay alive from day to day, as in the Stone Age or in wartime. When the going gets *less* tough, the tough have to make choices, now that they have more choices to make.

Go to the supermarket. Where your primitive ancestors would have been thrilled to have any kind of market, you shop in a market where, to find Wheat Thins, you must first paw through gluten-free Wheat Thins, low-sodium Wheat Thins, low-carb Wheat thins, low-sugar Wheat Thins, low-fructose-sugar Wheat thins, organic non-genetically-altered low-fructose-sugar Wheat Thins, and so on. The Age of Choice means the Age of humans becoming more human, since we are the animal that chooses. Giving all humans more freedom to choose, in every part of their lives – that is what Ayn Rand's philosophy, Objectivism, is all about. If she had not put that train of thought in motion, someone else would have, because it is implied in Man's nature. That's why today's world is increasingly Objectivist, with or without Rand.

And Rand does have a not inconsiderable influence. In the *Wall Street Journal* of October 12-13, 2013, Anne Kadet observed of the Empire State Building, "The vista from the 86th floor is dumbfounding. Folks simply gawk, gazing silently. Not to get all Ayn Rand about it, but it's amazing what Mankind can do. ... Later, I asked NYU urban planning prof Mitchell Moss to explain what makes the view so thrilling. He agreed it's about beholding human achievement." Earlier, in the April 27, 2013 issue, Kadet, reviewing New York's many walking tours, wrote: "Other themes include Jewish gangsters, food tours of Staten Island, shopping in the Garment District, and, for your inner Objectivist, 'Ayn Rand's New York'."

That line "Not to get all Ayn Rand about it ..." is priceless. It shows that Rand's name and theme are known, at least to the *Wall Street Journal*'s readership. It also means that Ms Kadet is a little embarrassed to effuse at Man's achievements. Being a New Yorker and a writer, and therefore an intellectual, Kadet has to make a show of blaséness.

Well, in some quarters it's still okay to "get all Ayn Rand" about Man's achievements. Go ahead and enthuse! Exult! Exalt! We just won't tell anyone. It's okay to say in earnest what Hamlet says in irony: What a piece of work is Man!

And cities are Man's temple ... especially the city of Ayn Rand and her century, New York.

CHAPTER 3
A TEMPLE MUST HAVE PROPHETS

Science Fiction writers! Yessiree Bob! They are the prophets prophesizing in the temple of Secular Man. Once they were crying in the wilderness, but now they are prophets with honor in their own land and time. They are prophets with profits! They predicted the future in the Twentieth Century and by god it all came true by the 21st. They were the high priests in the Temple of Progress when Progress was something we hoped *would* come. Today there is so much Progress so fast that we wish it would go away. At least can't it let up for a minute and let us catch our breath? What a rush, what a thrill it has been for us who have read science and science fiction all our lives – especially when our lives began in the long shadow of World War II. Triumph after triumph for the nerds, the geeks, the techies, and those who rejected the doom and gloom of the Bomb Age. Gene Roddenberry was right! Man did survive the 1960s, 70s, and so far up to 2016. Rand was right, too. Man has survived the collectivist vogue. Altruism is still riding high in the saddle on the underlying *moral* plane, so collectivism on the overlying *political* plane will return from time to time, maybe, but technology is dazzling everyone, young and old, with so many new tricks every year that "entrepreneur" is ceasing to be a dirty word. The minds of the young have changed on this point, not by reading *Atlas Shrugged*, but by seeing opportunities to start companies in industries that did not exist five minutes ago. After that, they will drool pious words about "giving back," but now at least there will be more money *for* them to give "back," and fewer poor people who need to be given to. Technology did it – not ideology. The problems pointed out by the Left, the reformers, the liberals and radicals – those problems keep going the way of the horse and buggy. Overpopulation, according to the "austerity preachers" (see Rand's introduction to *We The Living*, and her scorn for Jimmy Carter's plea to drive less, turn down the thermostat and give up), was supposed to have reduced us all to starvation by now. Instead, India is industrializing and building a middle class, and China is, too. Man the thinking animal *has* thought his way out of many problems since 1945.

I have just watched, online, Arthur C. Clarke, in 1963, talking about the art of predicting the future. He said that the only thing we can be sure of is that the future will be fantastic. If a prophet sounds level-headed and reasonable, in fifty years he will be seen as too timid. But if he makes predictions that threaten to land him in the loony bin, then his predictions might turn out to be almost as crazy as what will actually happen in fifty years.

Clarke then shows a model of a city of tomorrow. He says that the architecture of this city is already technically feasible now (1963). "But what about the day *after* tomorrow?" he asks. Will cities even exist? Will telecommunications make it unnecessary for humans to live close to each other in cities? Here he is thinking like a 20th Century Euro. How are WE going to live? It may not have occurred to Clarke that WE is not the question. How does *each individual choose* to live – that is the question. And some people choose to live in dense cities and some prefer the country. And people with money spend weekdays in town and weekends and summers at their "country seats," to use the 18th Century term. The future is not going to be collectivist. It is going to be humans acting more humanly then ever before, and human means *choosing*.

Freedom means balance. Some individuals will choose urban life, some suburban, some rural. Some will change their minds, and frequently. No Robert Moses will have the political power to try to turn cities into suburbs against their wills. Moses led urban Americans into the suburban wilderness for sixty or more years. Now let the idea of city living be reborn! It is okay to live in an apartment and walk to work and to market ... in Syracuse and Utica! Not just in New York City. Rand and her circle approved of Jane Jacobs, Moses's nemesis and author of *The Death and Life of Great American Cities.*

Think on that as you look at the plaque to Mary Lindley Murray, in the median on Park Avenue at 37th Street. I tell this story in *The Age of Rand.* This was the Murray family's country seat and the center of a working farm extending from about today's Lexington Avenue to Sixth Avenue, and about 30th Street to 50th Street. Now it is midtown, and Ayn Rand's old neighborhood. The country seats were chased clear out of Manhattan and the Bronx and almost up to Albany as New York City grew. New York and its northern suburbs, that is, since most people seem to end up splitting the difference between city and country and living in the burbs.

In *Voices From The Sky*, a collection of articles written between 1945 and 1965, Clarke predicted that someday each person will have his own personal phone number, so that when you call him, you won't know where in the world he might be. He will have a tiny phone on his person!

Of course, Clarke, born when and where he was, understandably speaks apologetically about anyone wanting to make money. He denies that "... only greed inspired the splendid tea clippers of the Nineteenth Century, or the Atlantic liners of today. Of course they were built to make money, but men put their hearts as well as their bank balances into them; and often they lost both." And then Clarke, an Englishman, and so a man who came by his love of ships honestly, makes the ship into a temple: "It is easy to see why ships have such an appeal to the human spirit. With their mobility, they symbolize freedom and adventure. ... The great ocean liners are the cathedrals of modern Man. Now he is about to build new shrines to later gods, for the ships of the future will be ships of space. ... For all but a brief moment near the dawn of history, the word "ship" will mean simply – spaceship."

Clarke expands on the spaceships of the future, calling them "bristling" because in the vacuum of space ships don't need to be streamlined, and describes them as "carrying the commerce of the future between the planets." So Clarke, no Luddite of course, does see the future as one of commerce, and he does see even capitalists as having hearts to put into projects, but still he never made the leap that Rand did. He sees the businessman as having a heart (sometimes) in *spite* of wanting to make money. Rand sees the businessman as having heart and spirit *because* he wants to make money; because he knows the difference between making money and just *getting* money. Clarke might retort, and most people today would, that businessmen up to now have not had Rand's exalted vision of business, and they have never known that distinction she makes between making and getting. Of course that is often true – but whose fault is that? Altruism, by telling us for centuries that we are scum, has helped to produce centuries of scum. The job of Objectivists in the years to come is to teach this generation – the generation that might settle Mars – the connection Clarke never knew: our spiritual goal and dream is to bring together the individual's love of his creative, productive work with a new rejection of cynicism about business, and show him how *that* is what will make him money in an intensely competitive economy, and will create projects that carry for him the meaning that temples and cathedrals and ships and skyscrapers carried for his ancestors. We will close the gap between the spiritual and the "materialistic." And we need never again snivel an apology for wanting to make money.

Materialism. Depend on it: The guy who accuses you of materialism is the guy who is about to take away your material ... especially the green material in your wallet. Here is Brooks Atkinson on Eugene O'Neill's 1929 play "Dynamo:" It's about "the death of an old god and the failure of science and materialism to give any satisfactory new god for our primitive need for ... a religious instinct to find a meaning for life." Here, though, Atkinson is complaining about Marxist materialism, not Capitalist materialism. Atkinson believes that we all have an instinctive need for a god, without which we will never be able to find a meaning for life. That is exactly the problem Rand solved, for millions. The meaning of life is doing all those things that make it possible for you to ask the meaning of life. Nice and simple.

Now let's talk about orchestral music, specifically, movie music. Get the DVD of the 1936 movie "Things to Come," by H. G. Wells, and look at the scene where Wings Over The World clears away the wreckage of war-torn Everytown and builds a new, futuristic city underground. John Cabal predicts "We will excavate the eternal hills!" (It's not made clear why the city should be underground, but artificial light, we are told, makes sunlight obsolete. Apparently, Wings Over the World builds things a certain way just because they *can* – like Frank Gehry.)

Now get the DVD of "Lord of the Rings, Part II: The Two Towers." Watch the scene where the camera swoops down into the mine of Eisengard. You see dramatic and sinister lighting, by torches. You see wooden waterwheels. You see a whole forest being clear-cut and each tree being dumped down into the giant mine hole, to be burned to stoke the forges where Sauroman's vassals are manufacturing weapons for his Orcs and Uruk-hai. He is turning a pleasant wood into a hellhole of heat, noise, mud, desolation – all to build an army to conquer Middle Earth. J. R. R. Tolkien's background, context, and subtext was World War I. "Eisen" means "iron" in German. "Gard" means "guard," or "border." Eisengard represents Tolkien's sinister image of Wilhelmine Germany, which, upon unification in 1871, went from agricultural to industrial overnight, and then armed for the conquest of Europe.

Compare the excavation of Everytown with the militarization of Eisengard. Here you see, side by side, two 20th Century British cinematic predictions of the urban/industrial future. In 1936, Wells, who supervised closely the filming of his novel, shows triumphant socialism sweeping away the oppression of the workers and the imperialism of the capitalists, and development – development of a super-city that is clean and pleasant and has a "rational" (socialist) economy, with jobs and security for all. Just a few years later, though, Tolkien shows the development of industry as hellish.

David Ramsey-Steele, a libertarian (a one-time Marxist in recovery) book editor at Open Court Publishing, born, raised, and educated in Britain, explained in a talk in the 1980s that the appeal of socialism before the 1960s was that socialism would develop a nation's economy, but that the appeal *since* the 1960s was that socialism would *prevent* development, and return us to a pre-industrial paradise. Actually, I find that the socialist professors are not loath to doing both, at the same time. In any case, it is fascinating today to see, in "Things to Come," the building of a city – an artificial environment – as part of the socialist ideal, after so many years now of the "back-to-nature" appeal. The New Everytown is a high-density place indeed. It looks like the Toronto City Hall. But clean; no smoking factories.

Now the music that helps to put these visual impressions across: The Eisengard music is frantic and threatening and makes you uncomfortable. The Everytown music is not threatening, but it is pounding. It is all about the pounding rhythm of heavy machinery. But, this being 1936, the pounding rhythm of heavy machinery mining out the eternal hills is shown as a good thing. It liberates the workers from the satanic, smoky mills of capitalism. That pounding, furthermore; that rhythm, sounds inexorable; inevitable. It gives a musical embodiment to the Marxist principle of the inevitability of future historical developments predicted by the infallible economic science of Marx. But if you don't buy the "inevitable" belief, you can still hear in that pounding music the sound of determination. The sky's the limit, or if you are mining, the Core's the limit. Nothing can stop us now, because we are Mankind and we have a goal and we have found out how to get there. Amazing what you can get over with an orchestral movie score.

In addition to prophets, do the temple of Ayn Rand and the god "Progress" have acolytes? Oh, boy do they! Two places where I have seen them scurry about like mice were the opening of the 34th Street/

Hudson Yards Number 7 Train station on Sunday, September 13, 2015, and a rare appearance of the observation car of the Twentieth Century Limited at Grand Central Terminal circa 2008.

One day, I was at Grand Central, in the concourse, holding up my "AYN RAND'S PARK AVENUE WALKING TOUR" sign, drumming up business, and chatted with a curious passerby. I showed him the picture of Rand waving from the cab of a train. He pointed at the locomotive and said "Ah! That is the 4000 Series E8 General Motors locomotive!" He was a train buff. He said he was at Grand Central that day because the observation car of the Twentieth Century Limited was being displayed to the public. I walked out onto the central platform, and there she was. Very Deco-styled. Looking brand new. People could board her. 1940s luxury. Ayn and Frank no doubt saw the scenery from this very car (or one just like it), as they moved from New York to Los Angeles in 1943 on the Twentieth Century Limited.

The platform and the car were swarming with people snapping photos of the car and each other with the car. (This was just before the Age of the Selfie.) They were enthused. They were chattering excitedly with each other about the car, its history, its excellent condition, its minutiae. They had found out somehow – no doubt there is a train buff network – that the MTA was rolling her out from whatever storage building in the train yards of New Jersey she was normally stored in. Or Amtrak or whoever it was. This experience would be repeated for me a year or two later with ships instead of train cars, when I met the Ship Lore Group, as they enthused and took many photos of three ocean liners making a rare joint appearance in New York Harbor.

Just a week ago, I saw the same enthusiasm yet again. The new Number 7 station, 34th Street/Hudson Yards, was opened. Again there were buffs. Enthusiasts. Photos being taken. One young man, with three cameras around his neck, was rushing to a spot where he could shoot the train entering the station, while another hobbyist shot one leaving the station.

From these incidents, and from historical re-enactors, I have conceived a great fondness for people who are "really, really into" something, no matter what it is, and no matter that the object of their lust does not happen to be one of mine. It is just great to see people loving something – something harmless, at least, but more likely something that has a creative, productive, life-contributing deeper meaning. Transportation is a big part of what man does to improve his life. It *should* tug at the emotions. The buffs are worshipers at the temple of Man.

CHAPTER 4
THE WORSHIP MACHINE

Google Maps. You can probably surf these maps while you read this book. Switch the app from Maps View to Satellite View. In the comfort of your own home you can look down on Man and his home planet from satellite altitude. Then you can zoom in until you seem to hover a hundred feet above the rooftops. There's your own home. There's the roof of 139 East 35th Street, Rand's home from 1941 to 1943, where she completed *The Fountainhead*. There's 36 East 36th Street, where she finished *Atlas Shrugged*, and the Villard Houses, east side of Madison Avenue from 49th to 50th Streets, where Random House published her magnum opus. And there's the Taj Mahal, the Eiffel Tower, Stonehenge, Disneyland, Macchu Picchu and everything else on the surface of the Earth. All for you to spy on at the touch of a button. There before you is all of Man's history and accomplishment – except for mines, and the International Space Station, and Voyager on its way out of the Solar System, but all those things and many more can be seen and read about online too.

Antoine de Saint-Exupery, author of *The Little Prince*, said that it is hard for an aviator to be democratic in spirit, because he spends his time looking down on humanity from airplanes. On the contrary, Google Earth makes you *more* democratic, because anyone can now (virtually) look down, godlike, on humanity. And you will look up to Man, by looking down at all his works.

Look down on deserts, on the arctic tundra, on jungles and on the bare rock of mountains. What do you see? Nothing – and so that is where tomorrow's cities will be built. Tomorrow's Dubais. Let's put one in Mexico's Gran Desierto, at the mouth of the Colorado River. Buildings covered with solar panel roofs. There's Man, finding, through high technology, uses for what was formerly unused, including whole deserts. Will that mean that Objectivists will remorselessly cut down, like Sauroman, the very last tree in the Amazon? No. People like trees, as urban amenities. They like small parks in cities and big parks outside of cities. And we are moving toward the paper-free office. And better-off, better-educated people have fewer babies, so we are moving toward a stable worldwide population. Technology means the spreading out of the population of the old tenement cities into dispersed, clean, new cities big and small, villages, suburbs, exurbs, isolated farms and villas; whatever the customer wants, so there will be more wide-open space at your doorstep, not less. The whole trend of civilization and technology and progress is toward learning to do more with less, so more industry will happen at the molecular level and take place in clean, quiet labs underground, leaving parkland open on the surface, like Everytown.

When you look down on Gran Desierto City circa 2100, you may see little that looks like a circa 2000 city, let alone a Dickensian one.

Will you ever be provincial in your attitudes again? Not if you look down upon Man's cities from above. Not if you sample his music and literature online. Not if you sample ethnic food from all over the world, and I suppose you'll be able to do that online soon. After Three Dimensional Printing must come materializing of food, just like Captain Picard when he says to his synthesizer "Earl Gray tea, ninety-eight degrees centigrade. Lemon." Will you fail to "get all Ayn Rand" about it when you look down on endless ribbons of concrete, flat-roofed factories (today more and more covered with solar panels for clean, efficient power!), and endless apartment buildings and suburban homes shaded by trees? "We will open the gates of our city to those who deserve to enter, a city of smokestacks, pipelines, orchards, markets and inviolable homes," says John Galt. Even without the reforms hoped for by Objectivists, you can see for yourself what Man has built so far. "Mankind will never destroy itself," says Howard Roark, "not so long as it does things such as this."

For the sake of the curmudgeons, those fearful of the conscious, reasoning self – even their own – I have to patiently explain that smokestacks are not ends in themselves. The City of Galt might not have any smokestacks at all, outside of a museum of the early Industrial Revolution. But it will be characterized by whatever advancing technology gives us to replace the now-obsolete burning of fuels for power. After all, Galt invents a machine that draws static electricity from the atmosphere and turns it into current, making possible cheaper and cleaner energy than that produced by Ken Danagger's coal or Ellis Wyatt's oil. Danagger and Wyatt will eventually have to find new uses for coal and oil, or go out of business. Progress does not suffer fuels gladly. There is always some more efficient way to power things. Come on, Anti-matter!

The Richardson Highway heading out of Anchorage – why does that highway in particular fascinate me? Because Alaska is still mostly empty of Man and his works. Also, most everything built in Alaska is under fifty years old, and much is under twenty, so buildings look new. When Alaska gets fully built up, if it ever does, and according to 2100's idea of what "fully built up" means, then we will see an industrialized state that does not have, and never did have, smokestacks – at least not many, and those inherited from the 20th Century will be torn down by then.

Mainly, though, my fascination lies in seeing a divided-lane, limited-access, cloverleafed highway that is *not* in southern California, or New Jersey, or in the Syracuse of my youth, but in Alaska! (They always spell it with an exclamation mark there.) The Richardson leads the driver not just to another city, but from the only Alaskan city of any consequence out into Terra Incognita – wilderness – the bush. Alaskans like to say "The nice thing about Anchorage is that it is only fifteen minutes from Alaska." As the city grew in the oil-fueled 1970s, old sourdoughs started calling the state's largest city "Los Anchorage." Google Earth your way up the Richardson and watch the urban sprawl gradually peter out. Each undeveloped tract of land is another chance to build a cleaner, more efficient, more prosperous civilization than our parents knew – but not by walking unprepared into the bush to be poisoned by an inedible plant, like that young cretin who got a book and a movie made about him for doing just that, so great was his fear and hatred of Man or decadent American capitalism, or whatever else his professors talked him into – Rand's "soft, safe assassins." Note that what I am celebrating here is not civilization over wilderness, or vice versa, but the total process of Man turning some of the wilderness into cities, so that he can henceforth have a choice – he can choose to live part time in the city, in the suburbs, or in the wilderness. His primitive ancestors had no choice about living in the wilderness – there was no place else for them to live.

The area of Alaska is 586, 412 square miles. Its 2014 population was 736,732. Only in recent years has the state finally gotten up to a population density of ONE – COUNT 'EM – ONE per square mile. One Alaskan put it this way: "You could put 50 million people up here and they would never find each other." Exaggerated, but not by much. A whopping 100 people per square mile, that would be. Alaska is two and a half times the size of Texas. Four times the size of California, with its 40 million thirsty people. Alaska has plenty of fresh water – no droughts in the Great Land. Isn't it fun to imagine Alaska's population and influence growing to match its acreage? Imagine Alaska the new California! Movies don't need strong sunlight anymore, as they did when D. W. Griffith and Cecil B. DeMille went west. Alaska could have a movie industry, and be a trend-setter state. Tourism would lead the way – go to Alaska to see wilderness ... from a heated bus or a country home of your own. Ellis Wyatt, in *Atlas Shrugged*, wondered why Colorado couldn't be the capital of a Second Renaissance. Why not a Dubai in Alaska?

These are the things I see when I follow the Richardson Highway north from Anchorage on my home worship machine, Google Earth.

I realize that not all share my priorities. Google "Alaska" and the news headline you get today – May 24, 2015 – is: DID BRISTOL PALIN SKIP HER FAMILY'S GET TOGETHER ON CANCELED WEDDING DATE? Inquiring minds want to know!

But the worship machine rolls on. If "worship" means extravagant respect and admiration, and "celebrate" means to mark, to honor, and to observe with festivities, in short, to enjoy, then I'm all set, sitting in my Queens, New York study, in front of my Mac, rolling up the Richardson. North to the Future! (The Alaska state motto.)

"I love those who do not know how to live, except by going under, for they are those who cross over." Nietzsche's Zarathustra gives a list of kinds of people he admires – his pastiche of Christ's Beatitudes. In that line, he means that the creative person knows that others will copy him, and so his achievements will no longer be unique. He will not be the only – he will be the first. He is Roark, telling the Dean "I stand at the end of no tradition. I may, perhaps, stand at the beginning of one." He is Andrew Stockton, in Galt's Gulch, training a man who might become his most dangerous competitor someday, because that is the only kind of man he likes to hire. He is Leonardo da Vinci, who, warned that other painters were copying his works, replied "That's alright. I will originate; they can copy." He becomes a bridge to the future, precisely because he is willing to create something greater than himself, and so go under. We will revisit this theme.

A title occurs to me as I Google Earth the Mohawk River Flats in Utica and Whitesboro, a neighboring village, where my mother and her mother grew up. I don't know what this should be a title for – a novel, a play, an opera: THE WAITING LAND. It must have been Aaron Copeland's opera "The Tender Land" that gave me the idea.

These flats are waiting for new uses. By default, they are currently a wildlife preserve. In other words, vacant lots. The backwash of the receding First Industrial Revolution. The second will be one of three-dimensional printing or God-knows-what.

In the 1970s, dispirited Soviet soldiers were telling each other that American spy satellites could tell whether your shoes were tied from 100 miles up. But now this military hardware has been commercialized. The consumer can buy apps that will aid his traveling – or even replace his traveling! You can drive – visually – around cities all over the world in the comfort of your living room, or on the subway. Much-maligned commercialism is the successor to militarism as a world-wide way of life.

Know where you can catch people in the act of bravely risking their capital and their time and taking a chance on a new business, as entrepreneurs? Look in the phone book, especially the Yellow Pages. Or their online equivalents. You can today find online the newspapers of yesteryear, with ads for shirt fronts, tooth powder, dropsy remedies, monkey glands, French Art, "Brilliantine and dime seegars" ("Hello Dolly"). And while you are reading the phone book, look under "A" for "Associations." See the ingenuity and energy human beings have brought to the non-profit, as well as the profit, sector of the economy.

If you want to see faces alight with excitement, put into your worship machine DVDs on the history of the space program. Astronaut Michael Collins, of Apollo 11, later wrote in his memoir *Carrying the Fire* that his favorite piece on Apollo 11 had been Ayn Rand's article in her own magazine *The Objectivist*. Her ecstatic description of the launch – she and her husband Frank were invited through Alan Greenspan's Nixon administration connections – makes that article a favorite among her readers. The line that sticks with me is her identifying the deeper meaning of the flight: This was the picture and the proof of Man's efficacy, a picture of Man "succeeding, succeeding, succeeding!" Look at the faces of the million people who had come to the Cape just to watch a minute or two of history in the making, and not even from the invitees' grandstand, but from the beach and the roads and the parking lots for miles around. Like Uluru, the rocket, on the pad and bathed in floodlights the night before launch, kept drawing everyone's eye. *There* is worship. There is *secular* worship. There is an emotional reaction usually reserved for art works of the highest order, as viewed by only the most sensitive esthetes. But these were not esthetes. These were not science geeks and nerds. This was Tennyson's "piebald parliament of Man." These were just folks, from all walks of life. But they were Homo Sapiens, savoring their species' proudest moment. And the fact that you can watch the event on your TV shows another great triumph of Man. Long after the people in the picture are all dead, their reaction can still be an emotional shot in the arm to later generations – even generations that were born on Luna, and Mars, and Titan. We, in the future, can share their ecstasy. Their moment of secular worship becomes ours, and our descendants', for all time. Man has, to that extent at least, defeated death. We are starting to beat the "pale Galilean" at his own game. (Google Roman Emperor Julian the Apostate.)

Occasionally you can see such looks of awe – pleased awe – on faces contemplating cities. One visitor from Hannover, Germany gave such a look when I took her to the observation deck of the Empire State Building in 1990 and pointed out that two hundred years before, this island was mostly farms and forest and one small city down at the southern tip. Her eyes sparkled. She tsked and shook her head in the way that says "Wow!" She reacted the same way when I told her about the Hubble Space Telescope, which was launching about then. It is great to not only react to your values yourself, but to find others who react the same way and enjoy their enjoyment. That is why Richard Halley, the composer in Galt's Gulch, explains to Dagny that he is not just trying to elicit emotions with his music, but to elicit the particular emotions he *wants* the audience to feel, and for the same reasons.

There is, though, one big difference between my Worship Machine and churches (the Worship Machines of the religious folks): The worshipers filling the naves of medieval cathedrals were looking up to the Sky Fella, through acres of glass: the translucent or tinted windows going up, up, up the high, buttressed walls of the building. They could see saints floating in the sky – because they had been painted on the windows. All that light and air must have been the reason that Rand said that she liked Gothic architecture, along with Modern, in 1935, as she began her research for *The Fountainhead.* The tall Gothic church tells the parishioners: You are the humble supplicant, helplessly shackled by gravity to the horizontal world of (practically) Flatland. But God floats above the clouds. He can fly!

But now, through the magic of Google Maps and the Internet, it is we who look down, as God used to do. Not so the people on the ground can worship us, but so that we can worship them – the builders of those cities we see spread out below us. In the Beginning – and still currently – they, in their millions, have created and create every day, all that makes life possible. And you can see that it is good.

THE WINTERS OF MY DISCONTENT

On April 11, 2013, comedian Jonathan Winters died. This was on the TV news in the morning. That afternoon, I was walking up Wall Street and was handed a half-price ticket for a comedy show by a 30ish man who mentioned that he himself was a comedian. I said "If you're a comedian, I feel I should offer my condolences."

Blank look.

"Jonathan Winters!"

Blank look.

"Jonathan Winters, the comedian, died. It was on the news this morning."

Blank look.

"You call yourself a comedian, sir?! Jonathan Winters was one of the great comic geniuses of all time!"

Being a 21st Century man, he said not a word to me, but just reached into his pocket, pulled out one of those electronic devices – Snotphones or Eyepatches or Boysenberries or Androgynes or whatever you call them – punched in the name JONATHAN WINTERS, and instantly had in his hand all the information ever recorded about the comedian I had seen on TV all my life.

So I guess the young people growing up in this century can be forgiven for thinking that they don't need to know anything about anything, since anything they will ever need to know they can just pull off the Internet in seconds. As each subject comes up, you just give yourself an instant shot of knowledge, like a shot of insulin. This anecdote should have gone in the UTOPIA chapter. As Zager & Evans said in their 1969 hit "In the Year 2525," "…your arms hanging limp at your sides … your legs got nothing to do – some machine is doing it for you." Yes, I am sure these handheld devices are a good thing, but it takes some getting used to. And deliberate, scheduled exercise. A more human way of life than before – a way of life that is all about choicemaking – means 90% of your time reading information on a screen and making decisions based on that information, and 10% of your time forcing yourself to get a planned number of minutes per day of a planned kind of exercise. Just like the astronauts on the space station, who have to force themselves to ride their excercycle a certain number of minutes per day so their legs don't atrophy. Welcome to Utopia.

By the way, for whom did I just write that story? Only for those as old and computer illiterate as I am. Unless there is a societal collapse to the Stone Age, you, the reader, will be on that young comedian's side and have no sympathy for those who have not yet mastered the Eyepatch or the Snotphone. Either that or I will send this book in a time machine back to 1960 to warn Gregory Peck and Ava Gardner, as they wait for the end On The Beach, that the world will end, not with a bang, but with a playlist. Like Star Trek's Talosians, youth will soon have overdeveloped brains, or underdeveloped brains full of overdeveloped chips, and have the power of illusion. At least self-illusion, but that's all you need – and who doesn't have plenty of it already? They will just sit and stare at whatever illusion they like, as the kids on the subway do even now, not looking up as you push them and their backpacks out of the doorway. You are disturbing them less by pushing them than by saying "Excuse me!" Taking out their earpieces and trying to grasp that they are blocking the train door would cost them more bother – more mental bandwidth – than being pushed out of my way, so they don't mind the pushing.

I did buy Ray Kurzweil's book *The Singularity is Near*, but there are so many books ahead of it on my reading list that by the time I get to it, I'm afraid the Singularity will have come and gone. You will all have disappeared into your black holes, whether physical or mental, and I will be left, like Burgess Meredith on "The Twilight Zone," reading piles of books made of paper, twine, cloth, pasteboard and glue. And we will see which of us is happier.

CHAPTER 5
IS NEW YORK THE QUINTESSENTIAL CITY?

The Establishment always wins.

In the Age of Altruism, that gave way to the Age of Rand late in the 21st Century (maybe), this was the sad fact, it seemed. Rome always wins. Money always wins, and the State ends up with all the money. We all have to render unto Caesar. The Establishment means the guys with the money and the power. No matter whether the money comes first and attracted the power or vice versa, both always attract the talent, who never bite the hand that feeds them. So the *New Yorker* Magazine writers would never champion a Jeremiah like Ayn Rand, who so wanted some Establishment figure to champion her.

But wait – Rome was not Athens or Persepolis. So the foregoing, like all generalizations, is true except when it isn't. Egypt, Persia, Greece, Babylon – all gave way to Rome, which gave way to London in the 19th Century and Washington/New York in the 20th. So Rome always wins, until it loses, and time marches on.

(Thanks to Washington, Hamilton and Jefferson, and a dinner at the latter's digs on Maiden Lane, the power got separated from the money: Foggy Bottom got the Federal Government, while New York got the banks and the New York Stock Exchange. Decentralization.)

In 410, Alaric and his Goths sacked Rome. Saint Jerome said "The world is beheaded." The destruction of Rome was the destruction of the world, because to Romans, Rome was the world. But this was not true at all. The world could and did get along without Rome. And Rome wasn't destroyed, just occupied for a few days.

New York likes to call itself the capital of the world. But we are seeing an age of decentralization, just like the Roman world after Roman government moved to Constantinople, Trier, Antioch, Londinium, Eburacum, Lugdunum, Lutetia, Rimini, Ravenna, or wherever emperors and attempted emperors made their headquarters.

Rome was the world, before Alaric, only because Rome was Man, writ large. Rome was Rule, Purpose, Order, Cosmos and not Chaos. But 21st Century Man now knows how to obtain and preserve all those values without an emperor and without a single city that is so dominant that even the sentry on Hadrian's Wall in Britannia and at Petra, in Arabia, could confuse it with the world.

Ray Bradbury wrote a story in which an isolated villager in Central America is puzzled when cars start streaming south on a new highway, their drivers raving in panic about a nuclear war having just broken out. "It's the end of the world!" they wail, and drive on south. The simple old villager wonders "What do they mean – the world?"

Poul Anderson, in *The War of Two Worlds*, has an Earth soldier returning to New York's rocket port after defeat in a war with Mars. He knows that New York and other major cities have been largely destroyed by nuclear missiles, but from cislunar space he can't yet see any difference in the broad, blue face of his home planet as his craft approaches it. He reflects that after all, men and Martians are small things, and space and time are so vast.

Distinguished British historian Piers Mackesy notes that General Howe's capture of Philadelphia did not bring an immediate end to America's war for independence. Since Philadelphia was the seat of Congress and America's largest city, once we take it that's it, right? "The capture of one's capital city would be enough to bring any European nation to terms," Mackesy explains. But American independence was an idea, not a bureaucracy. Philadelphia was not indispensible.

Mackesy's London has no rivals in Britain for the same reason that Paris has no rivals in France, and, most extreme case of all, Moscow in the Soviet Union. Government, in most nations, sucks the money, the talent, and everything else out of the rest of the country. Why is Paris, for Piaf, the city of lovers? Because it has all the college kids – numerous, sophisticated and liberal enough to live the single life longer than other French men and women in their twenties. See Hedrick Smith's *The Russians* for the extreme centralization of not only power, but the arts in Moscow in the Soviet period. Solzhenitsyn was the top writer in the Soviet Union before his exile, so his dacha was just down the road from President Brezhnev's!

But thanks to their Treaty of Maiden Lane, Hamilton and Jefferson made New York and Washington have to duke it out from 1790 to today for dominion over the life of the nation. Thanks to taxation, Washington will eventually win. It will suck the money out of Wall Street. Money will be taxed out of your paycheck and disposed of in Washington. Wall Street will no longer turn your saved money into more money. Congress will turn your money into popularity and re-election for themselves. Bread and circuses. Comrade Professor will tell you that that is democracy.

New York will become another Marseilles, or Liverpool. Just a workaday port. No glamor. No Broadway. Just Washington's Kennedy Center, showing plays that glorify the incumbent president, from whom all subsidies flow.

New York was largely a city of the railroad age. It was the 19th Century that saw the city's greatest growth, and it was, first, the Erie Canal, and after that, the railroads that did it. Cities of the ancient and medieval worlds, even Rome, worked less like a 19th and 20th Century city of intercity rail and subways and more like a 21st Century city of endless suburbs and cars. There was no mass transit in Augustan Rome. You got around on foot, on horseback, or by coach or wagon – private vehicles that could change direction at will. But in our time, tracked vehicles, and buses on fixed routes, add another level of density at the city core to the high level already caused by high land values, steel-framed buildings, and the invention of the elevator. No 20th Century city expressed this "density" theme as completely and as consciously and deliberately as New York – especially Art Deco New York, in the boom decade of the 1920s.

The RCA Building in Rockefeller Center typifies New York's insistence on verticality. Don't move to the suburbs. Just pile the company's offices on top of the TV studios, which are piled on top of the shopping concourse, which is piled on top of the subway station.

See how many pedestrians crowd the sidewalks and the atriums. We will pay those atriums tribute in the GREENLAND chapter below.

CANBERRA

My wife Belen and I flew to Australia in 2010. On the 24-hour trip from JFK to LAX to MEL, I made the mistake of reading Bill Bryson's book *In A Sunburned Country*. Most of the book seemed to be about Aussie snakes and spiders and crocodiles and jellyfish, and all the many different horrible ways they can kill you. There is a spider there with enough venom in one bite to kill an elephant. There aren't any elephants in Australia! Bryson plaintively asks why oh why do you NEED to pack enough venom to kill an animal you will never encounter in nature? Somewhere over Fiji I considered asking the pilot to turn the plane around and return to my familiar environment of mere rattlesnakes, Black Widows, alligators and grizzly bears. Then Bryson gave his impressions of Canberra, Australia's planned capital city.

On my walking tour "Skyscrapers of *The Fountainhead*," I show a picture of a house designed by George Grant Elmslie, on the rocky coast of Woods Hole, Massachusetts. That house may have been Rand's inspiration for Roark's Austen Heller house in the novel. Elmslie was a student of Louis Sullivan, as was Frank Lloyd Wright. I explain the often-exaggerated relationship between Wright and Rand's fictional architect Howard Roark. I mention that Walter Burley Griffin was another Sullivan student. These are two architects most people have never heard of. When people hear that Rand's hero in *The Fountainhead* is an American Modernist architect of the 20th Century, they say "Oh. Frank Lloyd Wright." – only because Wright is the only one in that category they can name. But Wright was not the only architect of that description.

If you happen to live in Canberra, though, you would be reminded of Griffin every day. He designed the city. The reservoir that forms the visual centerpiece of the city is called Lake Burley Griffin. Bryson, visiting Canberra circa 2000, writes that he could not understand Canberra. There did not seem to be much going on there.

But this is typical of planned capital cities. Washington was long considered a hardship post for foreign diplomats used to life in cities like London and Paris, where the political capital is also the business capital, the arts capital, and the everything else capital. That's why Ed Crane, president of the brand new Cato Institute, the Koch-funded libertarian think tank, arriving in Washington in the late 1970s, got this reaction from his cabbie: a "small-government" institute won't be popular in Washington, a company town where the government is the company.

What Bryson did not get was that the Australian government and Griffin and his successor-planners these hundred years were not building a city so much as a campus – a spread-out, car-friendly university campus for three hundred thousand. Lots of grassy margins around the thoroughfares – you can't call them streets, because they have no shops, only shoulders – and lots of bicycle paths in those margins. Go to Google Earth and compare Canberra with the Amherst campus of SUNY Buffalo and other 1960s-style major university campuses.

Not only were they planning a campus instead of a city, they were planning an *anti-city*. They have done everything they could to stop a normal, high-rise, high-density city from ever growing around the shores of Lake Burley Griffin. The CBD – the Central Business District – the city part of the city – is called "Civic," and it is pretty much a big mall, with a handful of five and ten story office buildings attached. But they have planned two other CBDs in the Australian Capital Territory; Belconnen, miles to the north, and Woden Valley, miles to the south, to pull office buildings away from Civic. They are just far enough away to compete with Civic and not far enough away to be independent cities. They are like tapeworms. And there is also a city called Queenbeyan, New South Wales, right on the boundary of the ACT to the east, pulling office towers out of the ACT altogether, as Arlington and Alexandria, Virginia pull office towers out of the District of Columbia.

As cities the world over spread by freeway and car and suburb, we say aloha to the vertical city and "Dude!" to the more recent, car-centric, horizontal, Los Angelized cities like Canberra; Astana, Kazakhstan; Abuja, Nigeria; Reston, Virginia; Columbia, Maryland; Chandigarh, India and Brasilia. On the other hand, there is that tower in Dubai, overtopping the Empire State Building and its successors by a wide margin, even though Dubai has nothing but empty desert all around for the taking. They built that tower not because of today's high land prices, but to anticipate tomorrow's. On the other other hand, I see a recent article online headlined "Luanda: Africa's New Dubai?" That's it, then – another matter of cycles, as we have seen before. No development ever means an end to history. Cycles of centralization and indispensability and verticality come and go and are followed by cycles of decentralization and dispensability and horizontal spread.

The funny thing is, though, that New Yorkers still see their city as the Skyscraper City, even though it has been a long time since New York had anything like a monopoly on supertall buildings. In the Age of Dubai, why do New York City businesses still put skylines on the sides of their trucks, as part of their logos?

Inertia, probably. New York has been associated for so long with skyscrapers that it would have to become associated with something else really, really important to make people change the company logos on their trucks from "Skyscraper Drycleaners" to something else. Maybe a volcano will erupt in the middle of Manhattan someday – didn't somebody already do that in a cable TV movie? – and the next drycleaning establishment will be called "Volcano Drycleaners." New York – Home of the world's newest volcano!

I did not make up that example of "Skyscraper Drycleaners," by the way. There is a truck I often see downtown with exactly that inscription. The artwork shows a hanger and a skyscraper skyline. I am collecting examples of company names and logos that use the skyline motif.

Gene Fowler was a reporter for the Hearst papers. He worked in New York from 1919 to about 1960. He wrote a very entertaining memoir about his days as a reporter, and called it *Skyline*. You can see why that word is particularly appropriate and evocative for a memoir of life in New York in the age of the Art Deco skyscraper, long before anyone here ever heard of Kuala Lumpur or Dubai. What is a memoir? A book telling, not every detail, but just the highlights of your past. Just the peaks, the most memorable moments … just the pinnacles on the skyline.

Skyscraper and skyline images, in words or in pictures, are natural in ads and logos for companies in the building trades. A lot of real estate companies have skyline logos. But the interesting thing is how many drycleaners and other companies unrelated to buildings use the same motif. We will return to this point throughout the present volume.

It may be that America's center of gravity will someday shift to the West Coast, at Los Angeles or San Francisco, or the Gulf Coast, at Houston or New Orleans. Harry Binswanger once predicted the former to Rand, who replied that she would never move. She would go down with New York! Now, that is funny, because at least one of her heroes in Atlas, Ellis Wyatt, differs. He says to Hank and Dagny "To hell with New York and the whole East Coast! This is the capital of the Second Renaissance!" ("This" being his shale oil operation in southwest Colorado) This is an example of the perils of taking Atlas, as so many do, both pro and con, as a manual of Objectivist dogma on every subject. How could such a New York partisan say that? It is also an example of how Rand the pre-1957 fiction writer changed into a very different person: the post-1957 non-fiction writer, public intellectual and leader of a movement. The bi-coastal Rand finally succumbed to the homing instinct, forsaking Hollywood for Midtown Manhattan. But Wyatt had put his finger on the decentralizing nature of a free society – see *The Age of Rand* on Hamilton and Jefferson and why the national capital ended up on the Potomac and not at New York (briefly mentioned three pages above).

Galt's motor would produce so much energy so cheaply that water desalination would permit vast, new industrial cities in dry prairie and mountain regions. *Anyplace* could be the capital of the Second Renaissance … Dubai comes to mind.

But if city life, to you, means walking and window shopping, New York is hard to beat … so far.

CHAPTER 6
REVIEWS OF *CELLULOID SKYLINE* AND *NEW YORK NIGHT*

CELLULOID SKYLINE: NEW YORK AND THE MOVIES,
by James Sanders

Celluloid Skyline is so close to the present volume in theme that it deserves to be "incorporated by reference," as the Wall Street lawyers say.

Sanders shows how the movie camera has shown New York City to worldwide audiences for over a century now. The book was published in 2001 – in fact, Sanders had to add an apologetic note at the beginning of the book, explaining that 9-11 had happened as the book was going to press. He also fascinates the reader with the story of how New York City gave birth to the movies. The Kinetoscope – a device for flipping cards behind an eyepiece for one customer – was introduced by Thomas Edison at Holland's Kinetoscope Parlor at 1155 Broadway, at 27th Street, on August 14, 1894. Lumiere, in Paris, got audiences to pay to sit in the dark next to strangers to see a *projected* moving picture in December, 1895, but Edison bounced back with the same attraction at Koster and Bial's Music Hall on April 22, 1896, thus marking the birth of the American movie industry. Frames on a reel were made possible by the invention of flexible film by Hannibal Goodwin in Newark, New Jersey.

The location of Koster and Bial's is marked today by a plaque on Macy's Department Store. It is next to an entrance to the store, on 34th Street, near the 7th Avenue end of the block-long building.

Hannibal Goodwin was an Episcopal priest. His church is still standing in Newark, on Broad Street, near the Broad Street Station, just north of downtown. A plaque credits him with the invention of flexible film.

What does Sanders find in the image of New York City projected on film? His epigraph, by Joan Didion, says it all, when she refers to

> ... New York – the *idea* of New York ... "Wall Street," "Fifth Avenue," "Madison Avenue" were not places at all but abstractions ("Money," and "High fashion," and "The Hucksters"), New York was no mere city. It was instead an infinitely romantic notion, the mysterious nexus of all love and money and power, the shining and perishable dream itself.

Why did she add "perishable"? Perhaps she was thinking of The Bomb, for which New York was a prime target. In Ian Fleming's *Live and Let Die*, James Bond, riding over the Triborough Bridge into Manhattan from Idlewild Airport (now JFK) says to his FBI contact Halloran, "I hate to say it, but this has to be the fattest atomic-bomb target on the whole face of the globe."

"Nothing to touch it," agrees Halloran. "Keeps me awake nights thinking what would happen."

Or maybe, to Joan Didion, and all the others who came to New York because their ambition told them that this is where they belonged, New York felt like a prize and a privilege, not just a map co-ordinate, that one had to earn and that could be withheld from the aspirant by Fate, or even worse, could be granted and later taken away, if you fell behind the pack. It wasn't that New York might perish, it's that Joan Didion might perish. "Wherever I am is Hell," said Mephistopheles, "because I am separated from God."

Didion is right. New York City is an idea; a dream some people have. Millions of people. I felt it, and you felt it too if you came to The Big Town to live. Wall Street became a street you walk on with your feet, instead of walking all over with your epithets.

Rand echoed Didion, or, rather, her husband Frank echoed Didion when he said that Ayn had created a glamorized version of New York City in her mind. Back in Russia, Ayn had enjoyed an operetta by Lehar called *Song of the Lark*. She remembered, many years later, how the characters in the show had worn "fashionable clothes in the latest foreign styles. The men wore top hats. I remember one scene of a ball, and a huge window showing a lighted street of a foreign city … Operettas saved my life … You know my love for city lights, city streets, skyscrapers … That's what I expected from abroad." (Barbara Branden, page 46) Glimpses, on stage and screen, of the wonders to be found "abroad" gave her hope.

Sanders surveys both the City of Dreams and the City of Tough Streets, the two general filmic faces that New York City presents to the rest of America. Movies also show pictures and impressions of America to the world and of Man to Man, and in all three cases the message is a dual one: "You are just like the people in the movies, and you are NOT just like the people in the movies." The moviegoer can identify with the good aspirations represented by New York City, by America, or by Man, and when the gritty streets and gangsters show up, and whatever the director sees as bad about America or Man is shown, then the viewer, as the lights come up, sits back, relaxes, smiles smugly, and says "But those violent or benighted days in New York are over now." Or: "I am not like those New York gangsters. I am like the talented transplant coming to New York to pursue his dream." Or: "I would have been against that American government policy." And finally: "Thank God it's only a movie. Real life isn't *that* bad. Man isn't that bad."

But Sanders, like everyone else, clearly has a special place in his heart, and in his book, for the Dream City – the exciting New York City, not the grit.

The secret of New York City's success as a setting for fiction is the ease of believing that in New York City anything is possible (see Chapter 14, below). Anything can happen, such as chance encounters, but especially, sudden rises and falls. Meteoric careers. Risk taking. Why? Because New York City employs the top people in most fields, and in the most conspicuous and fame-ogenic fields. That's why a few out-of-town *good* reviews of *Atlas Shrugged* in 1957 did not count for much against the New York *bad* reviews. Only the New York City, and mainly the *New York Times*, reviews "count" in book publishing.

Sanders points out that it is film makers, rather than writers, who have spread the Dream City to the world, because movies are seen by more people, in more different languages, than books are, and all at once.

There is a whole field within the movie-making process called "reference shots." Photographers are taking pictures of everything in the world, and collecting pictures others have taken, of different locales in different periods. These photos fill whole libraries in Hollywood. If the art director needs to create backings (what in theaters are called "flats" or "backdrops") of 9th Century Baghdad, or the set designer needs a street in 1899 Paris, he refers to the reference photos in the library. Guess which locale rates not just file cabinets full of reference shots, but the building of whole streets, not just for one movie, but as permanent sets, to be used in many movies for years to come.

If you rent the DVD of "Seven Days in May," you can hear John Frankenheimer giving his Director's Commentary on the film. He explains that so many movies involve either New York or LA or both that by 1962, when that film was made, it had become a convention among movie directors that when a scene is laid on a passenger plane going west, the passengers are facing left, and if flying east, right, just as two characters having a phone conversation will be shown with one facing left and the other right.

Sanders has a lot to say about the Fountainhead movie. It was made in 1948 and released in 1949, by Warner Brothers. He shows a photo of Raymond Massey (Gail Wynand, the Hearst-like newspaper publisher), in costume but out of character, relaxing at Wynand's desk between takes. Behind Massey, stagehands are installing backings. But they are the wrong backings. They are paintings made to look like giant, blown-up photos of the Plaza Hotel, the Sherry-Netherland, the Savoy Hotel, and Ely Jacques Kahn's Continental Building, all in Midtown. And it is a night scene. But when we first meet Wynand in his office, it is a daytime scene. We see a gigantic window behind his desk, and in the distance we see a *downtown* scene. We see the Citgo Building (later AIG), Farmers Trust, 40 Wall Street, 1 Wall, Equitable, and the Singer Building (demolished 1967). These views seem to have been shot – i.e., these paintings must have copied reference shots taken – from at or near the top of the Municipal Building. (Yes, they used to *paint* twenty or fifty-foot long paintings from reference photos. The technology to blow up a photo that big did not yet exist.) That means that King Vidor, the director, and Edward Carrere, the art director, were putting Wynand's New York *Banner* where it should be: on Park Row, which was Newspaper Row from about 1800 to about 1950. Was this deliberate accuracy? From Hollywood? Naw, couldn't be. Carrere must have just liked the look of the downtown shot better, because the skyscrapers are silhouetted against the sky.

What is Sanders' beef with the movie? "Most everyone knows the story," he says. I only wish it were true. After the obligatory, sarcastic dismissal of Rand's work as "fervid, peculiarly airless" and "comically surreal," and a "parable," Sanders misidentifies Roark as an International Style architect, and he lumps together the Eclectic and Art Deco styles as the Old, and the Glass Box of Roark and Corbusier as the New. What really happened to the movie was this: Edward Carrere designed Roark's buildings to look Glass Box, over Rand's objections, because this was

1948 and the UN Secretariat was what Carrere thought *you* thought was "modern architecture."

Then Sanders complains that the windows in many scenes, framing views of skyscrapers in the distance, undercut the movie's theme: that Roark is trying to revolutionize stodgy old architecture. Those big windows, letting in lots of light, show, he says, that New York City does not need Roark to give it big windows. This is not true. In the novel, it is mainly in the Dean's office that Rand complains of stingy little windows and stuffy, dark, gloomy rooms. The well-natural-lighted rooms Sanders refers to are in Roark's and Cameron's own small office and Roark's later fancy office, and in Roark's apartment in the Enright House, which Roark designed, and most importantly, in Wynand's office. Cameron's office has big windows only because it is a garret, like in *La Boheme*.

As for Wynand's office having big windows, Wynand is a conflicted hero – just the sort you have been told does not exist in Rand's novels – and he has the money and the taste to get an office built for himself with a great, refreshing sense of generous light and air. The office, designed by Carrere, but probably to Rand's specification – she gives no description of the office in the novel, except that it has a table big enough for Wynand to spread out newspapers and building plans on – has three foci: Wynand's vast desk, his vast windows of great views and skinny mullions, and his vast array of newspapers. Hanging on the wall before his reading chair are today's editions of each of the papers and magazines in the vast Wynand empire. (See Chapter 7 on Wynand's convex world map above the hanging papers.) We don't see, in the movie, Wynand's bedroom, which Rand makes much of in the book, so she uses his office instead in the movie, to proclaim the man. The book describes Wynand's penthouse as topped by an all-glass bedroom, so he can tell his mistresses "We are fornicating in the sight of six million people." Glass allows Wynand to imagine his readers salaciously leering at him – architecture reflecting his bad side: his contempt for the public that reads his paper, and for himself for publishing it. But switching from the literary Fountainhead to the celluloid one – shortening the sprawling story and "telling it in somewhat different terms," as she said – glass becomes Wynand's means of both looking up and looking down: up at the skyscrapers and down at the mob. There is a balcony outside his office windows. Wynand can imagine himself looking down on his subjects, the men in the street.

Here, as in her dark, bitter unpublished story "The Little Street," Rand uses the "street" as a metaphor for the mean, petty, envious mentality, that does not want to rise and that does want to pull down those who do.

The light and the vast, open space of Wynand's office suggest love of light and sight, just like Roark, and the uncluttered look suggests a strong sense of *purpose*, just like Roark. Looking down on the "men in the street" shows Wynand's negative side, but his Roarkish office interior suggests his good side. The man who ordered such an office interior must, underneath, in *his* interior, be Roark's kind of man. "Mr. Toohey, don't confuse me with my readers." "Do you think I pick art works by their signature?" "Whenever I saw a building I liked, and asked who had designed it, the answer was always Howard Roark," says Wynand.

"Any man who comes to me is my kind of man," says Roark. When the two men meet, they both instantly sense that they are meeting brothers in spirit. This throws Roark for a loop, because everything he has heard about Wynand has led him to think the opposite. There begins their journey together, which ends tragically, as it must because of Wynand's inner conflict.

Now back to Sanders' *good* insights on the *meaning* of New York City as seen through the lens of the movie lens. On page 274 he writes of "an Olympian convocation of Titans," namely, the *Queen Mary*, the *France*, and the *United States*, the ocean liners that evolved alongside the skyscrapers in the 19th and 20th Centuries as their horizontal version, along with bridges. All three have been called the modern analog to the cathedrals of the Late Middle Ages.

Sanders draws a distinction between skyscrapers and liners, on the one hand, and bridges and tunnels and dams, on the other. The latter are great engineering feats (How do bridge and ship engineers feel when Roark's mentor Henry Cameron calls skyscrapers "the greatest structural engineering feats of Man?), but skyscrapers and liners are built to support miniature cities in themselves; communities; societies. You will spend five or ten minutes crossing the George Washington Bridge, but you will live on a liner for days or work or reside in a skyscraper for years.

Sanders mentions several movies that celebrate both the tower and the ship together, the best pairing being in "Sabrina." The climax of the story sees Humphrey Bogart, a high-powered Dagny/Hank type, in his downtown skyscraper hearing the horn of a departing liner. He knows that his sweetheart, Audrey Hepburn, is on it. After four or five horn blasts, he can't stand it anymore. He takes elevator, cab and launch to the liner. We are made very aware in this scene of the skyscraper as viewing platform. Bogey can watch the streamlined liner slicing through the harbor's water, but however streamlined his Art Deco skyscraper may be, on a building the streamlining is only an artistic touch. The building is not going anywhere. As long as he stays in his tower, Bogey can only watch as his love sails away without him.

Of course, a streamlined, setback Art Deco skyscraper looks a lot like a rocket on a launch pad, doesn't it?

The still picture Sanders chooses to typify skyscrapers and liners in relation to each other is a photo from 1965. You see the thousand-foot liners interlaced with thousand-foot piers. The piers stretch the streets and the dry land out into the Hudson, while the liners bring the passengers of Le Havre and Southampton across the ocean and right up alongside the piers and gangways. On a waterfront, the ocean and the land and the street grid are brought together and knitted together like the fingers of two folded hands. The viewer thrills to this demonstration of Man's power to move things around and make travel possible.

The photo is looking south along the Westside Highway, from the ship terminals of the West 50s to the towers of Wall Street. The Midtown towers are just off screen to the left. Mist envelopes the skyscrapers in mystery, triggering the myth-making function in your hindbrain. What goes on in those buildings that can only peek at us through all that Sherlockian fog? And we also notice that something is missing. A lot of buildings are missing. A lot of tall buildings are missing, close to the Hell's Kitchen waterfront of the West 30s and indeed all the way up from the Financial District. This is a 1965 photo, so the latest two or three rounds of floor-count upgrading have yet to happen. There are crops of 10- and 20-floor towers visible in the Garment District, but the same photo today would show new residential towers on West 42nd Street rising 50 and 60 floors. Not to mention the new World Trade Center in the distance! And now the West Side Rail Yards around West 34th Street are being re-developed and by 2020 our perfect eyesight should see those yards disappearing under a new Rockefeller Center spawn. This spread of 50-floor-plus skyscrapers from their natural habitat right out to the edge of the island will get touched on again in Chapter 12.

Another insight the reader gets from Sanders is this: the 20th Century skyscrapers, liners, rockets, and other big engineering projects were *im*personal miracles – Olympians to admire with lifted heads, at a distance, from the ranks of the humble congregants in the nave. Think of young Ayn looking up at the Singer and Woolworth Buildings as the S.S. *DeGrasse* steered toward its berth at Jane Street in Greenwich Village in 1926, and Raymond Massey at the end of "Things To Come" watching a rocket carrying the first explorers toward Luna. The 21st Century miracle is *personal* – the pocket devices that put, or soon will put, all the information ever recorded in your hand, accessible in seconds.

And what do you see on that palm-sized screen? Other people, individuals like yourself, being interviewed or interviewing themselves – that's called "blogging" at the moment. The accomplishments they talk about may be as great as skyscrapers, rockets, liners, bridges, tunnels and canals, but they as individuals are more accessible to you. You can't get to know Othmar Amman or Brunelleschi or Imhotep very well, because they were born before sound and moving image recording. You can know them mostly by their big structures. *Circumspice*! Their structures are our Abu Simbels, or the giant ancient sculptures of Jupiter or Pallas Athena, or Diana of Ephesus, or Buddha or Christ the Redeemer. They are to be looked up at with awe, by all us puny humans sitting together in rows of pews, all equal in our smallness and anonymity. But now, as we all blog and are blogged by others (Facebooked, Tweeted, whatever), we can all see a little bit of divinity distributed over billions of us. What Aristotle's city does face to face, the computer, whether palm, lap or table sized, extends throughout space and time: James Stewart, in Alfred Hitchcock's "Rear Window," can watch his neighbors in their windows across his Greenwich Village courtyard. Through technology, we can now easily meet people all over the world and do business with them, and get to know them and enjoy their performances even when they are long dead. And so the Temple of Man does not have a nave – it has a hall of mirrors. By meeting our fellow humans, we can't help but reflect on the fact that their achievements reflect glory on *me*. After all, I'm human too. And if I can see a close up of Yo Yo Ma's face as he plays, then I can picture myself doing something great, too – if I can get to that level of concentration I see in his face. Cities are Temples of Man. The palm-sized city of seven billion is a temple … of me.

"Whiplash" is the name of a recent movie that shows a lot of close-ups of faces deep in concentration in a ferocious quest for perfection. In this case they are the faces of jazz musicians, but the quest for perfection can be and has been illustrated in any number of professions portrayed in movies and novels, such as architecture and railroad management. "Whiplash" is popular among Objectivists.

Twentieth Century Art Deco New York City and Twentieth Century movies – the perfect marriage of a medium and a message.

NEW YORK NIGHT: THE MYSTIQUE AND ITS HISTORY,
by Mark Caldwell

Mark Caldwell specializes in unusual foci for books. He previously wrote a history of rudeness, for example. This time (2005) he puts together the dual themes of night and New York City. He surveys nightlife – bars and arcades and such – from Dutch times up to Nine Eleven. Don't trust his dates and facts – he refers to the fire of 1789, when he means 1776 – and there are more mistakes of that kind as his book goes farther back in history.

But besides nightlife, he looks for New York City's life of the night – crimes, seeking night's cloak to hide them, and the love that dare not brave the daylight, newspaper hoaxes – mainly the Moon Hoax of 1835 – and fires that started at night because smoke detectors had yet to be invented. And sex clubs, abortionists, the Stonewall, Hoovervilles, and so on.

The theme, in both cases, is that city folks are more likely to be up all night than country folks. There are people doing honest work on the second and third shifts, there are people doing things that require secrecy, and there are people partying after work – trying to squeeze more waking and playing hours out of the 24 in a calendar day. This is made possible by electric lights and other inventions, and also by the mere fact of dense population: If there were not sufficient clientele, there would be no night clubs or other late night or all night services. Being up late implies that you a) live in the big city and are brave enough to face its challenges and rub elbows with VIPs, b) are rich and don't have to work tomorrow morning at all or are either in show business yourself or have enough money to see a Broadway show, and c) are in a city big and brightly lit enough that you can walk around at night unafraid of lions and tigers and bears as your ancestors would have been in the jungle. All these add up to modernity, glamor and prestige.

This last is a deeper meaning than a) or b). It is one that might not occur to most people. But it might occur to Arthur C. Clarke. In his novelization of "2001: A Space Odyssey," Clarke describes a band of man-apes cowering in their cave at night. They can hear a leopard killing their neighbors in the next cave, but they don't dare take on the leopard themselves. They can only keep quiet and hope the cat is sated ... for now. And it occurred to Ayn Rand. In Atlas, at Hank and Lillian Rearden's anniversary party, Francisco speaks to Hank about the thunderstorm that is raging outside Hank's warm, dry house. Francisco points out that it would never occur to most of his guests to thank Hank for the roof over their heads. It would not occur to them that Hank is the one who has made this party possible, along with this house and the steel mills behind it all. Man has kept the weather at bay, and the leopards, and the Huns – modern cities no longer have walls. With practice, you can learn to keep deeper meanings like that one close to your conscious level of consciousness. That means that you will enjoy and appreciate even mundane tasks more, by frequently relating each task to the deeper and deeper levels of meaning implied by those mundane tasks. Next time you cross Wall Street on Broadway after dark, notice that you did not have to show a pass to a Dutch soldier at the town gate, or fear that he will discover that you are a Catholic. Or fear an Indian attack.

Caldwell's book is mostly made up of stories, like Charles Dickens recoiling in disgust and fleeing a Five Points house in which his guide had shown him the depths of slum degradation, but at the beginning and end of his book he waxes eloquent on the deeper meaning of night and the big city:

"Office buildings empty. Fluorescent cubicles blaze on, and in the early darkness of late fall and winter afternoons the towers become geometric clouds of imprisoned light, winking off as the hours pass, as if lonely for their occupants, gone home to their apartments, suburbs and exurbs."

"Under night's canopy or shroud, everyone, happy or miserable, wanders for a while, emerges into a brief turmoil of crowd and light, then sinks back again into anonymity and darkness."

"So the photographic record creates as much mystery as it dissolves. In one respect photography is by nature ill-suited to night: it needs light, hence has to destroy darkness in order to represent it. Yet at the same time the momentary materialization of figures and faces from shadow into fleeting illumination is the night in its essence."

That line limns Caldwell's book in its essence.

In *The Age of Rand*, I wrote about the meaning of not just the big city skyline, but the meaning, specifically, of the night time skyline. Those lighted windows mean that we are safe from the leopards. Modern man can turn night into day. Caldwell's quotes, above, add to that deeper meaning. He expresses the realization that Man can use night and darkness; not just fear being used by it. Darkness is useful in choosing how much of ourselves to reveal and when, and to whom. There is that element of choice again – the very thing that makes us human. Caldwell may be very surprised to find that he has contributed a book-length hymn to the worship of Man that will characterize the Age of Rand in the future.

"Fluorescent cubicles" sounds odd, since it is the lights that are fluorescent and not the cubicles, but Caldwell must be painting a word picture of cubicles that seem to blaze with light all the more after dark for having blackness out the windows for contrast. Picturing the nightshift office, I seem to hear a different quality in the office's background noise, but that may be just my imagination. Do office noises sound any different after dark? Well, sometimes the office is just quieter then, if there are fewer people about, and you can hear the refrigerator door shutting in the office kitchen when someone gets his midnight snack.

Helen Keller claimed that she could feel a difference between day air and night air. The latter felt heavier. I don't know whether this was ever tested. I suspect it was just her imagination.

Imagination! That is the key to the meaning of night, especially in the big city, where anything can happen. The subtitle of Caldwell's book is *The Mystique and its History*. What is a "mystique"? Webster says that, in an older usage, a mystique was "an air or attitude of mystery and reverence developing around something or someone." More recently, it has meant "the special esoteric skill essential in a calling or activity." Abba Eban, Israel's Foreign Minister, said that in Israel's early years, the reception and support of immigrants became the national mystique. And a "mystery" is something that excites wonder, curiosity, or surprise. Caldwell's theme is the wonder, curiosity, and surprise of night time in the big city. Surprising things can jump out of the dark into the light at night. But modern electric street lights can make you feel at once adventurous and safe. As the leopards slink back out of the light and into the dark, you can breathe a sigh of relief and say "What a piece of work is Man!"

And there is the "reverence" element of "mystique." One look at Caldwell's dustcover tells the story: As the New York *Sun* masthead used to say, "The Sun It Shines For All." But artificial light does not. Whoever pays the CON ED bill has to have a reason to lavish money on lighting up the Empire State Building in green for Saint Patrick's Day. Light, at night, indicates the intentional, the chosen, the human. You feel reverence for the city because it is where there is so much human activity around the clock that it makes sense to light the streets around the clock. And the signs in Times Square are such money-makers that they are not only lit – they move! And have done for a hundred years. Truly "Signs and Wonders." (Google the Tama Starr book by that name.) The dome of the Chrysler Building, with its Art

Deco zigzags, the whole skin of the RCA (now GE) Building, with its relentlessly emphasized verticality, and the lights left on in offices late at night – mystery! What goes on in that office? The closing of a big deal, perhaps. Reverence! If it is important enough to warrant late hours for lawyers billing six hundred dollars per, then perhaps thousands of jobs depend on that deal closing. Perhaps YOUR job! Light, at night, indicates importance. Something is important to somebody. A city is where a lot of things are concentrated together that are important to a lot of somebodies.

Why the airplane lights on the spire of the Empire State building? Airplanes. The land here is so in demand, because the people here are so in demand, the landowners have to pile up offices until they puncture the air lanes above, so they need blinking lights to warn pilots off.

And that intentional lighting makes all the city a stage – a realization more vividly true than Shakespeare could have imagined, and on a bigger scale. City life becomes Art after dark, and art means the chosen, the intentional, the human.

Here is theater critic Brooks Atkinson:

"Whether Broadway was beautiful or ugly was beside the point. Broadway was never intended to be beautiful. All Broadway ever hoped for was that people should feel livelier when they plunged into its "tonic light-bath," as Stephen Graham called it. Night was its natural hour. By day, many of the lights were turned on impatiently as if the proprietors could not wait for the sun to get out of the way. Nature was in large part eliminated from this vast, clangorous bazaar. Even on clear nights, the stars were outdazzled by the great flare of light that leaped from Broadway, as if a supernatural furnace door had been opened. If you hunted long enough over the building tops, sometimes you could see a pale moon moving through its lonely orbit in the sky. Like a discarded mistress, it kept its distance. It looked reproachful and humiliated."

(*Broadway*, page 178)

I quote that whole paragraph because it is beautiful, and because it shows that it is not just Ayn Rand who can "get all Ayn Rand" about night in the city. The feelings are universal. Otherwise Caldwell could not, or at least would not, have devoted a whole book to the subject.

Pretty eloquent for a theater reviewer. Notice that Atkinson twice uses the formula "as if." We will see in my next book how Rand used that technique to point out a new and deeper meaning in an ordinary event. The line "could not wait for the sun to get out of the way" recalls Byron on "that tender light that Heaven to gaudy day denies." ("She Walks in Beauty") "Nature eliminated" recalls *We The Living* on St. Petersburg's parks being mere reluctant concessions. And Atkinson's "supernatural furnace door" recalls Rand's description of the entrance to Wynand's Banner building. Be warned as you approach the furnace: important things are being done here. You are among adults and are expected to behave. Here, nature is being smelted into the purposeful, the chosen, designed, altered, built; the human. Especially in the Theater District, where raw sound is smelted into music, and raw experience into drama.

Heinlein makes the moon a harsh mistress; Atkinson makes her a discarded one. Neat imagery! Next time you walk down the Great White Way, you can get all Brooks Atkinson about it.

Incidentally, I want to congratulate Caldwell on his courage for using the word "niggardly" on page 118. Niggardly is a Middle English (after 1066) word of Scandinavian origin meaning "stingy." A niggard means a miser; a skinflint. Caldwell might get away with using the word in print because the sharp-eyed reader may notice that the second vowel is an A and not an E. But if you pronounce this word aloud, everyone will think you have used an ethnic slur. I have seen this happen. You could exaggerate the A sound – nigg-AAAARD-ly – but then your listeners will think you both a racist and a pirate.

This bothers me because in "niggard" I see the death of an innocent word. I like the word. When you hear someone use it, and he scrunches up his face and pinches his thumb and forefinger together and draws out the N, you can just picture a tightwad pinching that penny till it screams. But now you don't dare use the word, because you know how your hearer will misinterpret it. So I say: Use it often and be damned! Tell people what it means and maybe they will become curious enough to crack open that dictionary on the shelf, if they can find it under its coating of dust. Don't use your computer's dictionary function – those computers are the reason everyone says "so me and huh went to like the mall."

Here lies Niggard. Killed through a case of mistaken identity.

Back to our theme of night and the city. Think "night and the city" and I'll bet you picture a wet pavement gleaming in the street lights after a rain. In the movies it always seems to rain in the city at night. Now add your own mental music score to the picture. You thought of jazz, didn't you? For me, it is either Henry Mancini or the Bossa Nova sound of Antonio Carlos Jobim.

Bob Lind was a singer-songwriter in the 1960s. He had only one hit, "Elusive Butterfly," in 1966. But in "Unlock the Door," Lind weaves an atmosphere of city, night, love and loneliness that is remarkable. In Lind's imagery, night and city and the girl he is meeting, and his own character as a lonely itinerant songwriter (I'm a refugee from stagnancy and no one knows my name ...) all melt together into a single set of images. It's almost hallucinogenic:

I'm a stranger with no one to give directions to my side ... (He means no one to give *the girl* directions to his side.)

Your city lights are blinding; my defenses have grown weak ...

Come and stand inside the shadows, call me to your arms ...

It's a cold and ugly city when you're lonely …

And the best one: "But now you've faded back into the crossword puzzle night/ And left no hint of how you feel to shield me from the light …

Isn't that a great image? The "crossword puzzle night." Picture the side of a residential high rise at night, with some windows lit and some dark. Like a crossword puzzle! Maybe you can see someone moving around behind one of those windows, but you can't hear anything, so it's a "dumb show" (a Vaudeville pantomime). Think of "Rear Window." Lind's drifting songwriter, in "Drifter's Sunrise," says "And you look through picture windows and see families in their homes/ But as long as there's a highway, you will walk alone." That is a rural or suburban scene, but same principle. Robert Frost painted the same scene in "Stopping by Woods on a Snowy Evening." A single farmhouse in the country, or a whole automat full of windows showing the infinite reality show of people in their homes, with only you, the stranger, just passing through, as an audience … that's night in the era of electric lights. "We bring good things to life!"

CHAPTER 7
GRAND CENTRAL TERMINAL

This book is, in part, addressed to the New York City tour guide of the Age of Rand; of 2050 or 2100. When tourists come from the new, free market cities of Dubai; Yupik, Alaska; West Siberia City; Nullarbor City, Western Australia; Jupiter City (today it's just a well in Western Australia); Amazon City, Kalahari City, and cities on Luna and Mars, to New York, and want to see where Ayn Rand, one of the liberators of Mankind, lived, then the New York City tour guide will want to find a Rand-related meaning in every building and street.

(A *false* Age of Rand, if certain zealots, by 2100, persuade Mankind that, since Atlas was published in 1957, and the world started getting better shortly after, then *Post hoc ergo propter hoc* – After that, therefore because of that.)

So let's play a game. What do all these constructions of asphalt and steel and concrete and glass *mean*?

Grand Central Terminal is where I entered New York City to live permanently in 1977, and it was very likely where young Frank O'Connor entered New York, too, about 1920, from his hometown of Lorain, Ohio, looking for work in the movies.

People say "Grand Central Station," but it is a terminal and not a station, and here's why: New York City passed an ordinance in the 19th Century that no trains be allowed south of 42nd Street. Coal-fired trains on the ground or elevated create noise, smoke and sparks. So the north side of 42nd Street was just exactly as far south – as deep into the city – as the New York Central Railroad could legally build their terminal. And the tracks and the trains all had to go north, in a vast trench later covered over and called Park Avenue. So your train trip either begins or it ends at Grand Central. Across town, Pennsylvania Station is a station, because the tracks go both east and west under it. You could board a Boston-bound train in San Francisco, pass under Pennsylvania Station, and continue east to Boston on the same ticket. (Those trains were underground and electrified from the start, so they could be put south of 42nd Street. Park Avenue was not yet covered over when the first Grand Central Terminal was built in 1873. That terminal was replaced by the present one in 1913.)

Now, you can see how this seemingly trivial difference between "station" and "terminal" sets the listener on my tours up for another New and Deeper Meaning. So let's slap a coat of NDM paint on Grand Central Terminal and see how it looks.

If a rail node is a station, then it is just one of many along the line. On the Alaska Railroad there are stations that consist of just a set of wooden steps. Hunters get on and off the train there – if they flag it down in time. But terminals are confined to big cities. When you got off the New York Central at Grand Central Terminal, you had *arrived.*

Go down onto the platforms of both the suburban trains and the subway trains under Grand Central and notice the pipes – electrical, water, any kind of pipes. Never noticed them before, did you? What do they mean?

Pipes mean purpose! Google pictures of oil refineries. What do you see? Pipes in great profusion, but not confusion. The deeper meaning you can see in pipes is that they imply careful planning and design. Every pipe is carrying something somewhere, and in such a way as to be profitable, unless the pipe is owned by government. This, I imagine, is why Ayn Rand had a picture of an industrial plant on the wall of her study while writing Atlas. Every brick in an industrial plant, she wrote, is an answer to the questions *why?* and *what for?* Why should this brick be exactly here, and that pipe exactly there? Go to the south end of the Lexington Avenue subway platforms under Grand Central, and you will see as fine a set of pipes as any since Ethel Merman. But you can do the same on many subway platforms, and in building basements, and other places. Notice and appreciate these things. They mean Man's rational mind at work. They are *saving* yo' ass.

It is a pity that future factories may not have as many pipes visible on the outside, and maybe not even on the inside, because manufacturing will all be done at the nano level. Finished products will just rise out of tanks of the fluid that nano-machines squirt, one atom at a time, into place to build a … anything. Even the biggest factories will be disguised as cute little Disney fairy tale cottages, if that is what passers by would rather look at. And even if the architect and his client *want* to make the factory look like a factory, what might a factory look like, if it is clean and quiet and tiny? The ornamental motifs on the outside of the building will have to look like chips and memory boards, assuming even *those* remain unchanged by 2100. Know who already designed architectural motifs in the 1920s that looked like printed circuits and silicon chips? Ely Jacques Kahn. Did he see the future?

Finding profound, and even reverable, meaning in workaday things like pipes: here's a funny one: Michael Kimmelman, "Urban Diamonds, Forged under Pressure," *New York Times*, Dec. 22, 2015: "But the real scene-stealer is the salt shed, a 69-foot tall enclosed cubist pavilion made of glacial-blue faceted concrete in the shape of a salt crystal. … the director of special projects for the Sanitation Department [said that] because of its six-foot-thick walls, the shed could survive whatever cataclysm befalls New York, leaving future civilizations to ponder why we worshiped salt." You might ask the people in Salt Lake City who built and named their "Salt Palace."

Across E. 42nd Street from the Terminal once stood a little Art Deco gem called the Airline Terminal Building. It was where you boarded buses to the airports. Built 1940 and demolished 1980. The architect's name was John B. Peterkin, so he must have been Rand's source for Roark's "Professor Peterkin." Since Dagny, returning from Galt's Gulch, flies to New York and takes a bus into town from the airport, this building is where she would have alighted. Over the 42nd Street entrance was a giant world map. It is convex – it wraps around the entryway. Compare it to Edward Carrere's world map in Wynand's office in the Fountainhead movie. Perhaps Carrere got the idea from this now-lost New York deco charmer.

Ten stories down under even the lower level of tracks at Grand Central, deep in the bedrock and heavily guarded, are the terminal's emergency generator and alternator. The air intake and exhaust pipes for the generator can be seen sticking up out of the median strip of Park Avenue between 48th and 49th Streets. Rand was taken down to this high-security area when she was given a tour of the whole terminal in 1947. The New York Central was thrilled to see a popular novelist (this was when *The Fountainhead* was climbing the charts and the movie of it was about to be made) show interest in railroads as the setting for a novel. Their publicity people showed her the non-public areas of the terminal and put her in a locomotive cab with the engineer and fireman. They even let her drive the train – it was the Twentieth Century Limited, the train that set the standard worldwide for luxury train travel for the fifty years of its run. I am not the only Objectivist to suspect that this visit may have given Rand the idea for Galt's motor. Or if not the idea for the motor, then at least the idea of Dagny securing the remnants of the motor in a vault by the side of the underground tracks may have come from this tour. But there were several other factors that must have fed into Rand's "motor" device. A device plot device.

When they showed Rand the alternator, they might have mentioned that it was Nikola Tesla who invented alternating current. Or Rand might have mentioned it herself: she had decided very early in the planning for Atlas that her hero would be an inventor. She must have read up on inventors. In Hollywood, she might have met Hedy Lamarr – movie star/inventor. She might have made a list of inventors and innovators. She must have thought of Albert Einstein, who was 26 when he published his Special Theory of Relativity. She has Galt invent his motor at 26. (John von Neumann, another math and physics genius, had a theory that math talent peaks at 26 and then declines.) She must have read about Edison, but it turns out that Edison was very much the bad guy of Tesla's alternating current story. Tesla was the chief engineer of the Westinghouse Electric & Manufacturing Company, which competed with Edison for the Niagara Falls contract. Westinghouse won, with its new alternating current system. Edison spread lies to the effect that direct current was safer than alternating. It wasn't. By the time Rand started making notes for Atlas, alternating current had swept the world. Tesla had died in 1943, so his obituary might have been fresh in Rand's mind on January 1, 1945, when she started making her notes. Driving from Los Angeles to New York in 1947, Ayn and Frank passed through not only Ouray, Colorado, the inspiration for Galt's Gulch, but also Colorado Springs, where Tesla had experimented on a possible new source of limitless electric power.

Tesla's theory was that the entire solid part of the Earth must have a certain average electric charge, and the entire atmosphere must have a certain average electric charge, and the two should be different. So all Man has to do is draw current from the difference, and he would have all the power he will need for centuries, clean and nearly free. Man could use the whole planet as a giant battery. It didn't work. It would have worked, Tesla concluded, but first you would have to isolate the solid part of the planet from the gaseous part by covering the entire surface of the Earth with a rubber insulator fifty feet thick. But for that small technical glitch, we would have free, clean power today.

But another possible source for Galt's motor was Yevgeny Zamyatin's novel *We*, available in *samizdat* – self-published form – in Russia while Rand still lived there. One interesting thing about that novel is that the author is painting a future (dystopian, but not nearly as bad as some fictional dystopian futures) that comes about because Henry Ford, or some fictional equivalent, becomes a world dictator. He calls himself "The Benefactor." One World dictatorship by the Ford Foundation. Think of it – Robert McNamara – the same man who brought you the Edsel and the Vietnam War. In Zamyatin's novel, there is an inventor who creates a device that draws static electricity from the air and turns it into current. That is not what Tesla's system promised – it is exactly what Galt's motor does.

Now, Rand was writing a novel, not a physics textbook, so she was not actually inventing a motor, she was creating a plot device. And it was one that lent itself to a neat metaphor. Dagny, seeing the key men in the economy disappear one by one, hypothesizes a man she calls the Destroyer, who is somehow getting these men to abandon the work they love. She is also trying to find the inventor of the motor. Of course she never dreams that they will turn out to be the same man. She says that the Destroyer seems like the opposite of the motor-builder: the one turns static into current, and the other turns current into static, and stops the motor of the world. Here Rand is applying the "energy" metaphor of her friend Isabel Paterson, in her book *The God of the Machine*, where Paterson writes of the world's "circuit of energy."

When we discuss the New York Stock Exchange below, you will once again see energy being at once metaphorical and literal.

A third possible inspiration for Galt's motor can be found under Frank Lloyd Wright's garage. On that same 1947 trip, Ayn and Frank spent a weekend with the Wrights at their estate, Taliesin, near Spring Green, Wisconsin. In a bunker under the garage of Taliesin, there was a generator. It was built by the Kohler Company of Kohler, Wisconsin. Kohler has a very nice website, and it tells a glowing story about the company and its company town. (I don't guarantee that the workers there would agree in every particular with the company website's version of history.) Rand may have heard of Kohler (mostly it makes bathroom fixtures) from Ely Jacques Kahn. He designed a pavilion for Kohler at a regional fair in Chicago. Leaving Spring Green, the O'Connors would have driven east to Madison and Milwaukee. (See *Working with Mr. Wright: What it was Like*, Curtis Besinger.)

Kohler was a little north of their route. They may not have visited it, but Hank and Dagny did. After their triumphant ride on the John Galt Line, and the start of their affair, they drive from Colorado to New York, and Dagny suggests that they take a swing up through Wisconsin to see the Twentieth Century Motor Company in its company town of Starnesville. It seems that after Jed Starnes, the founder, died, his two sons and a daughter mismanaged the company into bankruptcy under bizarre circumstances. And thereby hangs the tale of Galt's motor.

During the Fountainhead years, it is possible that Rand might have bumped into Tesla himself. Between Murray Hill, where Rand lived from 1934 to 1935 and again from 1941 to 1943, and Times Square and the studio offices where she read novels and plays and stories and evaluated them for movies, lies Bryant Park. Tesla could often be found there in his last years, feeding the pigeons. At the southwest corner of the park, which is now called Tesla Corner, there is a small stone structure where the park workers keep the lawnmower and the pruning shears. It struck me one day that this little stone box, if it bore Galt's oath over the heavy bronze door, could have been Rand's model for the stone powerhouse of Galt's Gulch.

A point about Atlas that many people not only fail to get, but flat refuse to get, is that it is a novel, not a tract, and it is to be taken as myth and not too literally, and that the characters come from principles, and therefore, in the real world, few people are likely to be thoroughgoing Dagny Taggarts or Jim Taggarts. Most people have a little of each.

It was, as so often, Nathaniel Branden who explained this, in my experience. He said that Rand learned novel-writing by growing up on Victor Hugo, Fyodor Dostoyevsky, Sir Walter Scott, Mark Twain,

Edmond Rostand, and the other 19th Century Romantic novelists and playwrights. The way they created a character was to first think of a principle – one that the plot needed, to propel it – and then they would build up a character around that principle. They would give that principle a name, a physical appearance, mannerisms, a backstory, and so on, all chosen by how well those details would reinforce the principle and the way that principle helps make the plot unfold.

The New York Central Railroad Building, across East 45th Street from the Pan Am (now Met Life) Building, is where Dagny, Jim, and Eddie all go to work every day. Picture Eddie arriving at work in the morning. You can, can't you? – because Rand had such a talent for creating characters you can remember. Who ever has any trouble telling her characters apart? Literary types say she is *too* clear in her characterizations.

No wonder Branden said once "I didn't live in the United States in the 1950s. I lived in *Atlas Shrugged*." The characters in the book became very real to the members of Rand's circle.

Let me show you the dark alley where Dagny hears Galt's footsteps. It is still there.

CHAPTER 8
THE WALDORF-ASTORIA HOTEL

I don't think I'm going way out on a limb, I explain on my walking tour "Atlas Shrugged," to guess that Rand had in mind the Waldorf-Astoria for the fictional Wayne-Falkland Hotel in *Atlas Shrugged*, and the Noyes-Belmont in *The Fountainhead*. Waldorf-Astoria is a hyphenated name starting with a W. Rand sometimes made up fictional names – including her own – with the same initials as the original. Alisa Rosenbaum became Ayn Rand. J. P. Morgan was probably the model for Midas Mulligan. Mr. Thompson was probably based on Harry Truman. "Writers and criminals keep their initials when they change their names," she said. The Wayne-Falkland is described as the top luxury hotel in New York, like the Waldorf. In 1945, as Rand was making notes for Atlas, she was living in Los Angeles, and a movie with Walter Pidgeon was released called "Weekend at the Waldorf." You can see the Xavier Cugat number from that movie looping endlessly in the lobby of the Waldorf today. Pidgeon had been one of those silent film stars who could not get into talkies. Then he appeared on Broadway in Rand's "Night of Jan. 16." It re-started his career, and he always gave Rand's play credit for that.

Told that the eastern seaboard was finished economically, and that the west coast was the land of the future, Rand swore she would go down with New York (mentioned above). What Kurt Vonnegut called "Skyscraper National Park" was her spiritual homeland. Symbols of wealth and luxury, like the Waldorf, meant something to her. And despite the altruists' posturing to the contrary, these things mean the same thing to them. To just about everyone, whether they admit it or not.

In 1947, the House Un-American Activities Committee (HUAC) held hearings in Washington on Communist Party influence in movies. After Rand, the other Friendly Witnesses, and the Communist Hollywood writers all testified, or refused to, the John Huston-led "Committee for the First Amendment" flew to New York for a victory party at "21." It turned into a wake, since it had come out at the hearings that the writers suspected of being CP members *really were* CP members, and the tide of public opinion turned abruptly against them. Huston's group had thought they would be seen as champions of free speech by flying, with great publicity, to Washington to be the cheering section for writers *wrongly* accused of being CP members (see Jeffrey Meyers, *Bogart: A Life in Hollywood*).

Meanwhile, a few blocks away, the Hollywood producers also held a get-together, at the Waldorf. It was not a party. It was a strategy meeting. What are we going to do now? Are the movie fans going to stop coming to see our movies because they don't like the politics of the writers, directors, and actors? Is it going to work both ways – are we going to lose customers because someone on the picture is too far Left? Too far Right? Both? They decided it was: both. Any reputation for being political was to be avoided. Any writer, director, or actor with a political reputation, Left or Right, was likely to be box office poison.

If only they had all listened to Ayn Rand. But in 1947, even Ayn Rand needed to listen to the Ayn Rand of thirteen years later. For *nobody* did the HUAC hearings turn out as planned. Rand was hoping to raise the level of debate to one of principles – democracy versus totalitarianism. Free Market competition versus a command economy. It did not happen. By 1960, Rand was embarrassed to have been used by HUAC and not given the chance to speak about principles. The Committee for the First Amendment was embarrassed by the Communists who had, as Humphrey Bogart complained, used them for big-name support they did not deserve. HUAC's chairman got caught breaking some unrelated law and went to the same prison as some of the Communists he himself had jailed for contempt. And the Communist Party started down the slope to irrelevance in America.

Besides the Waldorf and 21, the St. Regis hotel figures in the drama (southeast corner of 55th Street and Fifth Avenue). That is where Otto Preminger, in 1960, took the executives of United Artists to lunch and announced to them that he intended to not only hire blacklisted Dalton Trumbo to write "Spartacus," but to credit him openly. The execs said they would not try to stop him, but they would disagree with him publicly. Thirteen years had passed. Communist writers were becoming a non-issue. Time heals all wounds. This was one of the first cracks in the Blacklist.

In November, 1947, a month after testifying, Rand published "Screen Guide for Americans." It was meant as advice for the producers, not for the viewing public. Her advice was: Don't be so ignorant of ideas that writers can slip propaganda (of any kind) into *your* movies without you knowing, or caring. Ideas matter.

The Waldorf was the last of the big Art Deco projects in New York as the Great Depression set in (except for Rockefeller Center). It opened in 1931. The *AIA Guide to New York City* calls the building's appearance a "sedate version of the Art Deco style." The architects were Schultze and Weaver.

"AIA" stands for the American Institute of Architects, or, as Frank Lloyd Wright used to call it, the Arbitrary Institute of Appearances. Rand was introduced to Frank Lloyd Wright in the Waldorf ballroom by Ely Jacques Kahn.

In the Metropolitan Museum of Art you will see a model of the Parthenon. Take a good look at it, and then enter Rockefeller Plaza from Fifth Avenue, and then enter the Waldorf from Lexington Avenue, walk through the central lobby, and then the passage to the Park Avenue lobby. I suspect that Wallace K. Harrison and Raymond Hood and the other architects of Rockefeller center, and Schultze and Weaver at the Waldorf, were inspired by the entry corridor of the Parthenon. You would have entered the Temple of the Virgin Athena, between the columns, and walked down a corridor with torches sitting in torchieres angling out from the walls on either side of you. The passage in the Waldorf until recently had lights that looked just like those torches and torchieres. Entering Rockefeller Plaza from Fifth Avenue, you walk along a series of knee-high fountains and pools, with shops on either side. This passage is called "The Channel Gardens," because it is defined by La Maison Française on the south side and the British Empire Building on the north.

At the end of the torch corridor, waiting for you in the distance like the Wizard of Oz, is the central chamber of the Parthenon. If this were a Christian church, this would be called the sanctuary and the torch passage an elongated narthex. Or the passage is the nave and the central chamber is the space between the front row of pews and the altar. In the Waldorf it is the Park Avenue lobby. There are giant urns, which would hold burning incense in the Parthenon, but are just for decoration here. In front of you, the focus of the chamber and of every worshipper's attention in the chamber, is the god this temple was built to house. In the Wizard's palace it is the Wizard himself, a spectral image of a stern face floating amid the colored smoke of his incense pots. In the Waldorf it was (until a recent unfortunate remodeling) the very piano of Waldorf towers resident Cole Porter. Indeed a holy relic of New York in the age of jazz and Hollywood, of Noel and Cole, of Cugat, and the Count and the Duke, of Art Deco architecture, of this building and the glamor of the name Waldorf, of Kahn and Hood and Ralph Walker, and of Ayn Rand. In Rockefeller Center the god is the titan Prometheus, a golden sculpture by Paul Manship. I discuss his symbolism in *The Age of Rand*.

These spaces for worship – the central chamber of the Parthenon, the Park Avenue lobby of the Waldorf, and Rockefeller Plaza at the center of Rockefeller Center, all have to be defined by some sort of walls or perimeter. That brings us back to the definition of "temple" as a defined, delimited space set aside for worship. In the Parthenon, the space is measured by four walls of surrounding columns. In the Waldorf, it is paired square columns on three sides and on the focus side – the piano side – the Park Avenue side – it is a giant window. Three vertical strips of glass, partly blocked by metal grillwork on the outside. And Rockefeller Plaza has four walls composed of … buildings! The RCA Building (now GE) forms the focus-wall, and the other buildings of the Center form the other three, with the intersecting streets and walkways forming entrances to the central, sacred space from all four directions.

The only sacred space to outsize the skyscrapers of Rockefeller Center was the design, by Albert Speer, of the night time torchlight parade ground for the 1934 Party Day shindig of the Nazi Party at Nuremberg. (Sorry to use a Nazi example, but as a design idea, it fits this theme. Deco.) Speer borrowed over one hundred searchlights from the Air Ministry and set them up in a square or rectangle around the parade ground. He pointed them all straight up, and after the sun went down he turned them on. The columns of light shone straight up into the clear sky, and the beams spread and coalesced into a canopy of light at 20,000 feet. The effect was "a cathedral of light."

That's why Ellsworth Toohey, advising Church and State, says "Go heavy on the trimmings." A light show always impresses the local yokels.

Light is important. At the other end of St. Pat's from Atlas and Rockefeller Center, on Madison Avenue, are the Villard Houses. Henry Villard had Stanford White design a set of five mansions for him, built to look like one Florentine palazzo. (Later, the Villard Houses would house Random House, and so become the birthplace of *Atlas Shrugged*.) Villard was an immigrant, a Civil War reporter, and a railroad builder. He invested heavily in Thomas Edison's inventions. Electric light was the wave of the future. The two men were soulmates, both described by Villard's biographers as "filled with ambition and brashly self-confident …

innovators who thought on the grand scale. To each of them, capital (of which neither could get enough) was like a piano or an artist's brush, a tool for giving form to imagination; each included in his makeup a good deal of the salesman and the showman; and both had their eyes fixed on a vision of the future." Now, that is what Eddie Willers is talking about in Atlas: Ellis Wyatt reviving played-out oil fields reminded Eddie of "the stories he had read in school books and never quite believed, the stories of men who had lived in the days of the country's youth." Light implies understanding, and understanding makes it possible to do things that have never been done before, and America was meant to be a home for the doers.

I mentioned Abba Eban calling Israel's reception and support of immigrants the "national mystique." Looking through the looking glass of not just Atlas, but of magazines like *Black Entrepreneur*, we can see the day when the reception and support, and more importantly, the stimulating and enticing and encouraging of entrepreneurs will be the mystique of the whole world.

When writers call anyone connected with Ayn Rand her "acolyte," as they always do, they are sending you the innuendo that Rand was touting a new religion. My ideas are truth – your ideas are irrational superstition. My ideas are shared by all the talking heads on Charlie Rose and in the *New York Times* – all those endorsing your ideas constitute a cult. Well, at least we can say that the Enlightenment has won. Religion and all the words connected with it are now words of ridicule.

But in one sense they are right about Rand starting a new religion. In *Atlas Shrugged*, Rand was writing the founding myth of a new religion. Or, shall we say, the founding myth of a new civilization, or a new phase of civilization. That's because of something you will have noticed in Atlas. After giving his radio speech, Galt is arrested by the government and installed, in great luxury, in the Wayne-Falkland (read: Waldorf-Astoria) Hotel. There, in one of my favorite scenes in the novel, Galt is questioned by "Mr. Thompson, the Head of State." Mr. Thompson is given no first name. He is called the "Head of State," not the President. Congress is called the "Legislature." No dates are given in the novel. There is no reference to Russia, to World War Two, to the Cold War, or to the word "Communism." Rand did not want to write a topical book, but a timeless one. You read Atlas through a slight haze or soft focus. It is not quite the world we know. It is a sort of Twilight Zone. That was Rand's signal that the story's time and place don't matter. She was writing myth.

In 1927, Janet Gaynor, who would later be a friend and neighbor of Rand's, starred in a silent movie called "Sunrise." It was directed by F. W. Murnau, who had come out of the German Expressionist School of moviemaking. An intertitle at the beginning of the film says "This song of a man and his wife is of no place and every place; you might hear it anywhere, at any time." Their characterization of their movie as a "song" tells you that the story is to be taken more rhapsodically and symbolically than literally. Also, the characters have no names – they are called The Man, The Wife, The Woman from the City, The Obtrusive Gentleman, and so on. The village in the movie's first part looks more European – women in headscarves, braided hair on The Wife – while the city, later in the film, looks American. But then the restaurant interior looks more Berlin Art Deco or Vienna Secession or Bauhaus. All these choices, and the soft focus and other touches, keep you from seeing this story as taking place in Tilsit (now Sovietsk, in Kaliningrad), as in the original story, or in any other particular place or time, and they signal you as to how you should accept the fantasy. This German school also produced Fritz Lang, Rand's favorite director. This is how *Atlas Shrugged* should be read – and how any Atlas movie should be made.

By the way, the waitress in the restaurant scene might be Rand. In 1927 she was in fact working as a waitress and as an extra in Hollywood.

Ten thousand years from now, people will be reading Atlas alongside the Iliad and Odyssey, and being inspired by timeless values. Atlas is a vehicle for worship; a paper temple.

CHAPTER 9
FEDERAL HALL NATIONAL MEMORIAL

Marxist historian Howard Zinn is often gleefully quoted as saying that the government of the United States began on Wall Street and has never left. President Obama takes orders directly from the evil schemers of Wall Street, whose government protection insures that they always stay profitable and never have to worry about a bad quarter. Take Fanny and Freddie, AIG, Bear Stearns, Lehman Bros., Enron, General Motors, and Goldman Sachs … please! Nothing bad has ever happened to them! Zinn was enough of a historian, I hope, to know that what started on Wall Street was not the government of the United States but only government under the new Constitution of 1787. Tour guides always get that wrong. They tell confused tourists year after year that New York was the first capital of the United States. I have seen tourists reply "But I thought Philadelphia was the first capital." The tour guide does not know what to say to that.

The tourist is right. Philadelphia was where the Continental Congress declared independence on July 2, 1776. Congress soon agreed upon an operating system called the Articles of Confederation. That system ceased in early 1789 when the new Constitution went into effect and the newly-elected Congress met. The Continental Congress met mostly in Philadelphia from 1774, when it was first convened, to 1785, when they moved to New York. Historians and tour guides skip over the first thirteen years of independence as if they never happened when they claim that New York was the first capital.

The building the tour guides are talking about was called Federal Hall. The building you see today on that site is not Federal Hall. Federal Hall was torn down in 1812. The existing building is called Federal Hall National Memorial (FHNM). If it were the real Federal Hall, it would be called Federal Hall National Shrine. The present building went up in 1842 as New York's Custom House. Later it was called the Subtreasury – it was a branch of the Federal Treasury in Washington. Since 1954 it has been a museum of the site.

The first architects to work on the Custom House in 1842 were Ithiel Town and Alexander Jackson Davis, America's first architectural partnership; the first American architectural firm in the modern sense. But they resigned when their client, the Treasury Department, insisted on squashing their planned dome down into the attic of the building, instead of leaving it sticking up over the roof as domes are supposed to do. Davis was the designer, and what he had in mind was a combination of the Roman Pantheon and the Greek Parthenon – a big dome and lots of columns. The client prevailed, so when you enter the rotunda today, you are under a big dome, but when you go out on Wall Street and look at the building, you say "where's the dome?" There is just a small, glass cupola atop the dome that does stick up above the roof, but there is only one spot on the street from which it is visible, and since 9/11 you can't stand at that spot anymore. Davis, after this meddling, said "My design has been altered by vain and officious persons!"

Town & Davis were replaced by Samuel Thomson. Same thing happened. The Department made some change he didn't like. But when Thomson walked off the job, he took the blueprints with him! So the Department not only had to hire a third architect (John Frazee), they had to pay him to start the working drawings all over again.

You might call this "*The Fountainhead* as written by Aristotle instead of Rand." Aristotle would be advising Rand: "You see, Ayn, when the Cortlandt Homes committee brings in Toohey's boys to add their own irrelevant and stupid changes to Roark's design, Roark (acting secretly through Keating as his front) could have just swiped the blueprints. He did not have to dynamite the building itself. He needed to take what was his own contribution – the design, the blueprints, the Formal Cause of the building. He did not have to blow up the bricks and mortar. Those are the Material Cause of the building." Ayn would have argued back that walking out with the plans would not have been as dramatic as blowing up the joint. This is a novel, not a treatise on the Four Causes. Besides, the committee could just get another architect and perpetrate the same ugly mess, and that would not meet the condition Roark demanded for his work: that it be built exactly as he designed it.

Federal Hall began as New York City's City Hall in 1700. Since New York City was, until 1797, also the capital of New York Province/State, the City Hall also served as the Provincial/State Capitol. But for five years, 1785 to 1790, it also served as the national Capitol building. All three levels of government – federal, state, and local – used the same small (by today's standards) building on different days of the week for those five years. Most of that time it was the Continental Congress sitting under the Articles of Confederation, but from March, 1789 until August 1790 it was the Congress, the Executive Branch, and the Supreme Court using the building under the new Constitution.

Every tour guide tells tourists that the statue of Washington in front of FHNM is there because that is where he took the oath as President. But on the statue's marble pedestal are inscribed these words: "Erected by voluntary subscription under the auspices of the New York State Chamber of Commerce, November 26, 1883." On the base of the bronze is the artist's signature: "J. Q. A. Ward. 1883." On the other side is the foundry date, also 1883. This sculpture was unveiled to mark, not the centennial of Washington's inauguration on April 30, 1789, but his arrival in New York on Evacuation Day, November 25, 1783. New York was the British headquarters in America and the last place they evacuated at the end of the War for Independence. Evacuation Day was celebrated as a holiday in New York City until 1916.

Notice that the unveiling took place on November 26 although the date they were marking was November 25. That is because in 1883 November 25 happened to fall on a Sunday, and in those days people were very strict about avoiding civic occasions on the day when everyone was expected to be in church. They unveiled the sculpture the next day, Monday.

Tour guides say that Washington's right hand is held out, palm down, because he is placing his hand on the bible. But the sculpture has no bible under that hand. Objectivist art historian Dianne L. Durante, in her book *Outdoor Monuments of Manhattan, A Historical Guide*, says that the sculpture depicts GW turning, after taking the oath, to put his right hand on the railing of the Federal Hall balcony and to acknowledge the cheers of the crowd. But there is no railing there, either. I think these interpretations unlikely. Washington was probably facing west, not east, to take the oath, and so his left hand, not his right, would go to the railing on this south-facing balcony as he turned. Try this at home. Washington had his right hand on the Bible and his left hand on his heart. He was facing Chancellor (New York State Chief Judge) Robert Livingston, who administered the oath. The bible, on a pillow, was held between them by the Secretary of the Senate. Would they have GW facing east, with the Secretary standing with his back to the railing and the crowd, obscuring the bible, or would GW be facing west, with the Secretary to his right and the railing to his left, so the crowd could see GW's hand on the bible? Now turn to your left and put your hands on the railing. Doesn't your left hand want to move first?

When the Chamber of Commerce hired Ward, they must have discussed their plan for the sculpture, and someone must have pointed out that only six years after celebrating the centennial of Evacuation Day, they would be celebrating the centennial of GW's swearing-in. Also, at some point early or late in the planning process, it turned out that the steps of the Subtreasury building were available and that spot was chosen – the very site of the inauguration. Should they depict GW entering New York, or GW being sworn in?

Ward, being an ingenious artist, must have said (I am just speculating here) "No worries, gentlemen – I see a way of doing both. I can give you a sculpture that suggests *both* Evacuation Day and Washington's inauguration." Here's how he did it.

John Quincy Adams Ward has a place in American art history because he was the first American sculptor to *not* go to Europe to learn to sculpt. He learned his art from Henry Kirke Brown, who had already executed a Washington statue, in Union Square in 1856, depicting the General on Evacuation Day. In that sculpture, Washington is entering New York on his horse, leading his army down the Bowery, which was the main road into town in 1783. He has his hat tucked under his left arm and is raising his right hand high to greet the crowd. His fingers are splayed, exactly as Ward's GW fingers are on Wall street, but Ward has Washington's arm stretched out in front of him and to the right and palm downward. Washington, then, has been depicted at the edge of town by Ward's master, but now Ward is showing him as he has just stepped into the fort at the foot of Broadway. That fort, Fort George, was the very seat of British power in America, and had been for years. The earlier French and Indian War had been run, on the British side, out of that fort. Now the British are gone. As Washington leads his men, on foot, into the fort, the British flag is lowered and the American flag is raised. The Brown hand raised to say "Greetings!" is now lowered by Ward to say "Halt!"

(Fort George was demolished in the 1790s. In 1907, New York's later Customs House went up on that site on the Bowling Green. It is now used as the Museum of the American Indian.)

Ward has Washington's left foot way out ahead of his right, as if he has just taken a step. But he is not leaning forward to take another step. His weight is on his back foot, his right, as if he has just taken the last step of the Revolutionary War – the last step on a journey of eight and a half years back to New York City and its fort and back to peace and normalcy. His left hand is on the hilt of his sword, which disappears under his mantle, his cloak. His gaze is level, but his head is swiveling. At the moment he is looking to his right, toward the Stock Exchange, and toward the fort. He is looking in the same direction his splay-fingered right hand is gesturing. With his palm down, he looks as if he is saying "Parade rest. We made it. We are here. The British are gone, the war is over, and it is time to settle down to normal life again." The people of New York City certainly would have seen it that way – they had been suffering under British martial law, in a ruined city with little trade or business, for seven years. Brown's GW hand is raised in greeting from his horse; Ward's GW hand is lowered in finality, and in calming.

Now stand at the spot, in front of the Stock Exchange, where Washington's eyes and hand point. That's the best angle from which to view the sculpture.

(Science fiction novelist Robert Heinlein, in *Stranger in a Strange Land*, explained the difference between sculpture and a statue: "Sculpture is art. A statue is just a dead politician." But here, both are accurate.)

From this angle, you can see something in the sculpture that GW himself cannot see, because it is behind him and partly concealed under his mantle. So climb up the FHNM steps and look at the piece from behind. That, after all, is what sculpture is for; what makes it different from a painting. A painting is two-dimensional. A sculpture is three-dimensional. You can walk all the way around it and see a different picture from every angle. From behind, we see that Washington's mantle is sitting solidly on his left shoulder, but has slipped off his right, and is now draping down over a short pillar or column, on top of which rests a book. The pillar is a *fasces* – a bundle of rods held together with leather straps. This was the symbol of power and office carried before officials in ancient Roman processions. It has been used many times in art to symbolize the principle that "in unity there is strength." It represents the union of the states. The book on top of the fasces is thick and has a spine with seven ribs – just like the Masonic bible on display inside the museum. That bible is the very one Washington took his oath on. So clearly this part of the piece refers to Washington's inauguration. But he can't see it. So when we view the piece from the Stock Exchange, it is as if Ward is reminding us that as Washington enters New York in 1783, he does not know that six years in his future he will be back in New York to take up his duties as President.

The mantle is always symbolic in art. We speak of the mantle of office, the mantle of responsibility, the mantle of power, the mantle of heaven. By showing Washington's mantle concealing his sword, Ward is saying that the war is over – time for the sword to disappear. By showing the mantle slipping off Washington's right shoulder and coming to rest on the bible, and the bible on the fasces, Ward is saying that power, on Evacuation Day, is about to slip from the broad shoulders of one individual and come to rest on the impersonal institutions of church and state. One fasces under the inaugural bible means one nation under God.

The posture of the tourists taking in Grand Central Terminal look like that of the Washington sculpture at Federal Hall: their weight is on their back leg, other leg forward, and they are looking around. But their faces show a smile of admiration instead of the inscrutable look of His Excellency. Washington (assuming the sculpture were where it should be for Evacuation Day: in front of the fort) has the almost savage, almost grim, but certainly solemn look that William Daniels, as John Adams, shows, in the movie "1776," when the last state agrees to independence and casts its vote. Adams is overwhelmed with relief, because it had been such a close vote. In triumph, he says "It's DONE!" and then, taking a breath and calming down, "It's done." Washington must have felt the same sequence, of savage triumph followed by calm satisfaction, when he stepped into the fort and watched the British flag come down and the American flag go up.

Now go inside FHNM and see the bible, the railing, and the paving stone Washington stood on, and see the sunlight streaming in the cupola at the top of the dome, and try not to find yourself burning incense to Athena, the goddess of wisdom and patriotism.

Oh, yes – the Bill of Rights, by the way, was born here. Introduced in and passed by Congress and sent to the states for ratification.

There is a Fountainhead quote I am seeing online a lot these days. It is from the Dean Scene in Chapter 1. Roark speaks of his plans to design buildings by his own lights. The Dean says "My dear fellow, who will let you?"

"That's not the point. The point is, who will stop me?"

In a way, that is the bone of contention in any discussion of enumerated rights. The libertarian says that all that is not expressly forbidden is assumed to be allowed. The totalitarian says that all that is not expressly allowed is assumed to be forbidden. Whenever government enumerates certain rights, there is always a fear that that enumeration will be interpreted as denying or disparaging any rights that were *not* enumerated. That's why there is a Ninth Amendment.

Rights are entitlements we grant each other. After all, who is there but each other to *either* allow or stop us doing what we wish? We respect each other's rights out of our own self-interest. A threat to the rights of one is a threat to the rights of all. You should respect others' rights enthusiastically, not grudgingly. This is just one example of Rand's insight that your rights, and even interests, at the most fundamental level, buttress, and do not undermine or conflict with, another's. Keep those buttresses standing – and even flying!

Akhil Reed Amar, in *The Bill of Rights*, opens with these words: "The Bill of Rights stands as the high temple of our constitutional order – America's Parthenon – and yet we lack a clear view of it."

Town and Davis and Thomson and Frazee and Ward couldn't have said it any better. But say it they did – in marble and bronze.

CHAPTER 10
THE NEW YORK STOCK EXCHANGE

When I have foreign clients on my Wall Street tours, I make a point of explaining that the New York Stock Exchange is not the only stock exchange in New York. Today there is also the American Stock Exchange and the NASDAQ – the National Association of Securities Dealers Automated Quotations Stock Market. There used to be another exchange across Broad Street from NYSE called the Consolidated Exchange. The American Stock Exchange was formed by those stock brokers who could not afford seats on the NYSE. There is a perfect example of free enterprise: Nineteenth Century America protected the freedom of those stock brokers to form an alternative to the Big Board. If your kindly professors had their way, anyone trying to form alternatives to the government's "democratic" allotment of money to new enterprises would be jailed. Most nations have only one stock exchange, although they are increasing these days. I explain on my tours that an exchange is a company, not a government operation, that provides certain services to stock brokers, mainly, a place to meet; a roof over their heads, the latest electronic equipment, and most importantly, an agreement to trade only with each other and with a chance for everyone to bid on every offer.

Above all other sites and sights in New York City, the New York Stock Exchange (as the biggest one) embodies the meaning of this city, and all cities. It embodies the meaning of money, and to that extent, the meaning of Man. Anne Heller was inspired and intrigued enough to write the second biography of Ayn Rand (after Barbara Branden's) by reading Francisco's Money Speech in Atlas. Rand, typically, throws an old cliché back in the face of the Altruist world by having Francisco say that money is not the root of all evil, but the root of all good. But in her zeal to pull the old switcheroo, Rand exaggerated. Money is not exactly the root of all good. Thinking is. But you will get more thinking out of people if you pay them money. The money is the consequence of the thinking. Actually, Rand improved on that old Altruist cliché (and the old "Money can't buy happiness." chestnut, too) when she said: "Money will take you where you want to go – but it will not replace you as the driver."

Speaking of roots, you have heard the word "money-grubber." Look up the word "grub." It means to clear the land by digging up roots and stumps, or to dig for something that is hard to find. Or just to toil and drudge. In any case, it means to do productive work. If you hear someone calling you a money-grubber, ask him whether he is morally opposed to doing productive work for a living.

Banks and stock exchanges, and commodities exchanges and any other kind of exchanges, are where Man's hard-earned money is sent to be fruitful and multiply. You put your savings in these places, and there your money is turned into more money. The job of the finance industry is to put money into the hands that will increase it. The politician, having taken half of your income from you in taxes, will spend that money in ways that are *popular*. The finance industry will put your savings into enterprises that are *profitable*. Invested dollars create jobs. Tax dollars create what the 18th Century called "placemen" – men who occupy cushy government jobs. The trick for voters is to let the politicians know that the "public good" does not mean more government monopolies, but more of our money left in our own hands to spend, save, invest, and contribute in ways that are competitive, not complacent. If you want your savings to grow, put them in the hands of businesspeople who are under competitive pressure, not in the hands of placemen.

The finance industry, then, is the heart of Economic Man. Savings gather in and are pumped out again – out to productive enterprises that pump the blood back to you, the saver, increased. It is a cycle. Cycles are a good thing. Anything that does not cycle goes one way only, and then it piles up somewhere. Then you have too much of that thing in one place and none in other places where it is needed. Gaze across Wall Street at the Exchange and breathe a sigh of relief every day that you do *not* read in the news of any blood clots.

Does this mean that the Exchange is the ultimate temple of Man? The Ground Zero of the meaning of Ayn Rand's New York? The object of Future Man's reverence? You're damn right that's what it means. That money, cycling from your sensible, prudent, patient savings to the Hanks and Dagnys of the world, and back to you with interest, is what keeps you alive. And not only alive, but filled with hope for a better future – and you get to define "a better future" any way you want.

In "Hello, Dolly!" Dolly Levi says "Money is like manure. Doesn't do any good unless you spread it around." Put money where it will make more real wealth possible. More choices.

If we can get the Wall Street types to stand back for a moment, at the end of the day, at Miller Time, and feel the joy and satisfaction of non-sacrificially helping businesses start, then we will have driven the money changers *into* the temple.

THE PERSISTENCE OF MONEY

The Firesign Theater produced a comedy album called "The Tale of The Giant Rat of Sumatra." It is a take-off on Sherlock Holmes. A great new source of energy has been invented called the Zeppo Tube. One character excitedly calls the Tube's power "a power so great that it can only be used for good or evil!"

That line is meant to be funny, but the writer may be on to something. Actually, any amount of power – electrical, moral, or any other kind – can be used for good or evil, and usually does a little of both over time, but great power can do bigger deeds for good or evil. It's not the power that makes that choice. It is you and me. People sometimes foolishly blame the power. For centuries, the Altruists have tried to make you hate and fear money, or have contempt for it. Are you using money, or neglecting the flower and letting it die? Or are you letting it use you?

Money is the result of the thinking of creative, problem-solving minds. Money is Rational Man making life possible. Money fascinates us with its power, even when we misunderstand its nature. Everyone has always been able to see money make things happen. It remained for Rand to show why it does.

Time zones were established in the late 19th Century, for the convenience of London and Paris, because that is where the money was at that time.

At Madison Square, I explain to visitors that the American economy was much more centralized in the 1880s than it is today. Wherever your company was in the country, when it grew into a nationwide business, you moved to New York, to be near Wall Street and the banks that lent you money. You either moved your company headquarters or you moved just yourself and you ran your company by telegram, by remote control. John D. Rockefeller – oil refining – Cleveland. Andrew Carnegie – steel – Pittsburgh. Jim Hill – the Great Northern Railroad – St. Paul. All moved to New York. Western Union Telegraph was started in Rochester, but moved to New York when it went national. But by the 1970s, businesses in Los Angeles that used to go to Wall Street for loans found that they could now get enough money at home in LA. The Big Apple was being challenged as a source of investment by the Big Orange.

As Deep Throat advised, "Follow the money."

Why did Martin Luther King call Harlem the "capital of Negro America"? Why did Ian Fleming, in *Live and Let Die*, call Harlem the "capital of the Negro world"? Because Harlem was in New York, where the money was.

Why is English the richest language? Rich in vocabulary, I mean. Because it came from a mercantile empire, one that had just learned the first half of the gospel of wealth: trade, investment, expansion. The second half would be America's contribution: immigration, free enterprise, competition and entrepreneurship and innovation, instead of safe, complacent, unchanging, government subsidized corporations like Britain's East India Company. The English language, already hybridized by Norman French on top of Germanic Old English, now absorbs endless foreignisms, becoming ever more varied and subtle in expressions. Rich economy, rich language.

Why did Shanghai never take Communism very seriously? Because it was China's biggest, most commercial city; westernized, cosmopolitan. Regimes come and go. Business goes on as usual.

Why did twenty thousand people suddenly show up on the Golden Sands of Cape Nome, Alaska? Golden sands, that's why. And they planned to stay, too. They quickly built an opera house. Money, even the hope of money, makes things happen. Gold! The '49ers of California. Manaus, Brazil. Melbourne and Ballarat, Australia. Johannesburg, South Africa. Dubai.

Why, in the 1969 musical "1776," does the conservative Congressman John Dickenson say "Most men with nothing would rather protect the possibility of becoming rich than face the reality of being poor?" Because that musical was written (by Sherman Edwards and Peter Stone) to put a "liberal" spin on the Founders. The "conservatives" in Congress are shown goose stepping – the writers' way of saying that if you don't support redistribution of income you are a Nazi. One of those writers, years later in an interview, gleefully said "And that's as true now (after Reagan) as it was in 1969!" But okay, let's answer Edwards and Stone's point head on. By "face the reality" these "liberal" (meaning "illiberal") Broadway show writers mean that you can never hope to get ahead under "capitalism" and so you must support politicians who will tax the rich and give you the proceeds, while making sure that no one can ever again get rich. Meanwhile, millions of immigrants have fled Statist nations of all kinds to come here and get ahead. What I hear every day on the streets and subways and in the cafes is young entrepreneurs making fortunes with newly invented apps. They are failing to be as helplessly dependent on the politicians as the politicians tell them they are. They follow the money.

Why did songwriter Randy Newman explain his song "I Love L.A." by saying that everyone wants to live in Los Angeles, "believe it or not." I know what he's talking about. Everyone makes a big noise about hating L.A. and preferring San Francisco, because it is more soulful or something, but Los Angeles still attracts more people. Besides the weather, L.A. is the home of the movie industry. Money. Glamor.

Why do the Chinese burn a man's money after he dies? So he can spend it in the afterlife, just like the ancient Greeks and Romans and Hindus burned offerings. When you burn something, it turns to smoke and rises up to heaven and the gods and the Honorable Ancestors. Similarly, in the flashback in Atlas – to the youth of Dagny, Eddie and Jim – Francisco, asked why he wants to make money, says it is so, when he dies, he can afford the price of admission to Heaven. His excuse for that silliness is that he is only about twelve. But he is already on to something. He equates virtue with making money. As he grows up, he will learn more clearly what that means.

Rand wrote that it was Americans who coined the expression "to *make* money." I don't know whether that is literally true, but we can certainly say that the American attitude toward money is one of respect for the entrepreneur who thinks up a new way to create more real wealth – wealth that never existed before. Just getting money, or just moving money around, is not the same thing as creating new real wealth that didn't exist before an entrepreneur invented a new product or a new service or a new, more efficient way of doing something.

Why did Nathaniel Branden and his friends form a fascinated circle around Ayn Rand? Because she gave them a vision of the heroic. But her vision was different from all previous visions of the heroic. It involved, not self-sacrifice and dying gloriously on the barricades, like Enjolras in *Les Miserables*, but heroically following one's own truth against unthinking convention, and being rewarded with wealth and fame and honor and glamor.

What made the railroads, and the whole American economy, grow so much and for so long in the Nineteenth Century? The willingness of European bankers to invest here. Political stability did that, and those millions of immigrant entrepreneurs.

The other day, I got a $100.00 tip from a couple of visiting Ghanian gold miners – and I didn't even end up giving them a tour. We discussed a tour, but the guy said, "Whether we take your tour or not, this is for you." A Franklin. I'm getting on the next plane to Ghana and signing up as a gold miner, if the miners are throwing money around like that. But I'm afraid they may have been placemen, or something other than the ones who do the actual digging. If manufacturers are in a "race to the bottom," sending jobs to the poorest countries, where the labor is cheapest, and if Africa is the poorest continent, then the race to the bottom is going to end soon. There are already signs of growing manufacturing, as well as mining, in Africa. When this sleeping giant awakens ...

I have mentioned *The Barbarian Conversion*, by Richard Fletcher, 1997. One thing that struck me in that book was the attractive power of money and its role in getting pagans to embrace Christianity. For barbarian kings it was not much more complicated than: the Romans have the money and the power, so I will worship any god they have.

Christianity was impressive, even awesome. Just the bejeweled robes of the priests, and the silver candlesticks and golden chalices, were often enough to turn the heads of hardscrabble tribesmen and their chiefs. Barbarian kings sought conversion because it made them vassals to the Romans, or later, to the Franks or Byzantines, or the Muslims, if they were on the southern or eastern side of the Mediterranean. For my money, it was the Church Lady types who made the initial advances of Christianity into pagan lands, assisted by the Post-Roman Ladies Who Lunch. (Google both.) The records Fletcher researched are all about men – men organizing Christianity after it had already been introduced. He hints that it may have been the merchants who brought the new god into pagan lands along with their fancy manufactured goods from the Med, and their wine and olive oil and other luxury goods. But I'll bet it was Mrs. Merchant who showed off her jewelry to the local tribeswomen and got them in the door of the church. And then it was the Church Lady who took over, ensnaring the casual churchgoer with guilt.

Commerce and Christianity rode together. The new religion followed growth in population and wealth. It turns out the early Middle Ages were not as poor as we thought. Because the parishioners would contribute money to the local church, the Church opposed the local chief building and richly endowing a church if he was building it on his own land. That church's presence would raise the value of the land around it, and so the Church naturally wanted that appreciation to happen on land that *it* owned. Altruism was their weapon: they would tell the chief that he was being selfish to build a church on his own land, and that he should donate not only the new church building, but lots of land around it, to the Church. That is how the clergy began the process that resulted, a thousand years later, in their owning one third of England. They had guilt, but Henry VIII had swords, so he just confiscated all Church land.

For the chiefs, power and money were one. Become a Christian and get rich – that was the way to go. Christian rulers seemed to be rich and

97

powerful, and pagan chiefs poor and feeble. Kill pagans for Jesus and get good farmland, was the advice taken by recently-converted Saxon chiefs. One converted king was bugged by some Church Lady type for continuing to burn sacrificial offerings to his old gods while attending a Christian church and putting money in the plate. He replied that he was rich and well able to afford sacrifices to *all* the gods.

The Wendts were a Slavic people living on the Baltic coast of Germany in the eleven hundreds. They were more resistant to Christianity than other pagans because they had a widespread, wealthy, organized religion and clergy of their own – same as the Christians had. And a big, richly decorated main temple – their Vatican. Why throw out one clergy and tear down one temple for another? Unless, that is, the new god seems more powerful. And He did, because His Saxon followers, with their greater numbers and better weapons, defeated the Wendts in war and captured their temple and tore it down.

There were conversions by threat and by bribe, as well as by the Church Lady. All involve money or conquest. Later, as frontier areas were organized as bishoprics, the bishops wrote down tales of heroic conversion and other miracles. Scholars don't seem to worry too much about having to believe them.

In the Catholic, Mormon, and Episcopal churches, you can see the effects of money combined with old, dignified tradition in maintaining and spreading religious (or any other) ideas. In the Church of Scientology, you see the effect of money combined with the fact that some people will believe *anything*!

In all these examples, you see the power of money to attract human energy and make things happen. That is because money *is* human energy, made visible and tangible. When you see a penny, or a check for millions of dollars, take a moment to look at those numbers with respect. The penny was invented by Charlemagne, as the wages of a serf for one day's labor. Look at that penny and picture the serf working from sunup to sundown to earn it. Now look at the check for millions. That check represents, not more labor, but smarter labor. On factory walls you will sometimes see a poster that reads "DON'T WORK HARDER. WORK SMARTER. IT'S EASIER!" That is the whole meaning of human life, right there. When you handle money, you are handling the results of human ingenuity. You hold in your hands pieces of some person's life, his time and energy, but mostly his mind and ingenuity and his success at solving some problem. That penny in your hand is *the* "life force," if that New Age term has any real meaning. Think of it as you would the Host in the Catholic Mass – the very body and blood of the Savior. The mind is the savior of Man. The Sign of the Dollar is the sign of life.

Ralph Waldo Emerson wrote that if a man builds a better mousetrap, even if he builds his home in the woods, the world will beat a path to his door. They will follow the money.

WALL STREET AS GALT'S MOTOR

Here's the point: Rand quoted an old saying that there is nothing you guys on Wall Street can buy and sell that someone did not have to grow or fish or dig out of the ground first. And if we, in the 21st Century, can get people to keep that in mind, then Wall Street will become, in their minds, the place where Man turns less, old money into more, new real wealth, and "Wall Street" will become a positive buzz word in Man's mind instead of a negative one. The Wall Street broker should be proud to be one of those who put your money where it will grow, just like a farmer sowing seed. He should be taught to contrast his way of seeing money with the Medieval way of seeing it. Moving money, through guilt and taxes, from poor serf to Church and State does not increase capital and create more productive jobs. The much-maligned finance industry does.

In 1997, Hong Kong's prolific Jackie Chan made a movie called "Mr. Nice Guy." The climax involves a colossal truck flattening a luxury home. But why? Mr. Chan knows his audience. It is pretty much the lowest-common-denominator types who go to action movies. He must have figured that his audience would enjoy watching a luxury home get destroyed. And I'm sure that, in this Altruist world, people enjoy seeing the look on some rich bastard's face as he sees his mansion destroyed. But that world also gets their secret, guilty pleasure gratified too: they just want to see a mansion, period. Why do you think there have been TV shows like "Lifestyles of the Rich and Famous"?

In Atlas, Rearden says that Galt's motor, as an almost cost-free energy source, will mean about ten years added to every person's life. He does not mean that the motor will make a fifty-year old live to sixty. He means that every second and every activity of your life will be more efficient. Ten years, in increments of seconds, minutes, hours, over a lifetime, will be shifted from drudgery to more rewarding activities. More of your hours will move from the "have to" column to the "want to" column because of Galt's ingenuity. That ingenuity, and those ten years of life for you, turn into money, and then into more life. Just like the 1979 John Stewart song "Gold," that speaks of singer/songwriters turning music into gold.

The writers of "1776" would say: "You foolish proles will have to get your class consciousness raised! You will never get rich. The only way you can survive is to follow us, to the Left. Collectivize everything – starting with yourselves."

Gold, or politicians' promises. As the libertarian slogan says: "1776 – 1984. There is no middle ground."

MOTIVE POWER

J. Q. A. Ward also executed the sculpture group in the pediment over the columned façade of the Stock Exchange (designed by George B. Post, and opened in 1903). It is called "Integrity Protecting the Works of Man." It was Post's idea, carried out by Ward. It shows Integrity as a woman, taking a step forward, looking straight ahead, and holding her hands out in front of her. She is wearing a winged helmet, so she is Mrs. Mercury. She appears to be holding something in her hands, like a spear or a chain stretched across her front, but there is nothing there. Perhaps there was originally a spear in the sculpture and it has been removed for some reason. (The original marble figures of 1903 were replaced in 1936 with lead-coated copper replicas, so maybe the spear or whatever it was disappeared then.) On either side of her are men and women working. One woman is pregnant, and may be carrying a sheaf of wheat or corn. Integrity is stepping forward and barring us from approaching or threatening the workers. Perhaps Post and Ward meant there to be no spear in her hands deliberately, to convey the message that Integrity is an abstraction; an invisible quality. But whether physical or abstract, Integrity is protecting the savings of these humble workers. The Stock Exchange must protect those savings or else there is no point in anyone risking his savings there.

The workers together are labeled "Wealth Producing Sources." To the right of Integrity are "Agriculture" and "Mining," and to the left are "Scientific Appliances," "Motive Power," and "Designer and Mechanic." At both ends of the group are waves, symbolizing the ocean-to-ocean scope of the national economy. "From Ocean to Ocean" is the motto of Taggart Transcontinental, and Rand uses, several times in Atlas, the metaphor of the body's blood system to describe the nation's railroads servicing the national economy.

That "Motive Power" figure's body is wearing a leather apron and he stands in front of a wheel. It looks like part of a generator or electrical alternator. He has one hand on the wheel and the other is holding something – a tool, perhaps? "Leather Apron Men" is what the Livingstons and Delanceys called carpenters, ropemakers, and anyone who made things with his hands and tools. Those two leading families, talking in the taverns of Wall Street about the Stamp Act in 1765, had to wonder what the Leather Apron Men, and the farmers and the sailors, were going to do next in this crisis. "Motive Power" is facing east, across

Broad Street, but he has turned his head to his left, to glance north across Wall Street to meet the level gaze of Washington. In fact, he is the only one of the workers to be shown looking out of the picture. It is as if he is saying "General, you and your revolutionary generation freed the motive power of Man; now watch what we are going to do with it!"

Here is a line from Rand's article "Requiem for man," in *Capitalism: The Unknown Ideal*:

> Terms such as "greed" and "avarice" connote the caricature image of two individuals, one fat, the other lean, one indulging in mindless gluttony, the other starving over chests of hoarded gold – both symbols of the acquisition of riches for the sake of riches. Is that the motive-power of capitalism?

And even socialist Richard Wagner has his character Wotan, in "Das Rheingold," very logically ask Alberich what all his gold will buy him, since Nibelheim is "joyless" – in other words, what's the use of money if there is nothing to buy? Galt asks Mr. Thompson the same question.

And Eddie Willers tells the track worker in the Taggart cafeteria: "Motive power – you can't imagine how important that is. That's the heart of everything ... What are you smiling at?"

There are two senses here for the expression "motive power." What moves the world, and what moves you.

Just as "Motive Power" and "George Washington" look at each other and create another layer of meaning more than either conveys alone, so New York offers more pairs of sculptures and other things that play off each other. We will cover this in Chapter 13, under the subchapter *DYNAMIC DUOS*.

AGREEMENTS

I've been called an "Ayn Rand acolyte" and such so many times I have had to get over being irritated by it. "Acolyte" means "one who assists the clergyman in a liturgical service by performing minor duties." But the original Greek word meant "together-path." One who walks with the priest, literally, to the church, and figuratively, in his career path. If writing this and my previous book is a "minor duty," then I am an acolyte and proud of it. But not of Rand, particularly, rather, Rand and I are leading you, the public, in worship (or at least appreciation) of Man.

Because of his ability to think in the abstract – to handle concepts and not just percepts, as other animals do – to put concepts into words – Man is able to make agreements. Two or more humans can agree in written language to do or not do some defined action in the future. Agreements, therefore, are among the most human of all things. I make my living as a proofreader at a Wall Street law firm. I make sure the agreements say exactly what they are supposed to say.

Nathaniel Branden liked to talk about "the sense of life as a sacred mission." What could be more sacred, more human, more central to what makes life possible for Man, than the agreements affecting thousands of people and millions, nay, billions, of dollars? The lawyers who write, and the word processor operators and proofreaders and others who work on these documents of hundreds of pages, that we crank out every day – what is more important than that?

CHAPTER 11
BATTERY PARK

On October 24, 2008, Bill Moyers, on PBS, gave us all The Line: that the Great Recession had come about because Federal Reserve Chairman Alan Greenspan had faithfully followed Ayn Rand's laissez faire teachings and had let the banks do anything they wanted. There followed a torrent of Rand-bashing articles on the Internet (still going in 2016) and mentions of Rand in interviews and elsewhere. A new expression appeared: GOING GALT. Some Rand fans – perhaps not exactly Objectivists – made attempts, often strained, to portray themselves or others as Going Galt – bravely turning down the State's phony offers of help, and learning to live independently. Since 2012 or so, though, I have not been hearing the phrase. That's too bad, because that image – escape from the oppressive Leviathan State into a world of Purpose – is just the vision that could sell Objectivism & libertarianism to the public. It means the refusal to be co-opted by an offer of placeman status.

(Nowadays, I always wonder whether anything PBS says people say or do is actually being said or done by those people, or whether we just think it is happening because PBS reports it as being so. Or maybe people start doing whatever PBS tells them they are doing. That is, PBS, the *Times* (and I don't mean the Podunk Times), *The Nation*, *The New Republic*, *The New Yorker*, *Atlantic Monthly*, *Utne Reader*, *Mother Jones*, etc. The Professariat.)

And sell it, mind you, not just to dreamy college kids, either, but to the practical, sensible "Joe the Plumber" types, who at length find escape from State power a practical necessity.

Millions of Joes are all around us every day. They drive your taxi. They just got off a plane yesterday, from Pakistan, or Russia, or Haiti. To them, America, and New York City in particular, is Galt's Gulch, writ large. They fled hither from tyranny, corruption and war, to the land of Purpose.

Their best-known altar is Ellis Island, but there are others. Amity Shlaes writes, in *Germany: The Empire Within*, about a refugee camp in Friedland, in central Germany. It lies just west of the old East-West border, and was built to receive refugees from East Germany after World War II. But it was again doing a land office business in 1991, receiving not only East Germans, but Volga Germans, Silesian Germans, and in 1975, even Vietnamese. Today it handles Syrians. It has a monument that reads FORESWEAR HATRED.

In Fairbanks, Alaska there is a monument to The First Family, the hypothetical first family to cross the Bering Land Bridge – the ancestors of the Native Americans.

Pretoria, South Africa has its Voortrekker Monument, to the Boers, or Dutch farmers, who moved inland from Capetown and founded new republics.

Sydney, Australia has a monument to the First Fleet, that brought mostly convicts, but also some free settlers, to Sydney Cove, the founding point not only of today's city of Sydney, but of today's nation of Australia.

During the Civil War, Castle Clinton, the red stone fort in Battery Park, was the immigration station (this was thirty years before Ellis Island Immigrant Inspection Station was built), and nearby, in the Park, was a tent in which the Union Army was recruiting men right off the boat.

One day, two brothers from Sweden, Sven and Ole, got separated in the roiling crowds of confused, non-English-speaking immigrants coming out of processing in Castle Clinton. When Sven found Ole again, Ole was wearing a blue uniform. Sven said "Ole! Vhere'd ya get dat nice blue suit?" Ole replied "You yust go in dat tent over dere, Sven – dey got vun fer you, too!"

Besides Ellis Island, downtown New York celebrates the immigrant with monuments in and around Battery Park, sometimes indirectly.

Engineer and inventor of genius John Ericsson was doing land surveying in his native Sweden when he was fourteen and too short to reach the theodolite without a footstool. He left Sweden – why? Because the Swedish Army rejected some engineering design of his – and tried England. He invented a new fire engine. Rejected. Why? Because the London Fire Laddies didn't like it – it reduced the need for … you guessed it – Fire Laddies! But he did meet Commodore Robert F. Stockton of the U.S. Navy, who liked Ericsson's design for a 2-screw propeller for ships. Others had built 1-screw propellers, but two counter-rotating screws work better. So Ericsson came to America and – the thing he is remembered for today – built the ironclad *Monitor*. He gets a monument in Battery Park, and one in Washington. (Stockton became the second military governor of California – that's why there is a city called Stockton in that state.)

But here's the kicker: Commodore Stockton's grandfather, Judge Richard Stockton, represented New Jersey in the Continental Congress. He signed the Declaration of Independence. Only weeks later, while helping a friend move his family out of the path of the advancing British in New Jersey, Stockton was captured by loyalists and turned over to General Howe's Redcoats, who put him in New York's Provost Prison, formerly known as the New Gaol, on the town commons, now City Hall Park. Half dead from exposure, he signed a parole and was released.

The Commodore must have appreciated the fact that through himself America was getting another genius engineer, another designer and builder, another man of Purpose, another conqueror of Nature, whose inventions were better appreciated in the New World of creative, productive work than in the old world of Privilege and Placemen.

The biggest monument in Battery Park consists of huge slabs of stone that list the names of every single American seaman lost in the Atlantic in World War II – just in *coastal* defense! On this monument, and on war dead monuments in every town in America, you can read the history of American immigration. On monuments that list the town's war dead chronologically, back to the Civil War, or better still, the War for Independence, you will see English, Welsh, Scots, and, especially, Irish names predominating. By World War I, Italian names appear. World War II brings bigger numbers and more mixing of nationalities. Not till Korea and Vietnam do you see many Latinos. By the time of Iraq and Afghanistan you might see a Muslim (ironically) or Hindu name, or a name from anywhere on Earth.

The sculpture in Battery Park that affects me the most is *The Immigrants*, Luis Sanguino, 1981. Dianne Durante does not even include it in her book of Manhattan outdoor sculptures except in a list of works whose surface texture she does not like because they show Rodin's influence. Rodin started a trend toward rough texture on the surface of sculpture. But the very rough surface of The Immigrants suggests to me the roughness of the individuals it portrays, which is the whole point of immigration. Rich people don't immigrate. Poor, rough, uneducated people do, because they need to escape poverty and lack of opportunity in the old country. That's why these figures look ecstatic to see the towers of New York and the New World rising before them.

Cue Neil Diamond's "Coming to America."

And behind these immigrants stands "Liberty Enlightening the World." "Give me your tired, your poor, your huddled masses yearning to breathe free …" Free to do what? Anything they want, as long as it does not violate the right of the next guy to do what *he* wants. Mainly, to leave a better life for their children than they themselves had back in the old country. And better – by any criterion!

In Atlantis, Galt shows Dagny one of his gold coins. It reads "United States of America – One Dollar" on one side. On the other side of the coin is the head of "Liberty Enlightening the World." Dagny asks under whose authority these coins are issued, and Galt replies "That's stated on the coin – on both sides of it."

There was a movie called "Harry's War" about a tax protester, played by Edward Hermann (who also recorded a reading of *Atlas Shrugged* on audiotape). An overbearing Treasury official (David Ogden Stiers) sneers to Hermann "I'm the United States Treasury! Who are you?" Hermann's character has no reply, which is a pity. I would have replied "I'm the United States. And I employ you."

Since Congress, in 1792, defined the dollar as a certain weight of gold or silver, anyone could mint such a coin and it would be a U.S. dollar.

A certain weight of gold or silver – that indicates an economy based on real commodities and not on a politician's promise to give everybody everybody else's money, while making illegal all the things those people do to create real wealth. And liberty enlightening the world

– indicating humans leaving each other free to do creative things, even though creation (enlightenment – the Light Bulb moment – *seeing* a better way of doing something) means upsetting the government-protected monopoly of some friend of the King's

– and do notice it is "the world" – not just America: the role of America as, not the *only* free country, but merely the *first*

– all these things are implied by Galt's gold coin. Golden coin – golden door. "I lift my lamp beside the golden door."

On page 303-304 of the paperback *Capitalism: The Unknown Ideal*, in the article "Requiem For Man," Rand rhapsodizes on the look on a child's face when he solves a problem. That is the sacred – the best, the highest possible. She mentions, both here and in *The Ayn Rand Letter* ("Perry Mason Finally Loses"), the cartoonist's convention of the light bulb switching on over a character's head, symbolizing his having an idea or solving a problem. (I am collecting examples of the light bulb motif in art and commercial illustration.) The Standard Oil Building, 1926, at 26 Broadway, has a lantern on top that used to be alight with an oil flame. It certainly inspired Rand's Frink National Bank building in *The Fountainhead*, and perhaps Wyatt's Torch in Atlas. The latter recalls Liberty's torch, and when Galt has to spend a night holding lanterns up in the Taggart Terminal tunnels, Rand has Dagny liken Galt himself to the Statue of Liberty.

Today, Liberty's torch flame is metal electroplated with gold, with intense lamps shining on it. Enlightenment – ideas, and the freedom to turn them into gold. "...the defiantly stubborn flame of Wyatt's Torch ... not to be uprooted or extinguished."

Now, immigrants or native-borns, doing different things for a living, will inevitably mean that some will make more money than others. But the need to go where there is freedom – the right, the Dream – applies "on any level of ability" – that is a phrase that Rand used. That is important because one of the myths about Rand is that her ideas are only for the "Talented Tenth" (W. E. B. Dubois's famous phrase). The writer of a blurb for a novel about an architect called the book "a Fountainhead for Everyman" – as if the original was not. For the janitor as well as for the Edison, Ericsson and Einstein, you have to be free to participate in an economy of constant entrepreneurship and "creative destruction" – that is, no placemen or government-protected mercantilist monopolies – if you want to prosper.

Between Battery Park and Bowling Green Park (where people played Tenpins in the 18th Century) is the 1907 Customs House – the Alexander

Hamilton Customs House more recently, and more recently still, the Museum of the American Indian. It was designed by Cass Gilbert, of the Woolworth Building, a model (I'm guessing) for Ralston Holcombe in *The Fountainhead*. It is the site of the Dutch fort that protected Nieuw Amsterdam. After the Brits took over in 1664, they named the fort for whoever was on the throne currently, so during the Revolution it was Fort George (as mentioned above). The Royal Governor of New York Province had his office here and his house across the street at One Broadway, and so, during the war, did the Commander in Chief for North America.

The first crisis of the Revolution was the Stamp Act Crisis of 1765. When the hated stamps arrived from England, they were landed secretly and brought to the fort in the middle of the night by Royal Marines. The stamps never would have made it there if they had been brought in broad daylight and the Liberty Boys had known about it. The Act had been proclaimed in the spring, but did not take effect until November 1. On that day, a huge, angry crowd gathered in and around the Bowling Green, facing the gate of the fort. Gunners on the ramparts pointed cannon at the crowd. Stand on the steps of the Customs House and you will see that you are looking across the Green straight up Broadway. So were the gunners. If the officers had panicked and given the order to fire, hundreds would have been killed, but thousands would have stormed the fort, killed all the soldiers, and started the war ten years early. Fortunately, the officers thought better of it. Contrast that with Napoleon's "Whiff of Grapeshot." Life was cheaper in the Old World.

Later, the Royal Governor invited the most up-and-coming young men of the province to a fancy dinner at the fort. Among them was Philip van Cortlandt, later to make a distinguished record in the revolutionary army throughout the war. The Governor made these young men tempting offers of "preferment," that is, cushy government jobs, if they would remain loyal to the King.

That is what politics is about, and all it is about. Once you foolishly give a man a title like "King" and give him the power to tax, then, to stay in power, he bribes you with jobs. He makes you a placeman. Government is a business. You keep me in power, says the King, and I give you a job preventing the poor from practicing competitive free enterprise. Fort George, just from that little-known dinner anecdote alone, ought to be on every coin issued by a King ... or by a revolutionary government. That's why immigrants immigrate. That's why this *is* Galt's Gulch.

Inside little Bowling Green Park, New York's oldest and smallest, is a small stone that reads:

PETER CAESAR ALBERTI
FIRST ITALIAN SETTLER
LANDED IN NEW YORK
JUNE 2, 1635

Of course, the Italian Historical Society should have said "Nieuw Nederland" and not New York, for the colony, or "Nieuw Amsterdam" for the city.

(Update: That monument has now disappeared from the Bowling Green and re-appeared in front of an Italian restaurant on Grand Street in Little Italy. No kapish.)

In May of 2015, in Miami, I saw a TV commercial that sounded Objectivist, but maybe not perfectly so. I did not even catch what is was for – this happens a lot: many commercials are so artsy, and flash images so fast, that I don't get what it is they are advertising. It started with pictures of ordinary people. The voice-over says "These are the kings and queens of America. In this country, there is no royalty. Everything is out there. [something about ambitious and smart people seeing an opportunity] And when they see it, they take it."

In a century, perhaps it will not be necessary to make the point that being free to take opportunities makes you like a king of old. Some latter-day Huey Long will not even think of the "king" comparison. (Governor and Senator Long of Louisiana, in the 1930s, used the slogan "Every Man a King.") The glamor of royalty is fading even now. In the future, living like a king will just be called "normal." The expression "the conquest of space" has been used a lot over the years. It is another example of people using comparisons they get from old, familiar concepts such as monarchy and war. Exploring and settling space does not mean "conquering" it. You conquer, that is, you overcome, a specific problem in space travel, that's all.

Noel Coward made his first trip to the States in 1924. He knew no one here, and no one knew him. But the theater producers knew of his successful play in London, "The Vortex."

Wow. Imagine coming to a new country and having no one here to welcome you. No friends, no relatives. Just a calling card. But a calling card that says that you are a comer, and perhaps a genius. He got his play produced here, that is, after angrily walking out on the biggest producer in town because that producer wanted to completely change and water down Coward's play. Coward was no coward. This was his "Howard Roark Moment." Remember the scene where Roark turns down a career-making commission for a major bank building because the Board wants changes that will make his building look ridiculous? Also his "Galt Going on Strike Moment." I think of Coward's autobiography every time I'm in Battery Park. On that first trip, before things started going his way, the young playwright says he spent a lot of time sitting in parks, especially this one, wondering what in hell he was going to do to pay the rent. Years later, he remembered doing "a lot of shoulder-squaring" in Battery Park – because from the park benches he could see many ships – many more than today, almost a hundred years later – passing in and out of the harbor. Some of them would be going to England. He could not go home on one of those ships until he could justify the trip with a Broadway production with his name in lights.

If Coward was still sitting on that Battery Park bench a year and a half after arriving himself, he might have seen a ship of the French Line, the *DeGrasse*, steaming through the harbor between him and the Statue of Liberty, bringing another hopeful young writer and a future fan of his, Alisa Rosenbaum.

CHAPTER 12
THE GRID

Here's why the Grid rates a whole chapter for itself: It makes a city *of* the island, not just a city *on* an island. And more so as the skyscrapers spread from the Battery, and from the 1873 Grand Central Terminal near the center of Midtown, out to the edges of the island. That spread looks like Gordon Bunshaft's plaza of white Travertine marble spreading out from the walls of the Marine Midland Bank Building (Block of Broadway-Nassau-Cedar-Liberty Streets) all the way to the curbs on all four sides of the block.

Here is what Bunshaft was trying to do; the effect he was going for. The building was to take up a whole block, but the bank was willing to be wasteful of ground and not fill up its lot all the way out to the curb on all four sides. It was willing to have a wide sidewalk all around, especially on the Broadway side, where Bunshaft planned a broad plaza. But that sidewalk and plaza were to be visually part of the project: They were made of white Travertine marble, and that marble was to cover every inch of the block from the four walls of the building out to the four curbs. This creates the impression that the whole block is Bunshaft's canvas – it is white, although horizontal, unlike a canvas standing up on an easel – and by stretching out to the curb, that Travertine looks like a canvas stretched on the four curbs as on the wooden frame that a real canvas is stretched on. Bunshaft is saying: "Here is my blank canvas, and the building itself is my painting, except that being architecture and not real painting, it is bursting up out of the two-dimensional surface of the canvas into the third dimension."

Now hold that canvas-stretching picture in your head and expand it to the whole island of Manhattan. Two miles wide and twelve miles long. When I first laid eyes on the Grid, in the entry on New York City in the Golden Book Encyclopedia, circa 1960, what impressed the heck out of me was the fact that the Grid ran all the way out to the water in all directions. That's what I mean by a city of the island and not just on the island. The Street Commissioners of 1807 were taking no prisoners. There were parks, of course, but they were like Saint Petersburg's parks as Rand describes them in *We The Living*: "reluctant concessions."

Lately, people have been gathering on the 42nd Street viaduct of Park Avenue, in front of Grand Central Terminal, on certain days in the spring and fall, to watch the sun go down at the other end of 42nd street. They call this semiannual event "Manhattan Henge." It highlights something very special about the Grid: since the numbered streets go all the way across the island from river to river, you can see through all the skyscrapers, in one side of the borough and out the other. If you know to look for this effect, it helps to alleviate the sense of being lost in an endless city. Helen Mirren does not know about this. In an interview at the time she played the title role in the movie "The Passion of Ayn Rand," she gave her impression of coming to New York City. She said that you land in a plane, you get in a taxi, you get out of the taxi and you are in a building in midtown Manhattan. It feels to her as though she has been let into a castle and the gate has closed behind her. But that is because she has not used the Grid to see through the buildings. You don't have to feel completely enclosed by those buildings; that's the beauty of the long, straight streets and avenues of the Grid. She needs to do Manhattan Henge. She needs to look across to Weehawken from the fantail of the *Intrepid*. She needs to go to the Jersey side of the Hudson and look back. She needs to ride the 7 train at sunrise, with the rising sun at her back, lighting up Manhattan as seen from Queens. Helen should not mind coming to Queens; she has played so many of them.

The skyscraper skyline extends the grid up into the third dimension, just as Bunshaft did with Marine Midland. If you miss Helen Mirren's dawn train, take the 7 into Queens just before sundown. As you emerge from under the East River, you turn north briefly, and so you march along with the Grid. You can see exactly what the Manhattan Henge photographers are looking for: as you pass 48th Street, you will see the sunset right down on street level for just a second. You are looking clear across Manhattan Island, through the skyscrapers, on the line of 48th. And just as you locate an office or apartment in two dimensions on the Grid, you now see how the floors of the skyscrapers, and the elevators that service them, become another Grid: a vertical one. You are reminded that those buildings are that tall for purely dollars-and-sense reasons. They are built taller because the land under them is in more demand than other, less glamorous locations, and that land value, in turn, is caused by the demand for the services of the men and women who work there. These are the Atlases of the business world that sustains you and me, and to be close to them is worth a lot of money to other office workers, and makes them both able and willing to pay top dollar for the privilege of proximity – not to power, but to the power to build and create.

The skyscraperline has already been given a new layer of meaning in *The Age of Rand*, but here is a strange way of adding yet another. The skyline is the Anti-Holocaust. Just as that dark chapter in history showed Man the depths of which he might be capable, so the skyline shows us the heights – literally.

Olmstead and Vaux did not like the way the City conformed their Central Park to the Grid. A park is for strolling, relaxing, and maybe even getting lost in. It should be an escape from the Grid. Not that the Grid is bad, but while we are all depending on the Grid to ease our navigation, we need to have a periodic change of scenery. We have to, every weekend or so, get off the Grid, think outside the box, and be reminded of what life was like for our ancestors before the Grid. Olmstead and Vaux's favorite of all the city parks they designed around the country was Brooklyn's Prospect Park, because it has an irregular shape. As you walk deeper into the park, away from Prospect Park West and Grand Army Plaza at the park's northwest corner, you have trouble guessing which way you are headed, and which street you will emerge at on the south and east sides of the park. That's the whole point.

Want to see a model of a skyscraper city grid? Go out to your kitchen. Bring back your plastic ice cube tray. I'll wait.

Hold the tray upside down. There's your grid of numbered streets, seven of them, separating two rows of eight skyscrapers. These skyscrapers are short and stumpy, so they might have been designed by Ely Jacques Kahn, for reasons I explain in *The Age of Rand*. Separating the two rows of eight skyscrapers is a long, north-south avenue.

Now flex the tray. Yes, the ice cubes fell out, ya dummy – you should have used an empty tray. Hold the upside-down flexed tray up to the light. There is your Manhattan Henge.

Now turn the tray right side up. There you see the basements of invisible buildings, or the excavations for buildings yet to come. You can also see why archeology is almost impossible in the oldest, most archeologically rewarding part of the city – the site of old Nieuw Amsterdam. There is no original ground to do archeology *in*. It has all been dug and re-dug many times for four hundred years. What about under the streets themselves? Same problem – dug and re-dug, for the spaghetti bowl of water, sewage, electrical, pneumatic, fiber optic, and other lines. And subway tunnels.

If a series of gravel quarries, say, get re-developed as a city, then you might see those ice cube buckets become buildings, but buildings with only negative floor numbers. The building will scrape the granite pluton (the bedrock's bedrock), not the sky. On top will be all parkland. Next time you stroll through Central or any other well-used city park, imagine that all those other strollers just came up from buildings built entirely underground. And likewise the ice cream man and the piragua man and the juggler and the caricaturist.

That's why I don't think Isaac Asimov's "caves of steel" will come true. In that novel, written in 1953, Earth's office, factory, residential, and shopping buildings have grown into continuous malls – as we should have called them thirty years later. A whole city is enclosed in one big dome. Everyone is so used to living indoors that when a character is asked how he would like to have to walk for a whole mile out in the open, he shudders with horror.

Asimov himself was a self-described "claustrophile." He said that it took him a while to realize that not everyone would want to live indoors all the time. It's true – people like sunshine and trees and grass and the sound of the wind in the willows. Central Park in the summer, vast crowds enjoying the outdoors, milling around – now just picture fifty or a hundred stories of apartments under it. Like the first episode of "The Time Tunnel." Imagine walking down a flight of steps from Strawberry Fields, ringing for the elevator, and looking over a railing into a chasm a hundred stories deep, lined with apartments, and looking into the windows of those apartments, filled with Central Park underdwellers. Central Park all by itself is one of my favorite cities.

Now put those ice cube trays back in the freezer and take out an ear of corn. As you eat it, turn the ear up on one end. How many architects have thought about apartment high-rises, round, and with all bay windows – while eating corn on the cob? Maybe Chicago's Marina City?

(Marina City complex was designed by Bertrand Goldberg, a student of Mies van der Rohe, and opened in 1964. It was the first building in the United States built with tower cranes. It was financed largely by the unions of janitors and elevator operators, to discourage white flight to the low-rise suburbs. There was the rejection of class conflict theory, and a triumph of enlightened self-interest on the part of unions with some bucks.)

Now, while your ice cubes are freezing solid in their little buckets, let me take you to a synagogue, where the rabbi is pointing to the negative relief of the Ten Commandments, in Hebrew letters, incised into the wall behind him. He is explaining that when God is being worshipped, and the congregants are reading the Commandments, the spirit of God, or the spirit of His words, or something, comes down from Heaven and fills in those negative relief spaces in the wall. What was just a human construction, an art work, a mere representation of the Word, now becomes the actual Word itself. I heard that very explanation from a rabbi in Los Angeles.

Maybe I have been staring at maps too long, but somehow that image came to my mind when I was doodling a city plan. If a city begins as a crossroads, then it is starting life as a node ("node" means "knot") of radials. A grid of city streets might be planned around the crossroads if the place grows from village to city. But then more radial avenues might be added. No sooner does the city government lay out more radials, though, than more surrounding farmland has to be gridded up for residential side streets in the burgeoning metropolis. Radials, grid, radials, grid, expanding outwards in all directions. The original crossroads may be completely removed, to be replaced with wider streets. That has happened to Brooklyn. Where Adams, Joralemon, Willoughby and Fulton Streets come together – that's where the original five-way intersection stood, that was the whole village of Brooklyn in 1776.

Since those radials are bringing traffic into the city center, where are all those cars and pedestrians going to go? The radials can't just keep converging, with their traffic, into a black hole. So, to relieve the crowding, you distribute the traffic around a traffic circle, or roundabout, and you further distribute it around the grid. The grid then becomes the empty space that is filled in with the traffic, the bustle, the lives and, shall we say, the living Word of Man. Regular blocks preventing the great attracter, the city's CBD, from collapsing into infinite density.

The point where the Grid really starts to speak to the avid map-gazer about new and deeper meanings is the point where the city gets big enough to develop districts. The CBD, the Middle City, or residential zone, and the outer industrial belt and green belt and suburban belt – those are the basic, gross anatomy of the city. But the bigger cities will grow, at or near downtown, a theater district, a waterfront district (if there is a waterfront), a university district, a hospital district (Manhattan's First Avenue), a financial district (right at real estate value Ground Zero), and of course the Red Light District. There are ethnic neighborhoods, like Syracuse's Irish Tipperary Hill and Brooklyn's Vinegar Hill. A city may also grow a set of specialty districts all its own: Buffalo's Fruit Belt (a grid of streets with names of fruit trees), and the Hydraulics (Buffalo's first industrial district, 1827, where tanneries and grist mills were powered by the Hydraulic Canal), and Manhattan's Butter and Egg District, Meatpacking District, and Wholesale Flower District, all located along the Hudson River, because ferries would bring New Jersey farm produce across the river in the 19th Century. The development of specialized districts within a city is like the evolution of the structures within the cell, or the organs of the body. They make it possible for the tour guide to say "Park Row was Newspaper Row from about 1830 to about 1950. But why? Because Park Row was between the two big sources of news: City Hall, the courts and the jails, to the north, and the waterfront to the southeast, where ships came in bringing the latest newspapers from Europe."

I am still noticing today the widespread trope, or image, of the skyscraper and skyline in the commercial art on the sides of delivery trucks and store signs in New York. As if New York had a monopoly on skyscrapers, in this day of Dubai's Burj Khalifa and Kuala Lumpur's Petronas Towers! New York is no longer the only – but it was the first (except for Chicago).

CHAPTER 13
STATIONS OF THE DOLLAR SIGN

In Mecca the Haji makes the rounds of sites that teach the lessons of Islam. Here, we have paid particular attention to Grand Central, the Waldorf, Federal Hall National Memorial, the New York Stock Exchange, and Battery Park, and now we will briefly note some other sites that will bring a catch to the throats of all who worship Creative Man.

ROCKEFELLER CENTER

Rockefeller Center is one of the world's great Art Deco showpieces. Man worship is everywhere.

At the 6th Avenue entrance to the RCA Building (today the GE Building), the centerpiece of the Center, there is a mosaic over the door by Barry Faulkner called "Intelligence Awakening Mankind." Intelligence stands floating in the air, surrounded by smaller human figures doing things that require intelligence. Her eyes are looking down. Now that could suggest sadness, if this were a picture of tragedy, but since Faulkner's theme is Intelligence, I'm guessing that the downward glance is meant to suggest concentration and so, thought. Her arms are outstretched, palms up. That's interesting because that is the attitude of many representations of Christ, such as Christ the Redeemer, the giant Art Deco sculpture in Rio de Janeiro, on Corcovado Mountain. For Intelligence, the palms-up gesture might be interpreted as being what most people do when they are giving an explanation that they think, rightly or wrongly, is brilliant and answers all questions once and for all. "Q. E. D.!" But Christ, his followers tell us, offers us all redemption from sin. He is the great EMS of the universe – the Search and Rescue hero who has come to save us all from damnation. He offers us redemption for free … except for the quid pro quo of believing in him. The outstretched arms, palms up, are a gesture of offering, or of welcome. "Come home to me! Take the salvation I offer!"

Well, isn't Intelligence Awakening Mankind doing the same thing – secular style? "Use your own nature as the animal that thinks," she says, "and the whole world is yours. Take it!" She could be John Galt, saying, toward the end of his speech, "*The world you desired can be won, it exists, it is real, it is possible, it's yours.*" (a deservedly well-loved line)

Sculptor Lee Lawrie, who also did Atlas elsewhere in Rockefeller Center, sculpted a negative relief over the east entrance to the RCA Building, facing Rockefeller Plaza (the Parthenon sanctuary, see Chapter 8) and the Prometheus Fountain (by Paul Manship). The relief is called "Wisdom." Lawrie copied it from the frontispiece of William Blake's 1794 book *Europe: A Prophecy*. It shows an old man with a long white beard leaning out from behind and over a cloud. Blake drew the picture himself, and called it "The Ancient of Days." Blake: "The creator of the temporal world leaning out of the sphere of Eternity or the soul in order to measure out in the void a universe external to mind and intellect." The bearded figure is reaching out to measure, with a compass, a wall section of glass blocks.

Now that is really something – an ontology lesson in stone. This is just what Leonard Peikoff was talking about in his lecture on "Why Ancient Greece is my Favorite Civilization." (mentioned in the Introduction above.) The ancient Greeks had no interest in promoting, as Christians do, any sort of mysticism or talk about the ineffable or infinite or immeasurable. They *wanted* things to be measurable, and understandable. So the relief shows the Platonic, Kantian "noumenal" world represented by God in the clouds, and it also suggests the "phenomenal" world of finite, understandable, measurable phenomena that you and I live in.

Between the points of the compass is a quote from Isaiah: "Wisdom and knowledge shall be the stability of thy times." This means that Man's hope for peace, and as a consequence, prosperity, lies in understanding – and that implies following reason and the evidence of the senses wherever it may lead. Here we see Art Deco expressing exactly what Rand and Aristotle were saying about Man's nature, and not the Divine Right of Kings, as the basis, in ontology and epistemology, of ethics and politics. Objectivism carved in stone.

John D. Rockefeller Junior's Credo is also carved in stone here. To my annoyance, one of his beliefs was that the "dross of selfishness" should be burned out by the fire of self-sacrifice. Junior spent his whole life giving away his father's money. Rockefeller Center was his only profit-seeking project. Everything else he did was for burning out the dross of selfishness. An Objectivist Junior Rockefeller might have built or funded many of the same things – the Cloisters, Fort Tryon Park, Palisades Park – because they were beautiful and not because they were self-sacrificial. In fact, *were* they self-sacrificial? Didn't Junior himself get any enjoyment out of them?

One time, I got an angry look from a young Euro tourist in front of Junior's Credo, because Junior wrote that the individual is greater than the State. To the Euro, Junior was not self-sacrificial *enough*!

It is hard to resist guessing that Lee Lawrie's "Atlas" at Rockefeller Center inspired Rand's title *Atlas Shrugged*. So far, I have never been able to find any other outstanding contenders for the honor. There is one other Atlas in New York: He holds up the clock over the entrance of Tiffany's. The Lawrie Atlas holds up the sky, represented by an openwork sphere made of rings bearing the signs of the Zodiac. Lawrie was persuaded to make the sphere an open one so people coming out of the International Building would be able to see through it to Saint Patrick's Cathedral across Fifth Avenue. In the myth, it is the sky that Atlas holds on his shoulders. Rand makes it the Earth, to serve her own metaphor. To her, the Atlases of the world are the people who bear the weight and responsibility of the world on their shoulders. I don't know how many people realize that Rand's point here is scalable: It applies, not just to captains of industry, but to millions of people who accept millions of responsibilities, both great and small. You are one.

In *The Fountainhead*, Roark hires a sculptor named Steven Mallory. Keating sees a sculpture by Mallory called "Industry." "It was a slender naked body of a man who looked as if he could break through the steel plate of a battleship … It left a strange stamp on one's eyes. It made the people around it seem smaller and sadder than usual. For the first time in his life, looking at that statue, Keating thought he understood what was meant by the word 'heroic'." I wonder whether Rand might have been looking at Lee Lawrie's "Atlas" when she wrote those words.

Then there is also "Motive Power." But how many people even notice that one?

GODS IN THE PLACE OF MAN

I will pass over New York's many houses of worship briefly. Get off the beaten path, go to East 97th Street, and take a peek at the Russian Orthodox Cathedral of St. Nicholas and the Islamic Cultural Center of New York. I walked into that beautiful building one day, with its intricate Islamic geometric designs, took my shoes off, snooped around, and walked out and nothing bad happened to me. In fact, I chatted with a man who was either the head of the place or some official of the mosque, and he could not have been more welcoming. He was just as smiley and chatty as the head of the Hindu Temple in Flushing, Queens when I spent a whole day there for Lakshmi Puja. I thought, Okay, this is a constant: the president of the congregation, or the beadle, or rector, or whatever he is called, is trying to keep a non-profit organization afloat and is happy to have any visitor show some interest. He is always going to be the smiley, gladhanding type, in any religion, and I don't mean that as a put-down.

It was from Ayn Rand that I learned how to find common ground with even the most irreconcilable people. The clergy of every religion, and the learned elders of every philosophy, can all talk on the common ground of ethics. Notice that John Calvin's system of pre-destination has not been very influential lately. (Calvin got it from Augustine, but so did Rand's hero Aquinas and Martin Luther.) The clergy can't hold any threat of Hellfire over you if you are already pre-destined for Heaven or Hell anyway, no matter what you do. Without Predestination, bad conduct might have bad consequences, so it is in your self-interest to be good – the persistence of self-interest! The best dodge, though, was Rasputin's: "What must you do before you can be forgiven for your sins? You must sin! Therefore, go out and sin! It is the only way to salvation!" (approximate quote)

In front of the Time-Warner Center, at Columbus Circle, you will sometimes find a contingent from, shall we call it, Organized Atheism. They ask you to sign petitions on Church-State issues. They hand out flyers. I've been to maybe two of their meetings over the years. At one such, years ago, the chairman announced a surprise speaker – Dr. Albert Ellis, an old nemesis of Rand and Branden. At another, this year, the speaker described his efforts to erect a sculpture of Satan on the grounds of the Oklahoma State House. Just to prove a point, you see.

My introduction to atheism came from Nathaniel Branden. In the packet of information I got, in January, 1968, in response to a fan letter to Rand, there was an annual Report to Our Readers that mentioned some religious issue, after which Branden wrote "As uncompromising advocates of reason, Objectivists are, of course, atheists. But to become known as crusaders for atheism would be acutely embarrassing to us, because the foe is too unworthy." At that, I not only dropped religion with no agonizing, I began to gradually drop any anger *toward* religion.

Some people, brought up under strict religious rules, hold a grudge against religion for the rest of their lives. Thomas Jefferson was one. Frank O'Connor, Rand's husband, was another.

Currently, this is the new and deeper meaning that I find in religion, and it is Rand I credit with starting me on the search, always, for a deeper meaning that underlies both religion and philosophy: "God" is the name that many of the best people give to the source of their highest moral aspirations. The word "God" is an empty vessel into which people put their highest vision of the kind of person they want to be. That's kind of cute and quaint. But God is not the only name they could have given that source. A more accurate name would be "growing up" – becoming a man. That's why those aspirations are called "virtue." "Virtue" comes from the Latin "vir," meaning "man." As the whole human species grows up, we become more like your parents' idea of God.

Continue, from Columbus Circle, up the Upper West Side, to Columbia University, the Cathedral Church of Saint John the Divine, Grant's Tomb, and Riverside Church. Across the street from Riverside was, until 2013, the headquarters of the National Council of Churches, or, as Russell Means (founder of the American Indian Movement) called it, the God Box. It is a very plain, boring piece of postwar architecture. Toohey was right – if you want to inspire and motivate your followers, go heavy on the trimmings. This thing looks like a bank.

ZENGER

One meaning of Federal Hall National Memorial not covered in Chapter 9 is the John Peter Zenger trial of 1735. That trial helped to establish freedom of the press, and it took place in New York's City Hall, the future Federal Hall. Right now there are a lot of people getting a lot of air time, columns of print, bytes of the Internet, over the issue of Muslim attacks on cartoonists who draw disrespectful cartoons of the Prophet Mohammed.

The Zenger trial hinged on the fact that the things editor Zenger had written about Royal Governor William Cosby in the New York *Gazette* were *true*. That was the winning argument made by Zenger's lawyer. This helped to establish the principle that "the truth is your defense." Rand, in the 1970s, criticized the new principle in such cases: that your speech might be protected or not protected depending on whether the jury found that you <u>intended</u> to do harm or not; that by your intentions shall you be judged. Rand's comment was: "Try and prove it."

Zenger would not be impressed with those who, today, are deliberately disrespecting Muhammed, in cartoons and otherwise. Those people are thinking like lawyers and not like political, let alone moral, leaders. They publish disrespectful cartoons and then insist "I have a right to do that!" Yes, they do, but they are not in a moot court. They are in a competition for the support of a billion Muslims, and it is a life-or-death competition. If they disrespect Muhammed, they drive Muslims into the waiting arms of the extremists. They need to take a lesson from Gandhi. You will get public support from people around the world, including Muslims, if what you say is true and constructive. Offensive cartoons are not constructive. Cartoons attacking living evildoers are. So portray a terrorist because he is a terrorist. Don't attack Muhammed unless you are prepared to prove that Muhammed perpetrated or taught terrorism or some other crime. Just an offensive cartoon by itself is hooliganism, and while it may win you points in a law school class, it will not win you respect from the world. Gandhi would advise you, if you want to change minds and win supporters, to make sure that you choreograph every incident so that ALL the right is on your side and ALL the wrong is on the other side. Supporters of Muhammed-bashing cartoons are weakened, in their efforts to sell the pitch that the issue is one of the free expression of those cartoonists, by the fact that a disrespectful cartoonist is not someone we can wholeheartedly support, as New Yorkers could support Zenger as a reporter and Thomas Nast as a cartoonist, both exposing corrupt officials. Nast's cartoons helped bring down Boss Tweed.

Which is more inspiring? Defying the Prohibition laws in the 1920s, just for the sake of drinking, or defying the Fugitive Slave Act in the 1850s, to help slaves reach Canada and freedom?

William Tweed was the long-time leader of the Tammany Society, which began as an enlisted veteran's club after the Revolutionary War, but became the leading Democratic Party club in New York City in the 19th Century and a synonym for corruption. Tweed and his ring stole millions from the taxpayers. He was finally put in jail because Nast's cartoons turned even illiterate immigrants against him, and because dedicated prosecutors finally found witnesses willing to testify, and because Samuel J. Tilden, another Democratic politician, convened a meeting of other politicians in his home and laid their plans against The Boss and outmaneuvered him. Want to experience a really vivid moment of connection with history?

There was a panel discussion about Ayn Rand at the National Arts Club a couple of years ago. Anne Heller, Shoshana Milgram, and two or three others spoke. Alexandra York, a member of the Club, organized the panel, over the objections of some Rand-averse members. I arrived at the Club early and sat down to read a life of Boss Tweed before the panel began.

The National Arts Club is on Gramercy Park. It is right next to the Players Club building, a Stanford White-designed mansion for the club formed by Edwin Booth, Mark Twain and others for actors and non-actors to have a respectable place to mix. The National Arts Club is in a mansion, too – the mansion of Samuel J. Tilden. As I sat in the front parlor reading, I learned about the meeting of politicos that finally closed ranks against Tweed. I looked up in astonishment and said "Holy cow! I am sitting in the house, and probably in the very room, where this meeting took place a hundred and forty years ago!"

That's the ticket! Live in an old city, but turn on your computer – your Worship Machine – and Google Earth your way up to Alaska's Seward

Peninsula. Look at Tin City. See the village of Wales, out on the very point that forms the American side of the Bering Strait. Look down on the village of Inalik, on the west side of Little Diomede Island, facing Russia's Big Diomede Island across two and a half miles of water – a little longer than Central Park. See all that empty land; empty of everything but promise. North To The Future! Then go sit in Tilden's front parlor and commune with ghosts. Get a Players club member to show you Booth's apartment, up on the third floor of the house. The club has left it untouched since Booth died there in his bed in 1893. There you can REALLY commune with ghosts! Back and forth, from the past to the future, is how you keep everything in perspective.

Hold in your mind a picture including all the images I just painted: Blake's and Lawrie's measurable, understandable, Aristotelean universe of objective fact. The Zenger trial establishing the principle of "The truth is your defense." Gandhi building political support by showing facts and not just spinning theories – "Satyagraha" – the Force of Truth. Saying something in a political cartoon because it is *true* and not just because you legally *can* say it. Boss Tweed brought to justice by witnesses who could *prove* his acts of embezzlement. The facts of Man's nature expressed in art and historic sites in an old city as something you connect to even as you leave these old cities to start new ones on the frontiers of Alaska or the ocean or space. As I write, in about eight hours the New Horizons spacecraft is to make its closest approach to Pluto. What will be carved over the portals of some future Rockefeller Center, in some new New York City at the edge of the Solar System?

TWO PARK AVENUE

This was Ely Jacques Kahn's Art Deco masterpiece, so he moved his own office here when the building opened in January, 1928. It fills the west side of Park Avenue between 32nd and 33rd Streets. This is where Ayn Rand worked for him, unpaid, as a typist and file clerk, for six months in 1937-1938.

Kahn scoured the world looking for, sketching, and photographing examples of the art and architecture, and folk arts and crafts, of every ancient and modern culture he could find. Rand didn't think much of arts and crafts. She wrote in her working journal: "Kahn's insistence on the 'crafts' – too much. It is not part of architecture. … I'm not sure, but it seems to me that such a 'field' would, to Frank Lloyd Wright, be what writing for Hollywood is to a writer." What a great quote that is – for revealing Rand's personality! She was still under Wright's spell. She would later be disillusioned. She associated folk arts and crafts (and elsewhere, folk dancing) with the mediocre efforts of conformist Peter Keatings. You can tell that Rand was a dramatist at heart, because to her, there always had to be a hero and a dead hand of convention he was heroically struggling against. (The quote also shows what she thought of Hollywood writing. If she could have seen, in 1938, the TV writing of the 1960s, and some of the lowbrow guns-and-explosions movies, and the incomprehensible, pretentious, highbrow movies of today!)

Look at the ceiling mosaic in the entryway at Two Park. It kind of looks like electrical parts, but it also kind of looks like a Navajo rug. Kahn did that deliberately. He liked to bring together, for contrast, the ancient and the modern.

How did Rand discover Kahn, and why did she want to work for him? Perhaps she found, as I did, a book at the New York Public Library, called *New York: The Wonder City*. It was published in 1932. The library copy I found there may well have been the very one Rand held in her hands, unless it was the 1984 reprint. The book profiles New York's major buildings, businesses, institutions of all kinds, and prominent citizens. Under "Architects," Kahn's entry reads: "Ely Jacques Kahn is individual. He thinks for himself, and has the courage to back up any stand he takes."

Just the ticket.

DYNAMIC DUOS

We mentioned the RCA Building mosaic "Intelligence Awakening Mankind" (contrasted with Christ the Redeemer). Compare that title with that of the Statue of Liberty: "Liberty Enlightening the World." Awakening and Enlightening – this is modern Man worshiping that which makes his life possible. Man survives by using his mind. Awakening implies consciousness and thinking. Enlightenment implies seeing, perceiving, understanding, consciousness.

While we are looking for new and deeper meanings, it more than doubles the fun if we can find pairs of meanings – two sites in New York that play off each other.

Trinity Church, Episcopal, on Broadway at Wall, is Gothic Revival. St. Paul's Chapel, on Broadway at Fulton, is Georgian. The present Trinity, the third church on that site, opened in 1846. St. Paul's opened in 1765. So Trinity comes from the 19th Century, when Euros and Americans, having gotten out of the Middle Ages, became curious about what it was they had just escaped from. St. Paul's was built right smack in the middle of the Enlightenment, when people were rebelling against the Middle Ages and couldn't wait to get out of them. St. Paul's, therefore, is full of windows and light. Its ceiling is rounded, so there are no dark corners. Trinity is full of dark corners around the walls and ceiling, because of the pointed arches that are the main feature of the Gothic style. St. Paul's embodies light, understanding, clarity, definition, measurability. Trinity embodies mystery, uncertainty, infinity. Aristotle versus Plato.

If Rand gets you reading Victor Hugo, be aware that while Hugo's writing style is the glory of Mankind – timeless moral themes, timeless heroes and villains – his subject matter was sometimes the Middle Ages, mainly in *Notre Dame de Paris*. Likewise his fellow Romantic novelist Sir Walter Scott, with *Ivanhoe*. You aren't likely to be fascinated with a historical period while you are still in it. But as soon as you become aware of a great sea-change happening around you, such as industrialization, commercial empires spanning the globe, and representative government, then you want to read about what life was like in the bad old days, and you might start to delude yourself that the bad old days were better. You might get caught up in a nostalgia movement. That's what happened in the 19th Century. As Michael Corleone says, "Just when I think I'm out, they pull me back in again!"

In *The Age of Rand*, I cover the contrast between the verticality of Rockefeller Center, with its Radio City Music Hall, and NBC's Television City in Hollywood, which took advantage of cheaper land to spread out horizontally. Sometimes you want to be in the crowded, vertical city, and sometimes you want to get away from it all.

Likewise, on my "Skyscrapers of *The Fountainhead*" tour, I have people look straight up the height of Ralph Walker's One Wall Street, the Irving Trust Building (now Bank of New York), with its soaring vertical lines. Then I have them turn right around and look up the height of the Empire Building, 71 Broadway (1898), and what do they see? Cornice after stringcourse after cornice. All heavy horizontal lines – on a soaringly vertical building. This is what Roark is complaining about: horizontal lines that visually rob a tall building of its height. This building also has an Atlas connection: it was once the headquarters of US Steel – read Orren Boyle's "Associated Steel." And see Robert Hessen's *Steel Titan: The Life of Charles M. Schwab*. This building is where Schwab was ousted from the US Steel Board. So he went to Bethlehem, Pennsylvania and ran Bethlehem Steel instead. There, like Rearden, Schwab played the role of the feisty new entrepreneur challenging the complacent older company. He invested in new technology that enabled him to pour a large I-beam in one piece. He used the new beam to build Gimbel's Department Store. Gimbel's was his showcase for the new beam, just as the John Galt Line is Rearden's showcase for Rearden Metal. The scene where Hank and Dagny discuss this was a revelation to me. Hank charges Dagny a steep price for rails of Rearden Metal, saying that he knows how badly she needs that rail. Dagny fences back: She knows how badly Hank needs her rail line as a showcase for his new alloy. Hank laughs, delighted to bargain with someone as honest as he is. This dialogue, I thought, shows how two people talk to each other when neither is trying to fool or manipulate the other. This is how people talk when they respect each other. This is where I learned the frank and honest, sometimes brutally honest, way of speaking that Objectivists ought to not only learn, but teach the world. Branden pointed this out in a lecture: "Notice the respect with which Rand's heroes speak to people."

Today, the Empire Building, like so many other old office buildings, has gone residential. As we all get sucked into the Internet, will all the office buildings become apartment buildings, and all the factories be reduced to cute little thatched-roof cottages, where all manufacturing is done on the molecular level? Is this new technology of 3-D printing going to lead to a world with no big, smoky industrial plants? Will all manufacturing be quiet and clean? Will everyone work from home? Will there be no office buildings – and no stores, since we will do all our shopping online? With no commuting, and no shopping, will everyone on Earth abandon the cities to ruin and live in hobbit houses in the woods?

At Number One Wall Street, in Revolutionary times, there was a tavern. At that tavern, Lord Rawdon, an Anglo-Irish general in the British army, hung up a notice, in the winter of 1777, soon after the Redcoats took New York City. He was inviting the city's Irishmen to join up. He promised a big banquet at the King's expense. He got hundreds of takers. They signed their X, ate and drank copiously, and then most of them deserted and joined Washington's army. We will encounter his lordship again, in Chapter 17, below. His name, after the war, became attached to a gold-bearing range of hills in central Nova Scotia. Next time you pass One Wall Street, think of the Irish who gladly fought the Limeys for American freedom, and think of the Loyalist settlers in Nova Scotia digging for gold a century later. You are seeing another moral ideal at work: normalcy. Revolution and war, against Mercantilism, gave way to reform and peace, and Rawdon's name ended up representing productive work instead of political corruption. (See the chapter NORMALCY in *The Age of Rand*.) The Rawdon banquet and the Rawdon gold: a meaningful contrast.

Canada is one great big monument to the American Revolution. John Bull never wanted to face another Yorktown again, so he handled the Canadians with kid gloves through the 19th Century. The gradual, nice and legal independence of Canada represents a lesson learned, albeit slowly.

Here is a Dynamic Duo that requires a trip to Syracuse and another to Rio – or just switch on your Worship Machine and google Christ the Redeemer, in Rio, again, and this time contrast it with "The Spirit of Light" sculpture on the façade of the spectacular Art Deco Niagara Mohawk Building in Syracuse. Both stand with outstretched arms. Both are welcoming you to something and offering you something. Christ offers Redemption for the asking. Light offers you the ability to dispel the dark and see. And to see is to know and understand. Much like "Intelligence Awakening Mankind" and yet another: the mosaic over the portals of Bronx Science High School. This last hooded figure looks for all the world like Mr. Spock! Why not? He has his hands up in a Papal benediction, but I think he is measuring something, as the Ancient of Days is doing. Is there exactly one meter of space between his hands?

Look at all the places in Manhattan where the Grid has to work its way around natural obstacles. Look at Pearl Street, downtown. It bends a lot. But as you go from Pearl east toward the East River, you pass Water, Front, and South Streets, which bend hardly at all. That's because Pearl was, in Dutch times, the shore road. It followed the bends in the shore. But the other three streets were built later, on landfill. Go east on Wall Street, and you will see that the ground slopes down as far as Pearl, but then becomes dead flat – that's the landfill. Here you can see the concretization of a favorite maxim of Rand and Branden: Nature, to be commanded, must be obeyed. The grid regularizes the land a little, but the Grid has to yield a little, too. Ya gotta give a little, take a little …

Competition. The very meaning and purpose of the free market. The right of every buyer to shop around among competing sellers of all goods and services. For not only New Yorkers, but movie goers everywhere, this principle is symbolized and fondly remembered in the rhetorical question "Does Macy tell Gimbel?" – and the 1947 movie "Miracle on 34th Street." Another symbol of competition is the New York Stock Exchange at Broad and Wall, versus the American Stock Exchange, visible from that corner over the shoulder of Trinity Church. NASDAQ has moved from near Wall Street up to Times Square, but that also represents a famous dynamic duo of competition – the Midtown Central Business District rising after 1873 to challenge the original Downtown CBD. NASDAQ represented not only a third competing stock exchange, but a new *way* of trading stocks – by computer instead of by open outcry on an exchange floor. Competition within competition.

Just as Macy's and Gimbel's symbolize the competition of company versus company, so there is competition between the for-profit sector and the not-for-profit sector. And the government sector. This is what we see at the east end of 42nd Street, when we see the United Nations complex and the Ford Foundation, one of the biggest outfits in the Big Nonprofit world. And next to that, the Pfizer Company, makers of Viagra.

Around 1910, Abe Erlanger and the Frohman brothers headed the Theatrical Syndicate, which managed 75% of all the theaters in the country. It was challenged by the Shubert brothers, and soon it was the Shuberts who owned 75% of all the theaters in the country. Then other chains cut down that percentage, and the whole idea of going to a theater for entertainment was challenged by movies, then by radio, then by television, and today by the Internet. Competition within competition. How did the Shuberts get theaters and stars away from the Syndicate? By the Syndicate being obnoxious. Richard Mansfield was also obnoxious. Everyone on Broadway respected him as an actor, but as a manager, he was, not to put too fine a point on it, an asshole – as much as Abe Erlanger. So actors and audiences and other managers found ways around these guys. The Shuberts owned and managed. The Theater Guild managed without management. And then Playwrights Co. and the Group Theater provided alternatives to the alternatives. The very fact that some producers made themselves odious is what motivated others to create alternatives to them. That's competition. And the monuments to that process are to be found along Broadway today – but only if you have a tour guide with a picture book, as most of the theaters where these things happened were torn down long ago. The monument to their net result a hundred years later, though, is in your hand – your electronic device that gives you access to entertainment, and the history of that entertainment, on the Internet.

Look at the New Amsterdam Theater – it's still there – on West 42nd Street west of 7th Avenue. That was Erlanger's headquarters. The Shuberts' headquarters is still standing, too: the Lyceum, on West 45th Street east of Broadway. Before the Shuberts, Daniel Frohman, of the Syndicate, used the Lyceum. In Frohman's old office are the Shubert archives, so in one theater, built in 1903, you see a relic of both the earlier Syndicate era and, since they bought the theater in 1950, that of the Shuberts.

Fifth Avenue is legendary. Fifth Avenue was once where the mansions of the rich were. That's because it runs exactly up the center of Manhattan island, as far as the rich could get from the low-down waterfront districts on the Hudson shore to the west and the East River to the east. But later, by Rand's time, the mansions of Fifth Avenue were being demolished for the department stores of Fifth Avenue. Still symbols of wealth. John Galt, in his speech, purplishly declaims "You, who leap like a savage out of the jungle of your emotions onto the Fifth Avenue of our New York ..." Here, Rand is using "jungle" as a metaphor for emotion. (another "new and deeper meaning" to the images of jungle and savage) My rule of thumb, though, is to replace "emotions" everywhere it appears in Rand with "anxiety." Rand was not against emotions. But if you willfully evade facts and reality, the only emotion left to you is anxiety. And that's a jungle.

Fifth Avenue, in Rand's world, represents the rewards – mansions and stores – that await all mankind to the extent that individuals bravely face facts and reality. The pleasant emotions – joy and pride – also await you.

A related image Galt uses in his speech is "the Atlantic Skyline of New York." He contrasts that skyline with the temples of our primitive ancestors, which represented human sacrifice. But what does the word "Atlantic" represent? Why the "Atlantic" skyline? What difference does it make which ocean lies outside the Narrows? Wouldn't a "Pacific" skyline be just as much a temple to the brains and courage of the architects and high steel workers, and all the others who make skyscrapers possible? In Rand's era, yes, it did make a difference, because the Atlantic, and only the North Atlantic at that, was the glamor ocean. The North Atlantic washed the shores of Britain and France and America. In Rand's era the Pacific was still not as developed as the North Atlantic. Geopolitical scientists speak of the "Atlanticist" view of the world. In the 19th and 20th Centuries, the North Atlantic was where the power and the money was. The persistence of money again! This will require more and more explanation for the younger readers of Atlas as we durate deeper and deeper into the 21st Century – the century when the cutting edge of civilization could be anywhere and everywhere.

Rand may have slipped in a double, or triple, meaning here. The "Atlantic Ocean" means the ocean of Atlas, who holds up the western end of the sky at the Strait of Gibraltar. She also meant to imply the ocean of Atlantis, since some writers have placed it beyond that strait. In fact, in Atlas, one character calls Atlantis the Isle of the Blessed for the Greeks, and wonders whether what they had in mind was America, beyond the Western Ocean.

Just as the Washington sculpture at Federal Hall forms a pair with the one in Union Square (see Chapter 9), and "Motive Power" with the General, so the Union Square Washington was supposed to form a pair with the Lafayette sculpture nearby. Originally, the equestrian Washington was placed in the triangular traffic island where Fourth Avenue (part of the old Dutch Bowery Lane) meets East 14th Street. He was facing into Union Square Park, looking right at Lafayette. Lafayette (by Bartholdi, who designed "Liberty Enlightening the World" (the Statue of Liberty)) is shown standing on the bow of his ship as he travels to America to take part in what was not yet the War for Independence. The Marquis holds his sword over his heart, and holds out his other hand palm open. This reflects his statement that he had heard, from a passing ship in mid-Atlantic, that Congress had declared the thirteen states independent. "I stood on the bow of the ship, and pledged my sword and my fortune to the cause of American Independence," said the young idealist. The open palm symbolizes the open hand of generosity.

The Washington sculpture now faces south, down The Bowery, because that is the way he was riding on Evacuation Day, but in his original position, he appeared to be acknowledging Lafayette's pledge of assistance. To Washington, Lafayette (and Hamilton) became the son he never had.

Today, as we watch Washington facing south as he rides down The Bowery to take possession of New York City from the British, what do we see over his shoulder? It is twenty blocks north of him, as we look up Fifth Avenue. The Empire State Building! In *The Age of Rand*, I tell the story of how New York State got the nickname "The Empire State." It was GW who said it. As he waves his raised right hand in greeting to New York, he is bringing Empire in his train. "Look, New York, at what your revolutionary future holds!"

General William Alexander, who called himself Lord Stirling, commanded part of the American army at the Battle of Brooklyn (formerly called the Battle of Long Island). He commanded the

Maryland and Virginia regiments that counterattacked at the van Vechte house, holding back the Redcoats while the rest of the American army escaped across Gowanus Creek to the prepared positions on Brooklyn Heights. His heroic leadership is remembered today in a sculpture of Athena (goddess of wisdom and patriotism) in Greenwood Cemetery, on a hill looking down on the scene of battle and looking across the harbor to Miss Liberty. Athena has her right hand raised in greeting – and Liberty responds with her right hand holding up its torch. But not many people know this.

Go to 3rd Avenue between 7th and 9th Streets in Park Slope, Brooklyn. You are standing on the trenches, now buried under landfill and pavement, where the Redcoats buried over 200 Maryland soldiers who died in the Battle of Brooklyn, August 27th, 1776. The site was used, in the 19th Century, for a coal yard, and in the 20th for a paint factory. Some of the burial ground may be under the parking lot of an auto repair shop. Around the corner is American Legion Post 1636, which has a plaque facing the street, commemorating the soldiers who were buried there. These were the men who held back the Redcoats while the rest of the American army escaped by swimming across Gowanus Creek. The creek was later enlarged into the Gowanus Canal, which supplied many factories. In fact, Gowanus Canal and Newtown Creek, which separates Brooklyn and Queens, were, between the two of them, equal in industrial output to whole rivers, like Cleveland's Cuyahoga, for more than a century.

This area went from Revolutionary battlefield to industrial district. What could be more fitting? One of the things those men were fighting for was the freedom to start businesses in every industry and invent some new industries, and to build factories, and not to be restricted, by British imperial regulations, to being only a source of raw materials for British factories whose owners had friends at court. In the early Industrial Revolution, manufacturing was where the money was, so naturally the Mother Country wanted to keep all the manufacturing in England.

Regulations preventing the colonies from developing manufacturing, which means: from developing at all, is the very meaning of colonialism.

Now most of that manufacturing is gone, and Park Slope's trendy apartments and restaurants are creeping farther down the slope from Prospect Park to the canal. Someday the pollution in the canal will be cleaned up, the last factories will be torn down, and everyone in those new apartments will work from home. From muskets to muscles to minds, in three centuries.

Imagine standing at that Maryland soldier's side, as a ghost from his future, and whispering in his ear "What are you fighting for?" Look up the slope, to Greenwood Cemetery and Athena, Goddess of Wisdom and Patriotism, greeting Liberty.

We mentioned the mosaic on the ceiling of the entryway of Two Park Avenue, where Rand worked for Ely Jacques Kahn. Ancient and modern, together. It makes you think about the process of change, from past to future. Same thing downtown, in the entryway of Kahn's 120 Wall Street. This time it is a mural on the ceiling, and it shows a modern skyline of New York, and upside down to that picture is a picture of the 17th Century city, with sailing ships in the harbor. Old and New. Process.

When Kahn began designing Two Park, One Park was already there. It has an open entryway, a sort of cave you enter from the sidewalk before you push through the revolving doors and enter the lobby, and over those doors it has an arched transom. So Kahn designed his entry the same way, to create symmetry as you look back and forth across Park Avenue from One to Two. Sometimes an original touch can be given a building by doing the *same* thing as your neighbor. It's not Peter Keating-ish imitation – it's architectural dialogue.

Here's an unlikely pair. In Ridgewood, Queens there is a historic site called the Vander Ende-Onderdonk House. It was built in 1710 for the

Vander Ende family. But in the 1960s it was bought as a workshop for a small company that engraved metal plates. They engraved the plate that you can see today, next time you visit Tranquility Base Historic Park. It reads "HERE MEN FROM THE PLANET EARTH FIRST SET FOOT UPON THE MOON." Imagine my surprise when the manager of the site told me, in the midst of details about two Knickerbocker families who lived and farmed here three hundred years ago, that this was also a site from the history of the exploration of Space! Suppose the van der Endes and the Onderdoncks had had a chance to talk to Neil and Buzz. "Ve are settling in der New Vorld!"

"Yeah, we're exploring a new world too. Not settling, though, just exploring ... for now."

One site; two meanings. Past meets future.

More public art could be planned in pairs.

The statue of Horace Greeley might be moved up from City Hall Park to J. Hood Wright Park, which looks out over the George Washington Bridge. That Bridge is like Bifrost, the Rainbow Bridge that takes you to Asgard, the home of the Norse gods (and you thought Asgard was a piece of football equipment). It is the bridge to the west, with all its hope and promise. And Greeley, the most influential American of the 19th Century, the man who some say put Lincoln in the White House, was also the man who said that if you can't find a job, "Go west, and grow with the country." Greeley should be looking west, along the GWB and over the Hudson. In his day, there was such a word as "westering," because that is what people did. My computer put a red line under "westering," indicating that it does not recognize that word. There is a movie from the 1940s or so where an old pioneer shakes his grizzled head and moans "Westering has gone out of the people." You are being programed these days, by the Professariat, to see westering as the genocide of the Native Americans. I recommend a 2006 book by Alan Taylor called *The Divided Ground: Indians, Settlers and the Northern Borderland of the American Revolution.* Taylor makes the point that the Indians weren't dummies – they were not trying to stop all settlement; they were hoping to *manage* that settlement. If they could just maintain their sovereignty and independence, they could rent land to the settlers. The namesake of that bridge, as president, would have let them. He respected the independence of the Indian nations. Unfortunately his policies were not continued by subsequent presidents.

Maybe a sculpture of John Peter Zenger could be executed, and form a group around Park Row with the existing Franklin and Greeley – three newspapermen, for what was once Newspaper Row. Walter Winchell used to call newsmen "Park Rogues."

I'd love to pair Franklin with a re-creation of the George III sculpture that New Yorkers pulled down on July 9, 1776 and sent to a foundry for melting down into musket balls. It stood in the Bowling Green. On the base of the Franklin sculpture I would put "I'll have your little king for this." That story is in *The Age of Rand.* Why not pair Franklin, saying "Where there is liberty, there is my country," with Tom Paine saying "Where liberty is *not*, there is my country"? The wealthy Watts and DePeyster families financed sculptures of their ancestors John Watts and Abraham DePeyster. Watts is in Trinity churchyard, and DePeyster, after two moves, is currently in Thomas Paine Park. They were colonial Royal office holders, or "placemen," as discussed above. They were the very class that provoked our revolution. They should be put together in a group called "The Placemen" and paired, I should say juxtaposed, with sculptures of any number of New York City self-made men and women, like Madame C. J. Walker, or indeed like Eliza Jumel. Now *there* are a couple of stories for you to google!

Stand on Chambers Street, between Broadway and Elk Street. On the north side of Chambers is the former Emigrant Savings Bank. On the south side is the Tweed Courthouse – the only thing named after the Tammany boss who made "Tammany" a synonym for corruption. The Emigrant Savings bank was founded by and for the destitute Irish who got off ships in New York by the thousands, if they didn't die of starvation on the way. They took the jobs no one else wanted, like digging out the outhouses that stood in the back yard of every building before anyone had indoor plumbing. If these Irish workers made three pennies a day, they would save one of them. Now look at the stately Tweed Courthouse. You are seeing one million dollars (in 1870 dollars), in construction, out of the ten million taxed away from the people of New York for the job. The other nine million disappeared into the pockets of the Tweed Ring. Makes a heck of a pair, doesn't it? Contrast the workers who created wealth with the political bosses who stole it.

A very significant sculpture pair for our time would be Hamilton, the illegitimate and penniless son, with the Duke of York, who inherited his title and who took this commercial Dutch colony by force. Talent and Aristotelean self-actualization versus inherited power and the advantage of being born a king's brother. The New World versus the old. You might want to put such a sculpture-pair in front of the Hall of Records and surrogate's court, where genealogists do their research.

And how about the statue of Captain Nathan Hale in City Hall Park, and the Sugar House Window behind the Municipal Building across Centre Street? A barred window of the Rhinelander family's sugar warehouse has been preserved, because the Redcoats kept American POWs in those warehouses, where many died of exposure and disease. And as for the Prison Ships, go to Brooklyn's Fort Greene Park, after reading *Forgotten Patriots*, by Edwin G. Burrows. These monuments, and another in Trinity Churchyard, should be paired with the Placemen, since the men who died in the sugar warehouses and on the Prison Ships were liberating you and me from a world of placemen, and corruption. But today, dumpsters are often parked in front of the Window, and Hale should be at 3rd Avenue and 65th Street, where he was hanged, and not in City Hall Park, where, in any case, you can barely see him inside the high security grounds around City Hall, or as I call it, Fortress Giuliani.

Abraham Lincoln saw only one opera in his life: Verdi's "A Masked Ball," at New York's Academy of Music, on East 14ᵗʰ Street. The building was later torn down for Con Ed's headquarters. It was built by and for New York's old money crowd – the families whose money had come from shipping and land and retail selling in the 18ᵗʰ and early 19ᵗʰ Centuries. The new money crowd, in newfangled industries like oil, could not get boxes at the Academy, because those boxes had to be bought from the unwilling sellers of the old aristocracy. So the Nouveau Riche took their money farther uptown and built their own damn opera house at Broadway and 39ᵗʰ Street, the Met.

Moral: Class theory, like so many other theories, is a generalization, and generalizations are true except when they aren't. Some people will play the "old-money" game, but people make new fortunes every day, and they are the ones who will undercut the snob crowd. Think of that when you pass the sites of the Academy and the Met. You won't see either building, though: both are now long gone. Time, and new industrial fortunes, march on.

That phrase, "Time marches on!" comes from a CBS radio show of the 1930s and 40s called "The March of Time." It was produced by *Time* magazine at the CBS building, 485 Madison Avenue, one block up from Random House, where Atlas was published (in the old Villard Houses). Henry Luce, the founder of *Time* and *Life* magazines, was one of the models for Gail Wynand, in *The Fountainhead*, along with Joseph Pulitzer, although Rand's main model was William Randolph Hearst. When Wynand closes the Banner, Toohey finds a new job at a magazine, and starts right in asking the old-timers what the boss is like. Toohey is doing what Toohey does so well – he is looking for the key to his new boss, so he can manipulate him, as he had Wynand. As he asks about his new boss, a radio blares "Time marches on!"

In 1785, just a year after the British evacuated New York City and the War for Independence was over, New York saw the founding of the General Society of Mechanics and Tradesmen, on Wall Street. It moved its headquarters up to Union Square, as the city grew northward, and now it is on West 44th Street, between Fifth and Sixth Avenues. This was New York's first labor organization, and America's either first or second. Its main activity is that of a trade school. I find it fascinating because it shows what a labor organization was like before Marx and before class theory. Its aim was to turn unskilled workers into skilled ones, not into cannon fodder for the revolution and cowed proles after. Art classes are offered there. Labor history talks, theater world talks, architecture talks, and a membership library are offered. Victor Niederhoffer's Junto discussion club meets there every first Thursday. The American Revolution Round Table meets there for a dinner and a talk by a new Revolution book author five times a year. Several genealogical societies have offices there. And it is a quiet oasis in midtown.

Pair that with the old Communist Party building on West 23rd Street, across from the Chelsea Hotel. The General Society is still around, and the CPUSA is kaput. Theories come and go, but the workers of the world keep working, and uniting, and finding ways to better their lot, regardless.

In the eleven years since *The Age of Rand*, 2005, I have noticed another happy trend (besides the Gowanus Canal, three pages worth of digressions ago). Genealogy used to be used for snobbery and class distinction. No more. Because there is now so much more family history discoverable in documents, and those documents are so much easier to access, genealogy is becoming something that unites all mankind – after all, we all have ancestors – instead of something that divides us. I did observe in 2005 that the future is going to be the golden age of knowing the past – the future is going to know much more about the past than the past ever knew about itself – but that is coming true in more ways now than I foresaw. I wish I could go back in a time machine and show those old DAR biddies all the beaming, and crying, faces on the PBS show "Genealogy Roadshow." Faces of all colors.

And as the whole world becomes more and more the land of immigrants, every city is going to have to have a Liberty Enlightening the World and an Athena waving to each other.

SAY IT WITH A PLAQUE!

Under Grand Central Terminal is a big subway station. It is so busy and crowded at rush hour that I don't even remember what it looks like, since all I can see when I am there is the back of the person in front of me. That's a meaning all by itself – the culture of congestion. Dutch architect Rem Koolhaas wrote a book called *Delirious New York*, and coined that phrase. We walk in New York. Everyone else in the world drives. We build up; everyone else builds out. We live on the subway. Everyone else lives on the freeway. We see each other's clothes and we can see what the next guy is reading. If it is a Rand book, I give him my card. We look into each other's eyes. Everyone else looks into each other's windshields. Everyone in the suburbs is a beetle, looking at each other's carapace – his exoskeleton of steel.

Cue Stephen Sondheim's "Another Hundred People" From "Company."

On a certain stairway in the Grand Central subway station, one day at evening rush hour, there was a group of people, mostly older people, men and women, reciting the rosary together. There were five or six of them. They were at the foot of the stairs, so they were a little bit in the way, but not too much. I wouldn't say they were blocking the exit. I could step around them without much trouble. But in front of them was another older man. He was yelling at them 'MARY NEVER SAVED ANYONE! MARY NEVER SAVED ANYONE!" Now, he was obnoxious. He was far louder than they were. He was apparently taking a strong Protestant position about salvation by faith alone, a la Luther, but the point is: he was haranguing them and disturbing their unobjectionable public praying. This made me think of what H. L. Mencken said about freedom of speech.

Mencken (1880-1956) was a journalist. He covered the Monkey Trial in 1925. (Google it.) He becomes cynical reporter "E. K. Hornbeck," played by Gene Kelly, in "Inherit the Wind," with Spencer Tracy. He was one of the few who read Rand's first novel, *We The Living*, when it was first published in 1936. He wrote Rand a fan letter about it.

Mencken, in an interview in about 1950, said "I'm an extreme libertarian. I believe in extending freedom to the last limits of the endurable. I'm an agnostic, but I've had all kinds of believers and divines as friends and I get along fine with them. I assume they have a right to their beliefs as I do to mine. But what I don't have a right to do is to stand on the church steps and harangue the Catholics as they're coming out of high mass."

Precisely! So that stairway has become invested with a new and deeper meaning, for me, through this instructive experience.

Rand, in her essay "Requiem for Man," in *Capitalism: The Unknown Ideal*, quotes a friend as saying that "only the Vatican, the Kremlin, and the Empire State Building know the real issues of the modern world." In September, 1967, *The Objectivist* magazine and Nathaniel Branden Institute moved into the sub-basement of the Empire State Building, where they had eight thousand square feet – enough space for not only offices, but an auditorium. I often wonder what would have happened if Rand and Branden had not had their "Break," and if NBI had continued to grow the way it had been from 1958, when Branden started it. What if Nathaniel, who died in December 2014, and Barbara, who died in December 2013, had just kept doing the same thing, with Rand's support? NBI had by 1967 expanded into eighty cities in North America, and was about to blossom on other continents. Why, it might, today, be as big as the Church of Scientology! I saw a magazine of theirs recently, showing whole buildings they are building around the world. Frightening.

That trio – the Vatican, the Kremlin, and the Empire State Building – knowing the real issues, is an image that has stuck with me. What

Rand and her friend meant was this: The Vatican represents a moral system, and a long-term view, and the supernatural. (I love these lines in Rand's essay: "The Vatican is not the city room of a third-rate Marxist tabloid. It is an institution geared to a perspective of centuries, to scholarship and timeless philosophical deliberation.") The Kremlin represented, between 1917 and 1991, a long-term view, but no moral view (because Marxist theory had disposed of the whole concept of morality in favor of class struggle) and no supernatural claims, but a claim to an "iron law of history." NBI and *The Objectivist* magazine, in the Empire State Building (and their successors in 2016), represent a moral system, a long-term view, and free will rather than either a god or a historical theory of mechanical predictability. But the Communists could recruit Blacks, for example, while American conservatives could not, as well as women and other groups, because the Communists had freed themselves from certain false assumptions held by rich, straight white males. By seeing themselves as modern, the Communists were free from the medieval assumptions of the Church and what they called the Capitalists. And the church was free of certain Communist positions that were vulnerable. But being free of the trees that obscure most people's views, both could see the forest. The tiny Objectivist band of pioneers in the Empire State Building were free from the assumptions of all three.

Let's try that again. The Vatican could see the world issues more clearly than the average American because they knew the importance of a moral system. But the Church was crippled in its understanding by primitive faith. The Kremlin could see farther than the average American, because they had left behind racism and other prejudices in favor of universal human class struggle. But the Objectivists had rejected faith, racism, Marxism, and a whole bunch of other baggage and could see the world's issues more clearly than anyone. And those issues boiled down to: self-fulfillment versus collectivism, if by collectivism we mean imputing certain attributes to groups that really belong to individuals, like intelligence (contra the racists) and rights (contra the Marxists).

Like Rand and many others, I love the Empire State Building. I wish it were still the Vatican of Objectivism.

When you visit Madison Square, notice a very tall, skinny building called One Madison. Madison Avenue starts on that building's doorstep and runs miles north into the Bronx. The building looks something like Roark's Enright House in the Fountainhead movie, but what is really startling is that in the shot in the movie, the Enright House is standing, in relation to the Met Life clock tower building, exactly where One Madison stands today. Also startling is that Rupert Murdoch reportedly has bought the triplex penthouse on top, and if Rand were writing *The Fountainhead* today, Murdoch would be her main model for newspaper publisher Gail Wynand, as William Randolph Hearst actually was when she published the novel in 1943.

But Rand suggests in the novel that the Enright House is somewhere around today's UN location on the East River, in the East 30s or 40s. Her description of the building bases the design clearly on Frank Lloyd Wright's St. Mark's Project, three apartment towers that were never built. Both look like crystals stuck to the side of a rock, or rather, multi-faceted glass apartment masses stuck to the sides of a thin core tower of concrete. The plan of each floor of each St. Mark's building looks like a pinwheel of four apartments attached to the four sides of the concrete core. Wright did realize that design, in his famous Price Tower in Bartlesville, Oklahoma. The Price Company found their tower too skinny to be practical as an office tower – not very much space per floor, so you would have to take an elevator every time you wanted to go from tiny office to tiny office – so today it is used as a hotel and restaurant. That's why Ely Jacques Kahn got the last laugh on Wright in this case. His W. T. Grant building, now the Astor Plaza Building, at 7th Avenue and 45th Street, in the heart of Times Square, is much like Wright's Price tower design, only much broader. More acreage per floor, so better suited to an office building.

Rand liked party scenes. She put one in *We The Living*, one in the Enright House in *The Fountainhead*, and two in Atlas. The Enright scene made it into the movie. A couple of important points are made there. Dominique sees Roark for the first time after the so-called Rape Scene, but now she knows who he is. She's pretty surprised. Toohey sees Roark for the first time at this party. He does not know that this tall, self-assured man across the room is the Howard Roark he has heard tell of, the guest of honor, since this party has been thrown by Roger Enright to celebrate the opening of his apartment building and to showcase Roark's revolutionary design. Roark's self-assurance is exactly the thing Toohey has feared and hated in others all his life. He circles around Roark as if hunting or being hunted, and finally asks someone "Who is that man?" On hearing that he is Roark, Toohey sighs "Oh, yes, of course. It would be." He has seen the design of the Enright House, and now he is in it, and he knows that the design is the work of a genius, and Roark looks the part. Toohey knows the kind of man he must destroy when he sees one. Later, we see Toohey talking to a middle-aged business type, with a mustache, a cigar, a paunch, a vest, and a pocket watch. In fact, the actor in the movie scene looks exactly like the cover illustration of Sinclair Lewis's *Babbitt* (the Signet Classic paperback with a man with a cigar in his mouth and empty eye sockets). As Toohey spins his theories and opinions, the Babbitt figure says "Oh, I don't know about that intellectual stuff. I play the stock market." And that sets Toohey up for the best line in the whole picture: "I play the stock market of the spirit. And I sell short."

In that same party scene, a woman asks Enright "Don't you want to convince me?" (of the greatness of Roark's design for Enright's building) "No, madam. God gave you eyes and a mind, which you're to use. If you don't, the loss is yours, not mine."

Now, if the Rand bashers and smearers and mythmongers are to be believed, Rand's novels are not novels, but political tracts. And if Rand was an atheist, then a sympathetic character like Roger Enright should not be invoking God. But he does. Why? Because he is *not* a mouthpiece for Objectivism, he is a character in a work of fiction. There have been people, and well-read, smart people too, over the years, who have angrily insisted to me that Atlas is not a novel! Precisely because these people are smart, they like to argue, and so to them every book is a debate proposition. But the fact is that Enright is a fictional character with his own backstory, that of a self-made American businessman of the 1930s, and men of that type were certainly more often conventionally religious in their views than not.

And that goes for Dagny and Francisco in the long flashback to their teen years, in the chapter THE CLIMAX OF THE D'ANCONIAS. There is a scene where Dagny acts as an almost simpering coquette, and Frisco makes some statements that reflect youthful bravado. Do not take anything in that flashback as Rand's mature opinions or "settled Objectivist dogma." These are scenes that show the *development* of Dagny and Francisco as adolescents. Your professors told you that Rand is a bad writer because she never shows development in her characters. They were wrong.

Strolling around New York, looking for stations of the dollar sign, places with hidden meanings, we come to a building in Tribeca that isn't there anymore, so it's a good thing you are reading about it here. Moody's Investor Services was domiciled, until recent years, at 99 Church Street. Over the door was a bronze plaque that read "CREDIT – MAN'S CONFIDENCE IN MAN." The original is at the Harvard Business School, and there are other copies. Moody's reportedly has taken the plaque with them to their new digs at the new World Trade Center. The plaque shows a frontiersman, in coonskin hat and fringed hunting shirt, and holding a Kentucky long rifle in his hand, with a tree behind him, shaking hands with a factory worker, shirtless, wearing a leather apron (just like "Motive Power"), and holding a big, toothed gear in his hand, and with skyscrapers behind him instead of trees.

What is the artist telling us? He is saying that the frontier economy came before the industrial economy, and made it possible, because the frontiersmen, poor as they were in money, produced the raw materials that others turned into money ("Value added through manufacturing"), which was then saved, and those savings made the later industrial economy possible. And that the industrial economy of today will produce the savings that will open the frontiers of tomorrow. (It is now August, 2015 as I write. Every day I look online – my Worship Machine – for the next photos from Pluto, reached by the New Horizons probe on July 14.) Work makes possible savings, which make possible bigger and better work. Frontiers turn to industry, which makes possible the move to, and industrialization of, bigger and better frontiers. It's a cycle.

Under that picture is a quote by Senator Daniel Webster: "Commercial credit is the creation of modern times and belongs, in its highest perfection, only to the most enlightened and best-governed nations. Credit is the vital air of modern commerce. It has done more, a thousand times more, to enrich nations than all the mines of the world." I wish he had said "individuals" instead of nations, but Webster couldn't help living in the 19th Century and not in the era when the Internet destroyed the nation-state. (Oh, right – that hasn't happened yet. But stay tuned.)

Those words "the creation of modern times" echoes one of Rand's most intriguing lines in Galt's speech: "…I was an inventor. I was one of a profession that came last in human history and will be first to vanish on the way back to the sub-human." Last in human history? Rand must have been thinking of Thomas Edison, who pretty much invented the modern development laboratory. Come downtown with me and I will show you the plaque that marks Edison's first commercial power plant, on Fulton Street at Pearl, and his competitor the Excelsior Power Company, on Gold Street, and the HQ of his other competitor, George Westinghouse, where Tesla worked as the Chief Engineer, on Broadway at Liberty Street. The building still says "WESTINGHOUSE" over the door. The whole downtown stretch of Broadway shows the shift from 19th Century heavy industry – the economy of *Atlas Shrugged* – to today's economy of banking, investment and information. So does Rockefeller Center. Buildings there built for companies in oil, steel and rubber are now filled with law firms and handlers of money and data. Ely Jacques Kahn's great-grandson took my "Ayn Rand's Park Avenue" tour recently and told me he is in "Big Data."

The last profession to appear. As of 1957. A few have been added since then, though, like "astronaut." Time marches on.

Go to the State Street entrance of the train station in Schenectady, New York. You will find a plaque at the spot where Thomas Edison stepped off the train to build his manufacturing company in Schenectady, now General Electric. He did not come as a god or a conqueror, but as a businessman making a business decision as to which city in America to adopt for the manufacture of electric parts. But his arrival is celebrated with a plaque. That's how our species changes from a world of magic to a world of mastery by our dull, uninspired Babbitts of business. But that's what puts food on the table, and so that is what is worth sanctifying and setting apart as sacred.

On a building on Montgomery Street in Newburgh is a plaque identifying the time-worn edifice as "one of the world's earliest central electric stations, 1884." The day I discovered this plaque, the street was deserted, and in fact Newburgh is pretty much deserted, like all of America's old industrial cities. The plaque itself was rusty, and as down-at-heels as the building that bore it. I expected the Eloi and the Morlocks to appear around the corner. The wind moaned and the tumbleweeds would have tumbled if Newburgh were in Arizona. Isn't it great to be able to take miracles so for granted? If you seek his monument ...

I go out of my way to read plaques, partly because I might learn something, and partly because I am afraid no one else does. Not that the neglect of historic plaques does not have its upside: It is not good to take our forebear's achievements for granted, but it is good that we *can*. It means that those forebears succeeded in making a better world.

The Lower East Side is particularly rich in monuments, literal and figurative, to co-operation outside of government. The same Eastern European Jews who brought so much interest in socialism to New York also excelled in setting up non-governmental community groups, such as the Bialystoker Landsmanshaft, the Educational Alliance, and the Henry Street Settlement.

There is a plaque on Pitt Street at Grand Street. It is attached to a stone structure (and it is coming loose) that appears to be there to hold up that plaque and for no other reason. The plaque reads:

COOPERATION

Cooperation means concert for the diffusion of wealth. It leaves nobody out who helps to produce it. It touches no man's fortune; it seeks no plunder; it causes no disturbance in society ... It contemplates no violence; it subverts no order ... It accepts no gift nor asks any favor; it keeps no terms with the idle and it will break no faith with the industrious ... It means self-help, self-dependence and such share of the common competence as labor shall earn or thought can win.
–George Jacob Holyoake, London, England, 1885

Now, right here is an example of the utility of monuments, because as I write this, in August, 2015, I am googling George Jacob Holyoake, of whom I have never heard, and I am learning that he was a leading 19ᵗʰ Century British reformer, a lifelong champion of atheism (or "Secularism" he called it, so as to use a positive and not a negative term), a newspaper editor, and a "co-operator," that is, a promoter of voluntary co-operation. He coined the term "secularism" and the word "jingoism." He defined Secularism as concern with questions that can be tested by the experience of this life. American Revolution fans will note that Holyoake was the last British subject to be indicted for publishing an unstamped newspaper. He was also the last to be jailed for blasphemy. But he did not take on Altruism.

A block farther east, on Grand Street, you will see another plaque – another message someone spent some money to keep visible to the passerby. 'Graved there in characters clear are the words:

HILLMAN COOPERATIVE HOUSES
We want a better America, an America that will give its citizens,
first of all, a higher and higher standard of living so that no child
will cry for food in the midst of plenty. We want to have an America
where the inventions of science will be at the disposal of every
American family, not merely for the few who can afford them;
an America that will have no sense of insecurity and which will
make it possible for all groups, regardless of race, creed or color, to
live in friendship, to be real neighbors; an America that will carry
its great mission of helping other countries to help themselves.
TO PERPETUATE THE IDEALS FOR
WHICH HE LIVED AND DIED

You know what is really sad? Between Holyoake's time and now, the politicians have done such a good job of erasing any awareness of how much has been done by how many for how many worthy causes *outside* of the state. Today, Objectivists and libertarians should be giving the lie to all politicians, of whatever label, who claim that government "provides" anything. It does not provide – it just takes things over. Why isn't that message getting said, and getting over? Rand had at least part of the answer: the appeal has to be on the moral level, not on the political or economic level. The message must be "Politicians lie – and lying is wrong!"

Where's Rand's plaque?

Well, she almost got one. In about 2000, I got an email from a group called the Friends of Libraries, USA. They put plaques on buildings of literary significance. You will find one on Pete's Tavern, on Irving Place, because that is where O. Henry (a Rand favorite) did his drinking, and maybe some of his writing. They wanted to know where a plaque for

155

Rand should go and what it should say. I replied Two Park Avenue, because the plaque could mention *three* famous New Yorkers: This was where Rand worked as a typist for architect Ely Jacques Kahn, to do research for *The Fountainhead*, in Kahn's own masterpiece building, and Kahn's son, E.J. Kahn, Jr., who wrote for *The New Yorker* for fifty years, spoke at the inauguration of a lighting program there in 1987. For a few years, the owner lit up the façade of Two Park, with its multicolored Art Deco terra cotta, after dark. I saw it at that time and said "How beautiful!" – never dreaming that someday I would be giving Ayn Rand walking tours and would tell people that this was the very building where Rand researched the daily goings on in a real architect's office.

But the owners didn't go for it. They put their own plaque there, mentioning neither Rand nor Junior.

I am looking at a plan of the Cathedral Church of Saint John the Divine, Episcopal, on Amsterdam Avenue at West 110 Street. It is the fourth in size among Christian churches in the whole world. Six hundred and one feet long. The five subsidiary chapels radiate out from the High Altar, like the abstract figures in an Ely Jacques Kahn lobby ceiling. Like a peacock's tail. The two sides of the nave are lined with bays, each honoring a different profession or group or pursuit: Lawyers, Armed Forces, Sports. There are fourteen, seven on each side of the nave. Symmetry. Two lines of seven rectangular figures, all the same. Like mass produced cars coming off the assembly line. Simple figures repeated many times – that's how Kahn said you arrive at a style. But especially if that style is meant to celebrate modern, machine-like, efficient products of planning for the long term. Saint John's is a product of expanding horizons for New York. The cornerstone was laid in 1892. In a city this big, they had to plan for five small groups of worshipers at the same time, hence five chapels all the same. The plan accommodated a large population, and it also accommodated choice: maybe you are German, and you want to pray in the Chapel of Saint Boniface. Maybe you are a Scot and you want to pray in the Chapel of Saint Columba.

Ironic, isn't it? Even religion is touched by Rem Koolhaas's "Culture of Congestion." Saint John's is the General Motors of churches.

I have saved another layer of meaning from the discussion of the Washington sculpture in the above chapter on Federal Hall for this subchapter. Washington took the oath as President with his right hand on the Bible and his left hand on his heart (but not in this sculpture, for the reasons explained above). This was a Christianization of the Roman gesture used when taking an oath or giving testimony in court. The Roman citizen held his testes when he gave testimony – that's why it's called "testimony," and that's why a Roman woman could not legally give testimony. The Roman was swearing not only on his personal honor, but on the honor of his family – his descendants as well as his ancestors. The whole family, past, present, and future, would be disgraced if he lied under oath.

This replacement of the Roman family reference (testes) with the Christian reference to personal moral responsibility (heart) reflects not just the replacement of Jupiter-cum-ancestor worship with Christianity, but the advance of Modern Times through the American Revolution, which Washington represents. After this revolution, family starts to lose its importance. The individual is important as the seat of consciousness, free will, action, and moral responsibility. The whole family is not honored or dishonored by the action of one member. Go back up to Edwin Booth's apartment at the Players Club and ask the shade of Booth how he feels about that. He had to retire from the stage for two or three years after his brother John Wilkes Booth caused a little embarrassment for the family at Ford's theater in Washington. But he did return to the stage. In olden times the whole family would have been hunted down and killed, every man-jack of them. How's that for a deeper layer of meaning in a work of art – if you know a little context?

CHAPTER 14
BEAMS VERSUS CHERUBS, or
WHAT MAKES IT POSSIBLE VERSUS
WHAT IT MAKES POSSIBLE

The cherubs of Baroque and Rococo architecture and art show what Man's creative work makes possible. Showing the beams and other entrails of a building show what makes the cherubs possible. Both themes are perfectly valid in the arts, and one should not be neglected as the other one goes through its vogue.

The meaning of Art Deco architecture, at least its skyscrapers, was: Look at my piers! Inside my piers – my vertical members that can be seen from the street – are the steel beams whose tremendous strength makes my great height possible. Look at my horizontal visual members! They express the girders inside whose great tensile strength holds up my floors. Steel is what makes me possible.

The meaning of pre-Deco styles, especially Baroque and Rococo, was: The wealth that makes me possible is so prodigious and prodigal and bodacious and superabundant and overflowing that it makes possible all this effulgence of ornamentation. Froufrou! Over-the-top and bursting with splendiferous, riotous cascades of cherubs, flowers, leaves of acanthus and oak, gods, goddesses, caducei. As Rand describes Guy Francon's Frink National Bank Building in *The Fountainhead*, "It offered so many columns, pediments, friezes, tripods, gladiators, urns and volutes that it looked as if it had not been built of white marble, but squeezed out of a pastry tube."

You have seen Titian's famous painting "The School of Athens." Plato is pointing up to Heaven. Aristotle is gesturing down toward the Earth. For Plato, this life and this Earth are only imperfect reflections of a "Higher Reality" – the one he is pointing to. His architecture is one of cherubs and other symbols of the Christian Heaven. But for Aristotle, life is what you make it, here on Earth. In Galt's Gulch, Dagny makes a Freudian slip: She says something to Ellis Wyatt about "when you were on Earth." Meeting all these disappeared people gives Dagny the feeling that she is in Heaven. But Wyatt knows exactly what Dagny means, because he replies "You mean when I was in Hell? I'm on Earth now." Plato's choices were: imperfect Earth or perfect Heaven. Aristotle's, and Wyatt's, choices were: Hell, where you can't act, and Earth, where you can. And in his speech, Galt says "Do not remind me that it pertains only to this life on Earth. I am concerned with no other. Neither are you."

Rococo is the architecture of Utopia. Art Deco is about how you get there.

There was an article in REASON magazine once comparing the literary styles of Ayn Rand and Iris Murdoch. It was called "The Girder and the Trellis." Rand was the girder. (A girder means a horizontal beam only, because they gird the building. A vertical beam is called a column. Ayn would have preferred to be seen as a load-bearing column. An Atlas.)

Best to go to Europe to really overload on cherubs, and America's western cities for the forms that follow function. In New York, you can get some of both.

Now, here is what many dilettantes don't understand about Louis Sullivan's famous slogan.

("Dilettante" means someone who *delights* in the arts; who finds the arts *delectable* – from the Latin *dilectare*, meaning to delight in. Later, the word took on another layer of meaning: someone who has no business talking about arts he merely talks about and has no deep expertise in. I'm a dilettante in the older sense. Okay, both.)

By "Form Follows Function," Sullivan, Frank Lloyd Wright's mentor, and so to Wright what Henry Cameron is to Howard Roark, meant that the façade – often the only side of the building anyone can see, because the other three sides are hidden in the block – should not necessarily show its actual functioning parts, but artistic representations, or mere suggestions, *of* those functioning parts. This is why the Chanin Building will come up in a few more paragraphs. The columns inside the building hold it up and make its great height possible. But, for one thing, it is usually against fire codes to put the *real* columns on the outside, so you cover the column with a pier of metal, brick, stone, or some other cladding so the sidewalk critic can see where the columns are in the building, and he can see that you, the architect, choose to emphasize the vertical by representing each column inside the wall with a pier on the outside of the wall; a visual vertical element. Roark complains about the many early skyscrapers that have heavy horizontal elements that emphasize the horizontal and so rob these tall buildings of their visual height. A tall building should look tall, he says. But since *The Age of Rand*, 2005, there has come to be a skyscraper in Manhattan that is so tall and skinny, and plain and blah looking, too, that I have to amend Roark's rule.

It is on East 57th Street. No need to give you the address; you can't miss it. It is another of the "Oligarchs' Buildings," like the one next to Carnegie Hall. The Russians are coming! And boy are they loaded! They are putting their money here in the United States, where it is safe because we have political and economic stability. The oligarchs don't understand *why* we do, but they understand *that* we do. This building is white. Period. Just a plain white box. New Yorkers of 1970 complained that the World Trade Center towers were the box the Empire State

Building came in. But compared to the 57th Street job, the Twin Towers were filled with detail and personality, and it almost seems, cherubs. At least they had a shiny strip at the top, to show you that the workers knew which floor was to *be* the top.

Now for the Chanin Building. This one is high Art Deco. It is on East 42nd Street, across from Grand Central and the Chrysler Building. Sloan & Robertson built it for the Chanin Brothers in 1928/9. The brothers built and managed theaters and hotels. This was their own headquarters office building. It shows both "what it makes possible" and "what makes it possible."

From the third to the fifth stories, in the recess between two corner masses, there is a row of nine piers or pylons or pillars or columns or buttresses or call them what you will. They look like nine identical model skyscrapers, like the miniature of the Cities Service Oil Company Building you see as an ornament over the door of that building at 70 Pine Street downtown. These nine wooden soldiers all in a row look like Deco versions of Gothic buttresses, but they don't look like they are buttressing the wall as buttresses any more than they are holding the upper floors up as columns. They are, therefore, piers: expressions on the outside of the load-bearing columns on the inside. They remind us of the great steel columns making the building's height possible, though they are not the columns themselves. They aren't even where the columns are – the columns are evenly distributed around the building, while these faux buttresses are massed in one place. They are one step less literal, as art works, than the rising scale of Halley's Fifth Concerto in Atlas: "They [the notes] spoke of rising, and they were the rising itself." The buttresses speak of rising, but only as an ornament.

These nine buttresses on the base of the building are repeated at the very top – and that's the point. The actual columns holding up the building are unseen, buried inside the walls, but the buttresses at the summit suggest the idea that the columns have burst through the roof to reveal themselves in all their naked glory. They suggest, then, both the purely ornamental flourish of the Baroque and the purely functional members of, say, Chicago's John Hancock Building, with its diagonal beams visible outside the building's glass skin, or Paris's Pompidou Center, with its skinside inside and all its innards outside.

And, with the third floor preview, and the 53rd floor big finish – the TA-DA! – the buttresses frame the experience. You always assume that the sidewalk critic's eyes will start at eye level and sweep upward. That way, the base of the skyscraper is the first movement, the Allegro, of the concerto, the shaft is the slow, quiet, middle movement, the Adagio, and the crown is the big finish, the Furioso, repeating the theme of the third floor, but with more zest and a sense of completion. Just as Rand's paragraph describing Halley's Fifth Concerto appears in Chapter 1 and is repeated word for word on the novel's penultimate page.

AIRPORTS

A skyscraper and an airport are like cherubs. They are crowning developments that imply a head, which implies shoulders, which imply a spine, and legs and feet. The whole king under the crown, and his retainers, and the peasants who feed them. What the careful reader of Atlas gets from Rand's heroes, especially Dagny, is that these are people who never take for granted all the steps that made today possible. You can't hear the word of the Lord from the head bone unless it is supported by all the connected bones down to the toe bone.

An airport implies a city big enough to support it. It implies a business class whose time is so valuable that they must get to that meeting by air today and not three days more slowly by bus, cost what it may. ("...the words of a businessman's language: *price no object*." – *Atlas Shrugged*) It implies leisure travellers who have worked hard and earned a vacation on another continent. Such a long trip requires a jet. If you are one of the *idle* rich, you could take your private railcar from New York to LA, then sail your yacht to Tahiti. But air travel implies that you, who are not idle, no matter how rich you are, rate a two or three week vacation at the antipodes, but you have every intention of coming back to the work you love and the responsibilities you have freely chosen.

Airports are the easiest part of a city to spot on your Worship Machine. Zoom in on any modern city and you will see this giant form, with its runways, just outside the built-up metro area. Think of the land that airport takes up! That's where the mines of the future should go. Might as well dig out any mineral wealth under all that flat land. The Netherlands is so desperate for land that they even farm the land between the runways of their airports! The farmer has to get clearance from the tower before starting out on his tractor to plow. Picture mineral wealth coming up from the particle beam disintegrators, to a processing plant, and right to the shop counters where you buy your Dramamine before boarding your plane – and all concealed under the runways themselves. A large part of tomorrow's cities may lie underground. Shortens the taxi ride from plane to hotel room. "Driver, just take me straight down three blocks, from the terminal to my hotel."

It is the capitalists who have achieved collectivism: Markets are collective entities. No one individual sets prices; the aggregate of all the transactions in the market do. And while a city has its skyscrapers and airports to show the head on the body, or the cupids on the ceiling, it is not, in our dynamic 21st Century economy, the same individuals or families on top in all ways or for all time. The Old World's mistake was to assign individuals – nay, whole families for generations – to a "station in life" by force. And they *needed* force to keep that peasant family down on the farm, because they were ignoring Man's nature. Man is an individual, with skills and ambitions that differ from individual to individual, not from family to family. Church and State are failing to obey Nature, so they fail to command it. And so they "always fall."

(In the "Gandhi" movie, Bapu says "There have been tyrants and murderers, and for a time they can seem invincible, but in the end they always fall.")

So a free society is *not* just like a man's body. Individuals come and go. Companies and whole industries come and go. The Dow Industrial companies of today, and even whole Dow industries of today, are not the same ones of fifty, or sometimes even five, years ago. Look at a city on Google Earth and try to find the original town site and orthographic center – but don't expect the same families to fill its ballrooms for generations on end. "Society" in the snobbish sense of the New York 400 has gone the way of the dodo. With or without Rand's influence, the world really is coming to value individual achievement rather than old money – and the resulting fountain of the products of the human mind is too powerful and varied for the old money types to count for much anymore. We are becoming more collegial.

In Atlas, Dagny asks Ellis Wyatt why he wants to live so far away from "everything." You can tell that Dagny is a New Yorker. "Everythng" means New York. In fact, just parts of Manhattan. Wyatt retorts "I'm just a few steps away from everything." He means his oilfield – he lives right next to it. To him, his own creative work is everything. Dagny's question is out of character for her: she is also married to her career. She should understand.

This is the worldview of the Age of Rand. Snobbery will give way to context (a favorite Rand word). For you, in your personal context, the things you will want to see out your front door every day are the things that make you a living, and more: that you think of as giving you your identity. For Ellis Wyatt, that would be the oilfield where he "mixes his labor with the land." This is an old, played-out field that he figured out some way of reviving. It's not just work, you see, it is the ingenuity with which Wyatt has learned to produce more with *less* work. Cities are where this effect tends to take place anyway. It's hard to hide things in a city. Living in a city makes Jane Jacobses of us all. In the country a factory can be missed by travelers driving by on the Interstate. But in the city the homes of the rich at Fifth Avenue and 90th Street are only ten blocks down and one over from the bodegas at Madison and 100th. And the factories are only a little farther away than that. An

Objectivist factory owner will want to live within sight of his factory and the homes of his employees. He will not fear his workers or what they do to the neighborhood. Esthetically, and spiritually, he wants to see the integration – the whole process of his life, his city, his industry, his workers and customers, all laid out before him like a Thomas Hart Benton mural. The cherubs will be alighting on the beams.

CHAPTER 15
IT'S MITHRAS TIME IN THE CITY

Who invented Christmas?

Pope Liberius, in 354, decreed that Christians would celebrate Christ's Mass on December 25th. That does not jibe with shepherds watching their flocks by night, since shepherds do that only in the spring lambing season, so why did Liberius choose that date — so close to the winter solstice? He was stealing the birthday that Mithraists had assigned to their incarnation of Ahuramazda, the god of light: Mithras. Liberius was simply trying to undercut a rival religion.

But much of what we think of when we hear the word "Christmas" was invented in 19th Century New York – mainly Santa Claus – or in London, Philadelphia, or Boston. "Jingle Bells" was written in the Boston area, but the sheet music was published on Frankfort Street, New York, in the printing and publishing district. London saw the invention of the Christmas card, and of course Dickens' "A Christmas Carol." The Christmas tree stand was in invented in Philadelphia, and Christmas tree lights in New York.

The publishing firm of Inskeep & Bradford, on Broadway between Cedar and Liberty, published Washington Irving's *A History of New York* on Saint Nicholas Day, December 6, 1809. There Irving introduced American, and then world, readers to Saint Nicholas flying in a wagon over the rooftops, delivering "his yearly presents to children." Half a block up Broadway is the site of Alexander Hamilton's newspaper the *Post*, which ran the world's first Christmas advertising. Two more blocks brings the Christmas pilgrim to 10 John Street, where Henry M. Onderdonck published an 1848 illustrated collection of the poems of Clement Clarke Moore, including "A Visit from Saint Nicholas." Four more blocks brings us to the site of *Harper's Weekly*, whose cartoonist Thomas Nast put Santa Claus at the North Pole, and Joseph Pulitzer's New York *World*, whose cartoonists added Mrs. Claus. Down at Wall Street and Pearl Street, northeast corner, James Rivington, owner of the New York *Gazette*, wrote at yuletide in about 1770 that "Christmas is being celebrated here with the usual Dutch festivities, including the appearance of St. A Claus." This was the very first rendering of the name Santa Claus in print.

The winter solstice is the day when the nights finally stop shortening and start lengthening. This meant hope and rejoicing to all our ancestors, and they all associated the event with whatever other beliefs they had. Jesus was born. Mithras was born. Baldur, the Norse sun god, died and was reborn. Our ancestors lit bonfires, or retold the story of oil lamps miraculously staying lit for eight days. Our ancestors gathered the boughs of the holly tree because they remained green through the winter — a sign of hope for the spring. The word "holly" comes from "holy." The holly tree was the holy tree. It was always about the return of light, of the sun, of spring and of life.

After the success of "Star Wars" in 1978, a Star Wars Christmas special was televised. But since the story takes place a long time ago, in a presumably non-Christian galaxy far, far away, they could not have Luke Skywalker celebrating Christmas, so the writers posited a "Life Day" holiday observed in Luke's galaxy. They weren't far off.

I lost interest in "Star Wars" before the prequels appeared, twenty-odd years after the originals. I even outgrew "Star Trek." I had looked forward eagerly to the movies and "Star Trek: The Next Generation," but when "Deep Space Nine" premiered, I was dismayed to find myself bereft of interest. Some stories appeal only if they trigger nostalgia for childhood.

Religion works the same way. The only hold religion has on most people is childhood nostalgia, and habit. "A long habit of not thinking a thing wrong gives it the superficial appearance of being right," said Sir Francis Bacon, "Time makes more converts than reason." There are some exceptions: seekers, who go from religion to religion, looking for whatever turns them on, but most people follow a religion only because it was the one they were brought up in.

H. L. Mencken said "I've always been an agnostic, and my father before me and his father before him." He added that like other born-and-raised atheists (he used the word "agnostic," but I gather he meant atheist) he had no worries about whether the admonitions of any religion should be followed. He felt perfectly comfortable ignoring them all alike. But those brought up in a given religion who declared themselves atheists later in life, Mencken said, could never escape the nagging fear that they might be wrong and go to Hell for it.

If you were born and raised a Christian and not a Hindu, do you *worry* that you might never escape the cycle of death and rebirth and never reach Moksha? Of course not. If you were born to Hinduism, do you *worry* that you might go to Christian Hell for failure to give your life to Christ? Of course not. And you will never, let's face it, get around to reading the Gita, the Koran, the Book of Mormon, and all the other sacred texts just to make sure you're in the right religion. If you are like most people, you worry only about the religion you were born to, and all the others you dismiss as silly.

A long time ago, I decided that if I were not prepared to take *every* religion seriously, then why should I take *any* of them seriously? Why should I take my parents' religion any more seriously than I would the idea of asking Zeus or Woden for luck in business, or love or crops?

With all that understood, let me wish all atheists a merry Christmas. The magic of Christmas lies in its ability to break all barriers and simply absorb anything that history throws at it. Today's modern, American, secular, universal and above all, commercialized Christmas absorbed everything from the Norse mistletoe myth to the Roman Saturnalia.

(It then absorbed commercialism. Within three years of the invention of the light bulb, the president of the New York Edison Company became the first to hang his Christmas tree with electric lights — which saved many lives after that: the original German custom had been to light a tree with tapers: tiny candles. Open flames on a dead, dry tree.)

Our ancestors burned the Yule log, lighting it with a brand from last year's, to invoke the spirit of light. Eventually Thomas Edison and others did in fact what Prometheus did in myth: they "gave men a gift they had not conceived, and lifted darkness off the earth." (*The Fountainhead*)

Kudos (Greek for "honor") to A. T. Stewart and Rogers Peet and Tiffany's and Sloane Carpets and the Washington Market and all the other stores around Broadway and City Hall Park in the early 19th Century who pioneered the Christmas greens and Christmas tree lights and Christmas music and department store Santas and all the other happy reminders of the return of the sun! All the "crass commercialization" of Christmas in the city that brings joy to the hearts of Altruism's Scrooges of self-sacrifice and suffering! (Even if they won't admit it.)

Cue "Silver Bells – It's Christmas Time in the City." (By Jay Livingston and Ray Evans. First performed by Bob Hope and Marilyn Maxwell in "The Lemon Drop Kid," 1950.) A hymn to the commercialization of Christmas.

We have not taken enough advantage, in this volume, of the sense of smell for worship purposes, so let's try this: Remember the special multi-colored Scotch Tape that used to appear only at Christmas time, for wrapping presents? It had a distinctive, metallic smell. John Galt explains that legends like Atlantis or the Garden of Eden exist because there *was* a time of perfect happiness in the past. But it was not in Man's past – it was in yours and mine and everyone's past. Childhood. That colored tape smell is one of the time machines that will transport you back there, for a moment. Maybe Thomas Wolfe was wrong, and you can go home again. "I'll be home for Christmas, if only in my dreams." (Lyrics by Kim Gannon, music by Walter Kent, recorded 1943 by Bing Crosby for Decca, as Side B for "White Christmas." Dedicated to servicemen overseas. Beloved. Commercial.) What's Christmas without Bing?

If you were brought up Christian, use Christmas to recapture the wonder of childhood, and be fascinated learning the beliefs and folkways of your own remote ancestors, who were short on facts, but long on imagination, when it came to explaining the world around them. Revel in nostalgia for Man's childhood and your own. It is true that you can't go home again, but you can carry a little of it with you into the future.

CHAPTER 16
THE BLUE PLACE

We now return to the topic of night and the city as glamor. You may be surprised to learn that "glamor" is an Irish word meaning "a magic charm," as in: I'm lucky because a witch put the glamor on me.

Picture the scene: The Metropolitan Room is a small night club (in the 1920s sense, not for "clubbing" with the Millennials) on West 22nd Street between Fifth and Sixth. It's where I go to hear the songs of Noel and Cole. Stephen Holden, reviewing music for the *Times* of September 9, 2015, writes:

"A royal-blue night sky and twinkling stars: the perfect moment." With those words, the complicated jazz singer Nancy Harms introduced her rendition of "Prelude to a Kiss" on Sunday evening at the Metropolitan Room, where she sang a program of Duke Ellington-related songs titled "Ellington at Night."

Got the picture? Got the mood? What more do you need, to get the mood, than the words "blue," "Ellington," "evening," and "metropolitan"?

"Infamous" – the 2006 movie about Truman Capote (Toby Jones) writing *In Cold Blood*, features soliloquies by some of Capote's Park Avenue friends of the 1950s and 60s. The speeches are performed in front of a backdrop of the Manhattan skyline at night, and there is another such background on the cover of the DVD. Why that background? Because that was Capote's world – the world of New York ... no, of

Manhattan, and only the parts around Central Park at that, at night, the meaning of which we have examined previously (here and in *The Age of Rand*, in the chapter THE ART DECO PHILOSOPHER).

Why is blue my magic color? Why not black – the color of night? Because blue is not the color of night, but of evening, when the sunshine of gaudy day and the black of night *even* out. That's why they call it evening. And evening represents a good day's work done. Time to enjoy the fruits of your labor. Or, blue can mean dawn – the promise of a new day. Or, blue can mean the black of night softened by Man's ingenious electric light.

At this point, google the Blue Grotto on the Isle of Capri. Besides the cave entrance at sea level, where you enter in a small boat, there is another entrance, all underwater, that lets sunlight into the cave, and that sunlight comes up through the water to illuminate the airspace of the cave in deep blue. That color is what I'm talking about. But in this case, the blue light is natural. When it is man-made, it carries another meaning.

I am looking at four recent print ads that show variations on my "Blue Place" visual theme. The first is a Harry Winston Jewelry ad. (No, the word "jewel" is not related to the word "Jew." Jewel comes from the French *jeu*: game; play, which comes from the Latin *jocus*: game; joke.) The background is a blue night view of Manhattan skyscrapers. The Chrysler Building is plainly visible, but fragmented, seen through the window glass. Three multi-jeweled rings are sitting on a table in the foreground. The picture is a little dark and blurry. It's on newsprint, probably from one of the free morning papers. Not high-quality printing. But that just adds to the shimmering. The jewels look like they are on a glass tabletop in front of a window, with some mirrors here and there, fragmenting the skyline view. This fragmenting of the view is not because the photographer was imitating Picasso – Rand forbid! – but because the windows, the glass tabletop, and the mirrors all suggest the shiny, reflective, refractive qualities of diamonds.

The second ad is from *Playbill*. It is an ad for "An American in Paris," by the Gershwin boys. It shows a young couple strolling, arms around each other's waists, past a kiosk and toward the Eiffel Tower. The sky is shaded from light blue at the ground to dark blue and starry above the point of the Tower. Need we say more?

The third is from the back cover of *Time Out* magazine, February 25, 2010. It advertises One Brooklyn Bridge Park – a luxury condo building. M'lady is dressed in a shimmering maroon gown that flows down to the floor and halfway across it. She wears a jeweled necklace that goes on for days. She carries a small chandelier, and a bigger one hangs nearby. Behind her is a wall that is all glass, and through it we see a nighttime skyline of lighted skyscraper windows. Stars dot the sky. The sky is all dark blue; no shading. At the bottom of the buildings out the window is a green band that undulates roundly – it is the treeline of Central Park. The caption reads: "Bored with handbags, Catherine noted her extravagant 13' ceilings and began a chandelier collection."

The style of the cartoon – that's what it is – and of the caption suggests that the ad is meant to both appeal to the *New Yorker* magazine crowd and poke gentle fun at it. We can take a little kidding, can't we? We must be big about these things. It's like the cartoon in the *New Yorker* itself that shows a smart (in both senses) young couple in their smart-looking living room, filled with art books. The woman says to the man "I wish you'd stop saying 'Scarlatti, of course'."

The fourth ad in this collection of Blue Places is not blue. Again, there is a nighttime skyline view. Again it is a real estate ad. Again there is a smart-looking couple in evening dress. Again there is a full-wall window. The couple are looking southeast past the UN Secretariat and across the East river to Long Island City, Queens. The young woman holds a wine glass and the man holds her. But they, unlike the Americans in Paris, are not making eyes at each other. They are both looking at the view and they are both rapt. They could be Hank and Dagny – especially since the woman wears an off-the-shoulder gown, as Dagny does at

173

Hank and Lillian's anniversary party. In fact she is wearing a shiny metal bracelet, and the man's hand is on her forearm, just touching the bracelet. Maybe they *are* supposed to be Hank and Dagny. But their sky is brown. Well, maybe brown is in this year for interior decorating, and the photographer had little of the condo's interior to show, so he made the sky and the river look like a restful, brown interior instead. He gives the window frames and the windowless north edge of the Secretariat a golden glow, to accent his brown nightscape. A curious strategy, but it sells the image of a condo for subtle, sophisticated buyers. Nathanial Branden did the same thing, come to think of it, by putting his NBI records in brown jackets with the look and texture of old, brown leather textbooks, or classics. Brown is the color of deep thoughts.

(The ad is for 50 United Nations Plaza, in the *New York Times Magazine* of May 3, 2015.)

Know what else is blue? Air. Why is the sky blue? Because the air absorbs the longer red light waves from the sun, and reflects the shorter blue ones, so blue is what we see (to simplify a bit). Leonardo da Vinci once wrote in his diary "I have discovered a new perspective!" He meant that he had discovered another way, besides parallax, to indicate in a painting the way things look different at a greater distance than at a lesser: they get bluer. There is more air between the viewer and a distant object than a close one. So the distant object is bluer, and fuzzier.

BLUE NOTES

In 1926, when Rand was alighting in New York from the S.S. *DeGrasse*, George Gershwin was basking in the reception of his "Rhapsody in Blue" just two years before. He had started to make his mark as a Broadway songwriter, but his Rhapsody made him a force in the concert music field too. Brother Ira made up the title. It showed jazz influence (!) in the concert hall!! One writer of record jacket notes said that the Rhapsody is not exactly jazz, but just an "enthusiastic whoop from the 20s." "Jazz is music," George explained, "It uses the same notes that Bach used. Jazz is the result of the energy stored in America." There's that "energy" theme again. Motive power. You can't imagine how important that is. Legend has it that he wrote the piece for a blind girl, so she could hear an aural impression of his visual impression of the New York skyline. Why "blue?" Perhaps because the skyline is distant and being distant, it often looks blue.

I tend to think of red as the color of energy, because of fire, I suppose. In ancient Chinese philosophy, the Yang is red, hot, male, positive, canine, obvious. Yin is blue, cool, female, negative, feline, subtle. But actually, blue is the short-wave, more energetic end of the spectrum. But that does not work in poetry, because it is counter-intuitive.

A whole state can be blue, if it is an archipelago in the blue ocean: Elvis Presley's "Blue Hawaii."

The countryside has musical charms: Aaron Copeland's "Appalachian Spring." But cities have a vast library of music all their own, and it often involves evening and nightlife and blue dusk and the blues being played in slightly dangerous blues joints. Leopold Stokowski once stopped his rehearsal of a Rachmaninoff piece for a little musical history lesson for his orchestra. "Look at number 27," he said. "See the jazz influence? Rachmaninoff used to go down to the bad parts of town and listen to the music, and it began to creep into his work."

City songs: tick them off in your head. Shuffle off to Buffalo. Chicago: On State Street, that great street, they do things they don't do on Broadway. You can leave your heart in San Francisco, if you wear a flower in your hair. I'm looking at a record called "Madrid After Dark." Arrivaderci, Roma! Silver rain was falling down upon the dirty ground of London Town. London Pride is a flower that's free. Moscow Nights. Rio by the sea-o. Boston, my home town. Back in old Napoli that's *amore*! Saigon, the Paris of the East. They're dancing in Chicago! Down in New Orleans! Philadelphia, PA! Baltimore and DC now. Don't forget the Motor City! They'll be swingin', swayin' and dancin' in the street ...

There is a Tijuana Brass number called "Memories of Madrid." It is a sad, sentimental song, as all pleasant memories are a little sad, since you are remembering joys that are now past. Many such songs concern a city itself, rather than, say, a girl you met *in* Madrid. The city you once visited means to you a trip, or a move you thought might be permanent but wasn't, to a certain city, and all kinds of circumstances of that trip, including memories of sights, sounds, smells, and tastes – George Takei, at a Star Trek convention, recalled filming in San Francisco: "We did some good eating in San Francisco; some *very* good eating."

But here's a lesser known musical piece, and one that celebrates New York and the skyscraper in particular. It's called "Manhattan Tower," composed and conducted by Gordon Jenkins. It is an orchestral setting for an ecstatic spoken poem about the residential tower the composer lives in. He suggests the street sounds – horns, bustling cars and cabs – and the sheer excitement of just being in the city where so much life goes on around you. The cover photo – by Sammy Davis, Jr., no less (he was a noted photographer, among his many talents) – is an evening view from the top of the RCA Building, looking toward the East River, and lots of blue sky and clouds lit by the setting sun, the Chrysler building, the UN, the New York Central (read: Taggart Transcontinental) Building, Raymond Hood's Daily News building, and others. Who is doing the looking? A young couple. Their heads are tilted toward each other, but they only have eyes for New York. Davis has captured one of those sunset moments when da Vinci's aerial perspective turns the grey limestone, brown brick and white tile of the buildings gold, even as the sky turns a darker and darker blue each minute. On the back of the cover is a sketch of some typical Manhattan towers, the Chrysler and Empire State among them. The artist fills in the tops of the towers more fully than the bottoms – shows more detail – and more darkly, with heavier strokes. This is the technique that Ilona Royce Smithkin used in her sketch portrait of Rand that you see on the backs of many of Rand's paperbacks, and by Rand's painter friend José Manuel Capuletti. The painter fills in more fully the part of the portrait that he wants the viewer to focus on, and he lets the sketch dwindle down to a few strokes and then to nothing, farther from the focus. In Royce Smithkin's case, the focus is Rand's eyes. Here it is the tops of the towers: Like Roark, the artist wants to emphasize the tallness of these tall buildings by making us notice their tops more than their bottoms.

(Google Ilona Royce Smithkin. She is the subject of a book and two documentaries! She's a character – still going strong in her nineties!)

Look at the Leonard Maltin annual Movie Guide. Turn to the "B's." Note how many movie titles use the word "blue." The mystery and adventure of cities in the evening – works every time.

YOU ONLY LIVE TWICE: ONCE WHEN YOU ARE BORN, AND ONCE WHEN YOU LOOK DEATH IN THE FACE.

Oh, I think we can do better than that, Mr. Ian Fleming. Why bother getting born, and why bother facing death, if there are not plenty of moments in the middle that you are glad to experience for their own sakes? Wynand's "typewriter" moments? (In *The Fountainhead*, Wynand asks Roark, "When you think back on your life, does it all roll forward evenly, like a sort of typing exercise, all the same? Or were there stops – points reached – and then the typing rolled on again?"

"There were stops.")

At Hank and Lillian's party, Dagny says "...celebrations should be only for those who have something to celebrate." Now, before the Rand-bashers cry *Elitist!* we should add that Rand makes it clear that Dagny is criticizing those people who go to parties to go through the *motions* of celebration and joy but who have created nothing that brings joy. It is as if they are trying to reverse causality: If we celebrate, that will give us something to celebrate. Kind of like the Cargo Cult. Or it will help us fool ourselves that we have something to celebrate. She tells Hank that she has at length permitted herself a break and wants to celebrate the completion of the first sixty miles of Rearden Metal track for the John Galt line. (Think there might be a subtext here? Like maybe Dagny just wants an excuse to be with Hank, and maybe scope out Lillian?) Hank's party, in his house outside Philadelphia, and within walking distance of his mills, is, for the occasion, Dagny's Blue Place. It is her Miller Time. An evening spent doing something other than work. Reward time.

Hobbies are something to do in your Blue Place. Rand wrote an article on why she liked stamp collecting. She gave a very sensible account, as only she would think of doing, of why Man needs hobbies. When you quit working at the end of the day, you don't just drop off to sleep, you take some leisure time. But what is "leisure"? A leisure time activity is like your work – it is problem solving – but it is work in miniature. It is not how you make your living. The problems you solve are not fraught with grave consequences. So you are using your mind, but in a more relaxed way. The problem solving makes the activity fun, and the lack of dire consequences makes it a relaxed activity instead of a tense one.

"What does your mind go to in the evening, by itself?"

That is a question Branden asked in one of his lectures. It may be the most important line in all his lectures and books on psychology. The purpose of that question is career choice. If you want to know, in your teen years, what you should do with the rest of your life, consult the Blue Place in your mind. When you come home from work and are spending the evening relaxing, where does your mind go, unbidden? Follow it, and that is where you will find fulfillment and happiness.

John Galt refers to a man "in love with himself and life." Rand means a man who had self-esteem early in life – that is, he started life assuming, until proven otherwise, that his life was worth at least the old college try. And so he tried. And whatever the struggle, he loves the struggle, as well as the instrument luck gave him for that struggle. Thus he loves both himself and life.

I gave a long and difficult walking tour once. It was my "Ely Jacques Kahn's Art Deco New York" tour, which runs at least three hours even with a small group. (The bigger the group, the slower, because they straggle, and they ask questions, and not always relevant ones.) I build in a bathroom break in the middle of this tour. And this was no ordinary group. These were about twenty attendees of the International Congress of Art Deco Societies, meeting here in New York, and coming from all over the world. They were experts. They had some technical questions that I did not know the answer to. But they had a good time. We adjourned the tour, after four hours or more, at a restaurant, and dined and chatted. I was hot, sweaty, sun-struck, dizzy and exhausted. My throat was bricky dry and sore from projecting to twenty people, outdoors, for four hours. After dinner, though, I couldn't help walking back over the tour route, re-living the experience. Here I remembered something I was afraid I would forget, and there vice versa. Here I got a good question, there, I got an irrelevant or even incoherent one. Here I said something that got a laugh. There I was asked a question I could not answer.

The sun was down. The sky was bluing. A good day's work was done. In my head, I was hearing the theme to the James Bond movie "You Only Live Twice." The gently descending notes of the intro suggest gently falling into an easy chair, or into a swimming pool on a hot, sweaty, sunny day, after the day's tension and work and responsibility are done. You hear much the same gently descending sound in the theme of the movie "Midnight Cowboy."

My first remembered picture of the idea of glamor was an ad in a *Life* magazine from around 1960. It was a car ad, and it showed a big, new car and a well-dressed man helping a well-dressed woman into it. Both were smiling, and it was clear that they had a lot to smile about. But for some reason the entrancing, fascinating, charming, magical, exciting, glamorous thing about the scene was that it was laid at night, and in front of either an airport driveway or something. I have not located the exact *Life* issue and ad. Googling "1950s and 1960s car ads," I am seeing

179

several illustrations that are at least in the ballpark of this distant visual memory. I may be conflating multiple images. I seem to remember that this picture, or one of those pictures, showed the car parked at or in a grotto; a cave half filled with a lagoon, and filled with a diffuse blue light. And maybe the woman is stepping out of or into the water, while the suited man stands leaning on the car, or something like that. That may have been another ad besides the airport scene. Anyway, that was my Blue Place. It has stuck in the back of my head for fifty years. It was a magical place for grownups, though, not for children. There were no leprechauns in this cave, as you see in the Disney movie "Darby O'Gill and the Little People." Grownups drive cars and fly on jetliners. When the secular child asks for some glamor, he is praying (remember: "pray" means "ask") to his future self to do whatever it takes to realize his childhood dreams. What he does not realize is that his future self is also praying to him. The child is father to the man. Please be the child who had the courage to start on the path that would bring me, in adulthood, to the Blue Place.

CHAPTER 17
FOLLOW THE RIVER TO ITS SOURCE

To write a book about cities is not to deny or disparage the hinterlands. As a born Upstater, I took a long time getting over my resentment of New York City. I learned that, like it or not, even the biggest of the Upstate cities, Buffalo, cannot hope to compete with the Big Town. An inland lake port will never be as big and rich as an ocean port. (See *The Age of Rand* for the role of the Erie Canal here.) Buffalo made the steel, Niagara Falls the electricity, Aurora the toys, Akron the gumballs and gumball machines, Lockport the car radiators, Jamestown the crescent wrenches and the voting machines, Rochester the cameras and lenses, Hornell the snowmobiles and subway cars, Trumansburg the Moog synthesizers, Syracuse the air conditioners, candles, china and traffic signals, Fulton the Nestle's chocolate, Watertown the safety pins, Little Trees air fresheners and the first portable steam engines, Rome the copper goods, Utica and Amsterdam the textiles, Corning the glassware, Cortland the typewriters, Binghamton the flight simulators, Johnson City the shoes, Norwich the aspirin, Glens Falls and Oswego and Newton Falls the paper, Kingston the bluestone and the natural cement, Poughkeepsie the computers, Yonkers the Otis elevators, Lowville the cream cheese and bowling pins, and Schenectady the electric devices and locomotives, but New York City, with its harbor, sent the goods to worldwide buyers, collected the money, and put that money where it would make more money. The harbor begat the shipping, the shipping the insurance, the insurance the banks and the banks the stock and commodities exchanges. And all these things together begat the population base that begat the universities, the publishing, the radio and movies and TV …

But the child of the Age of Rand will see economics not just in practical terms, but in poetic terms. "Economic Geography" is not only the title of a book Rand took out of the New York Public Library to learn about business, continent-wide, as part of her Atlas research, it means something. It is a moral ideal, like "value added through manufacturing." It is a theme that has been rhapsodized in movies. Old movies, mostly, before the zombies and vampires. It is what Richard Dreyfus's character meant in "The Apprenticeship of Duddy Kravitz," when he looks out, appreciatively, at his hometown, Montreal, and says "Biggest inland port in the world." Another character, in "Lucky Man," looks over the skyline of London and says "Biggest money market in the world." It is exactly what Walt Whitman meant by "Hog butcher to the world! City of big shoulders!" And my Australian friend Max, when he proudly averred, of his hometown, Melbourne, "World's most livable city!"

Poetic terms, and what may seem like dry bizman terms or corny adman terms, but which mean something. Follow the Hudson and Mohawk up to the village of Scotia, across the river from the big GE plant in Schenectady. There you will find a corporate park ingeniously named "Corporations Park." In this small office development, "Access Boulevard," "Business Boulevard," and "Capital Boulevard" cross "Patent, Potential, and Prestige Parkways." Contrast those names with the street names of the old world: King This, and Duke That: titles from ancient, stagnant military aristocracies. (Francisco, in Atlas, speaks of how the coats of arms of the rotting aristocracies of Europe have given way to the trademarks of American companies, as war as a way of life gives way to production and consumer choice as a moral ideal.) Or, since the Enlightenment, streets named after authors, composers, painters and such. Admirable at first glance, but check whether the city or national government that named those streets might be pulling the trick Rand warned against in her "Racism" article: a government and a people trying to give itself credit for "producing" artistic and scientific geniuses. What is implied by the street name "Access Boulevard"? *Access to Capital*: in other words, how the poor of the world are about to get all the prosperity the socialist politicians promise will come … once they hold all the strings. By their street names shall you know them.

But here is a real gem. Nugget, rather. Stan Rogers, the late, great Canadian folksinger/songwriter, wrote a song called "The Rawdon Hills." It is a sad requiem for a gold mining district in Nova Scotia that just ran out of gold. Or did it? "Grandsons of the mining men, you can see it in your dreams. Beneath your fathers' bones still lies the undiscovered seam/ Of quartzite in a serpentine vein that marks the greatest yield … The Rawdon Hills once were touched by gold." How about that, for giving meaning and emotion to a dry, technical geologist's phrase like "quartzite in a serpentine vein that marks the greatest yield?" And what emotion would that be? Hope, if hope is an emotion. Those placers and smaller seams and that pannable gold dust had to come from somewhere. Whatever ancient supernova spewed a chunk of transmuted, alchemized gold, however that chunk coalesced with others to form a chunk called Nova Scotia, and however that chunk joined with others to form the Earth, it might have been a million tons just as easily as a thousand ounces. Maybe. There's always hope. Dig deeper. For the meaning, I mean, *and* for the gold.

You can tell what people value by what they dig up and put in museums. I'm just barely old enough, at 62, to remember some industrial and other pre-war buildings, mostly in the Upstate cities. And I have spent a lifetime watching the decline of the Rustbelt. But now I am fascinated to watch the process of transformation of the Industrial Age from a living culture and way of life to a memory preserved in amber and in amber-tinted tintypes.

A glance at the *Society for Industrial Archeology Newsletter*, Winter 2014, at the library of the General Society of Mechanics and Tradesmen, yielded these notes:

*Borglum Fountain Honoring Sewing Machine Manufacturer Restored –
Bridgeport, Connecticut – Nathaniel Wheeler, 1820-1893 – Commissioned
by Wheeler family as gift to city after his death. Completed 1912, restored
2014. Mermaid in the sculpture holds up light globe. Wheeler & Wilson
Manuf. Co. First U.S. patent pool: W & W, Singer, Howe, and Grover
& Baker.*

*Petrolia, Ontario. World's oldest producing oil field. Oil Springs, Ontario.
Sarnia. Still uses 1863 pumping technology, so now both a museum and
a working oilfield.*

*Tahawus, New York. Iron contaminated with titanium, 1840. Revived for
paint pigment, 1940-1990. Currently there is some interest in processing
the tailings to recover titanium.*

*Eckhart G. Grohmann "Man At Work" collection of paintings of workers
and workplaces. Milwaukee School of Engineering.*

*DVD "Echoes of Forgotten Places." Abandoned factories set to music.
Includes footage from 1936 film "Steel: A Symphony of Industry."*

Just a glance!

There is a bunch of stuff we can learn from just the few minutes I
spent with this newsletter. There is the theme of using the light bulb to
symbolize having a creative idea – a favorite image of Rand's. That's one
for my Light Bulb Motif collection. There is the theme of businessmen
in a free market banding together, without government coercion, in
things like patent pools. There is the promise of history being preserved
and taught while an industrial plant is still being used. There you see the
past – and the future of the past! There is the eternal search for new uses
for things, like titanium, that used to be waste. There is no such thing
as waste – there are only resources you have not yet learned the use of.
And there is the art that Man creates to celebrate his own inventiveness.
If a composer is setting abandoned factories to music, and making films

with titles like "Steel: A Symphony of Industry," then if I am crazy and "getting all Ayn Rand about it," then at least I have company.

If you spend all your time in New York City or other capitals, you eventually start reading *The New Yorker* (there must be a Paris and a London equivalent) and you start to turn into Percy (the *New Yorker's* cartoon mascot, a fop looking through his pince nez), looking down your long, aristocratic nose at those benighted peasants who don't live in New York (gasp!), or not in Manhattan, or not on the Upper East or Upper West sides, or on those sides but outboard of First and Eleventh Avenues, or Second and Tenth, Third and Ninth and so on to simply not having a Central Park view. (Can't you just picture the resulting *New Yorker* cartoon?)

The more mature person, no matter how rich or important he is, knows to go camping once a year or so, to keep his perspective and appreciate the comforts of civilization, and likewise he needs to spend time in cities that are not New York. He needs to remind himself that other cities and small towns and rural areas produce the things he needs. It may be that most people in the 21st Century are more receptive to this idea than their grandfathers of the early 20th Century or the 19th. Your grandfathers came from small towns, from farms, from branch cities, and having made it to Fifth Avenue did not want to be reminded that they came from humble beginnings. But you, the great grandson, will have gotten over this. You will enjoy and feel uplifted by the process of reviewing, and retelling to your children, *how* your ancestors came from humble beginnings and have improved their lot. The secret lies not in where you are at the moment, but in being constantly aware of the whole *process* of improving lots. Your inspiration will be Dagny, in Atlas, who is very good at keeping her whole historical context near or at her conscious level of awareness at all times. That is the meaning of her "morning after" scene with Hank. But Galt is even better at this. This constant awareness of *process*, of context, is why many people say they are willing to take on a tough job if it is for only six months. They know that the labors and the wounds are not vain. (see "Say Not the Struggle

Nought Availeth" by Arthur Hugh Clough) After a short time, things will get better. We live in hope. And it is why Rand used to say "Those who live for the future live in it today," and "To hold an unchanging youth is to reach at the end the vision with which one started."

To embrace Nature does not have to mean to reject civilization. It depends on *why* you embrace nature, to what extent, and what particular aspect of nature you embrace, and what "embrace" means. Go upriver. Smell the grass and the Wonderbread and the fresh sheets on the clothesline (three childhood smells of mine, on Collamer Road at Fremont Road, East Syracuse; yours may be different). Cycle back and forth between Collamer Road and 120 East 34th Street – nature and city – childhood imagination and grownup responsibility – resources and value added – what makes it possible and what it makes possible. Fill the cup and then empty it again, like Zarathustra. Watch the factories go up, and then go down – down into the ground, to free up ground space for parks, and down in size, to the unobtrusive scale of Galt's small powerhouse. Remember how, in Chapter 3, we contrasted "The Two Towers" with "Things to Come." High technology is clean technology. By the time of Star Trek, 2166, you will be able to smell the fresh air of the country and enjoy the street life of the city at the same time, through clean, miniaturized manufacturing and fast transportation.

Ayn Rand is ridiculed for speaking well of smokestacks. In *Capitalism: The Unknown Ideal*, she explained that the only time in history that you see a dramatic increase in population is in the early years of industrialization. Factory life in Britain's cities meant survival for people whose ancestors had been subsistence and tenant farmers for centuries. But now, through industrialization, many could spend just enough years in factory work to save up money and open shops – thus making Britain a "nation of shopkeepers." And the jobs that were most miserable in those years turn out to be the surviving pre-industrial jobs, like chimney sweeping, and not the factory jobs themselves. The factory years were the years when women and children could, for the first time in history, not *have* to work. A man could at last begin to support a whole family.

And the population grew, because not so many people were starving or decimated by plagues as had been the case back on the subsistence farms. Rand wrote that anyone over the age of 35 should say a silent "Thank you" to the nearest, grimiest factory smokestack – just for their role in getting Man off the subsistence farm, not because factories need have smokestacks in the future. Go to Bethlehem, Pennsylvania and look at steel mills like Hank Rearden's, preserved as historic sites; relics of one stage in Man's progress toward ease, abundance, safety and cleanliness. Eddie says "You can't imagine how important motive power is," and the unnamed track worker across the lunch table smiles ...

Guess why The Soviet Union was first to put a satellite in orbit (on October 4, 1957 – six days before Atlas was published). Was it, as most Americans feared, that Soviet technology was ahead of ours and their rockets were therefore more powerful? No, it turns out that the only reason the Soviets had more powerful rockets on the shelf already is that their H-bombs were more primitive than ours and therefore heavier, and so their rockets were more powerful because they *had* to be. Motive power is important – unless you don't need it.

As you learn to appreciate motive power, high technology, trains feeding New York City with the produce and raw materials of a continent, and the inspiration that comes from holding the cause and the effect in a single glance, you will also learn to appreciate city parks. They are not there to carry the message and meaning of the evil of cities and the moral superiority of the rural countryside, but to present a miniature model of both. Parks are nature as artifice. Parks are models of the hinterland for port city dwellers, like model train sets, landscape paintings, and Beléns (a nativity scene model in a Spanish-speaking church is a *Belén*; a Bethlehem), and in an abstract way, they are like toy soldiers, model ships, and Barbie Dolls: whatever you expect of adulthood in childhood, and whatever you wish to remember of adulthood in old age, you surround yourself with pictures and models of.

One fine piece of nature as artifice as nature is the watercourse in Brooklyn's 1866 Prospect Park. We discussed this park in the Grid chapter. The watercourse ends at a pond. But where does it begin? Pretend you are Burton and Speke and follow the stream back and back until you find its source. You find a small pool, with water cascading down from a pile of rocks. A spring! But then, if you read about the park, you find that the water coming from this spring is artificially pumped up from the pond. Remember the line in *We The Living*?

"How beautiful! It's almost real."

"How beautiful! It's almost artificial."

In *The Fountainhead*, Rand has Roark design Monadnock, a resort made up of small bungalows built on the ledges of hills, "in such a way that the houses became inevitable, and one could no longer imagine the hills as beautiful without them." And Roark's Heller house is built of the same granite as the seaside rock mass it is built on. These are examples of Frank Lloyd Wright's principle of "organic architecture." Let the building look like it belongs there. "When in doubt," advised Wright, "plant a tree."

And there is beauty in the mental picture of the same water endlessly cycling from pump to cascade to pool to brook to pond to pump. Unseen until Olmstead and Vaux wish it to be seen. The water struts its hour on the stage, performing its act for the human spectators, then it goes backstage to its dressing room again. It is the designers' act of design – an act of human will – even though its purpose is to present, just as in a painting or sculpture, a picture of nature. A pretty bit of nature, though – Olmstead could have given us a picture of a hyena chewing on an adorable little lamb, but that's not the aspect of nature the audience usually likes to contemplate for its beauty. If you did, though, you might get away with it by reminding the audience that animals eating other animals is also an example of the cyclical nature of Nature.

In this day of Interstate Highways, we often forget the watercourses around us. We often forget that water courses around us. Our ancestors did not, though. Look at a map of Westchester County, New York. It is on the east shore of the Hudson, above New York City. "Above" meaning upriver. When British Major John Andre was stopped by three New York State militiamen at North Tarrytown (about to ride across a bridge that spanned what is now called Andre's Creek, just before it emptied into the Hudson), he assumed that they were "Cowboys" (Loyalist militia), but they turned out to be "Skinners" (Patriot militia). Andre thought he had already ridden too far south to encounter Patriot militia. Farther down the Hudson, on New York Island (Manhattan) was the first outpost of safe Redcoat territory. In No Man's Land there were constant raids by the Cowboys, so for all Andre knew, these could very well be three of them. Fatal mistake, though. A few more feet, across that bridge, and he might have made it the rest of the way down the Hudson shore to the first British checkpoint. Smiling, Andre said "Gentlemen! I hope you belong to our party."

"What party?" parried the leader.

"The lower party."

This had to be explained to me the first time I read it. "Lower?" Andre meant *lower down the river*. In other words, New York City – the British headquarters and his own. Who would understand that way of putting it today? The joke today is "You're from New Jersey? What exit?" I know otherwise well-informed people who wonder why Manhattan is called an island, not ever having noticed, on maps, narrow little Harlem River, separating the island from the Bronx mainland, among the divided lane highways on both of its shores. The highways have overwhelmed the natural landscape. That short line "The lower party" speaks volumes about how our ancestors saw the world and their place in it. No wonder we need parks, as models of vanishing continents.

Hoboken, New Jersey is like Prospect Park. It is a miniature continent. It calls itself the "Mile Square City" because it is just about a mile square. If you get there by ferry, you are Columbus, sailing west, and landing on a land mass that continues flatly for a mile and then ends abruptly at a bluff a hundred feet high. Now you are Lewis and Clark, and Zebulon Pike, and John C. "The Pathfinder" Fremont, bumping up against the Rocky Mountains. Any gold nuggets in that gravel? And what lies beyond?

Once, in Denver, I sat on the ground, facing west, in City Park, Denver's Central Park. I became suddenly aware that a mile of rock separated my keester from sea level. Syracuse, my hometown, is 380 feet above sea level, and I had gotten used to living not more than about fifty feet up in the air in Brooklyn. I pictured the rise of that mile of altitude telescoped down from two thousand miles horizontally to one. Brooklyn's Coney Island beach to Denver, the "Mile High City." In my mind's eye I looked over my shoulder, eastward, and down a mile long, forty-five degree slope to the Atlantic surf. On Page 1 and 2 of *The Fountainhead*, Roark looks at the rocks around his swimming hole. He sees a streak of rust, and thinks of iron ore in the bedrock, waiting for his hand to give it a new form and meaning, as steel beams in a building. Pioneers did just that – they looked for streaks of rust in the rocks wherever they roamed. When they saw it, they dug for iron ore. Iron oxide – it's in our blood.

I just got back from a pilgrimage to one of my sacred mountains. No, not Sinai or Olympus or the Acropolis or the Temple Mount or Capitol Hill or Ararat or the Tien Shan (the Mountains of Heaven – to China what the Rockies are to American "Westering") or the lava pits of Pele the volcano goddess or the one in Sudan that a pharaoh carved his image on or Ship Rock or Devil's Tower or …

No, I mean Fresh Kills Landfill on Staten Island. The mountain of garbage. It is across Richmond Avenue from Staten Island Mall. There's another pairing. Garbage to goods, to be sold in the mall and go home with you as food or furniture or a beloved keepsake. And then back to garbage again, days or decades later. Nature is all about recycling, and Nature, to be commanded, must be obeyed (a favorite Rand maxim). Even the universe as a whole will get recycled someday – the Big Crunch. We will all go together when we go.

Garbage, in the 21st Century, is just another resource … an unnatural resource, but a resource. Invent a use for garbage and it instantly becomes what economists call a "scarce good." That's just because someone will pay money for it, now that someone has discovered a use for it. If what you have a lot of is peanuts, like George Washington Carver, then you look for new uses for peanuts. If you have garbage, ditto. Thirty years ago, I found, in *Popular Science* or some such magazine, an article about particle beams that can chip carbon atoms, one by one, off a diamond and deposit them on a surface you want coated with diamond. Soon this invention found its way into an Isaac Asimov novel, *Nemesis*. Even made the front page of the *Times*: DIAMOND ERA BEGINS. But not much since then. I remain hopeful, though, that particle beams will someday be pointed into landfills and will chip out atoms of different elements, and those elements will be collected for re-use. Then the landfill will be just one station along the way from Nature to use to re-use. The landfills of 21st Century cities are so big right now only because of a temporary delay in the use of particle beams or other technologies for breaking garbage down. Soon the landfills will shrink and all but disappear, and the cycle will become more even and not so lumpy. Cargoes are today sometimes left unloaded on ships in New York's harbor because they are not going to be sold for a while, and in the meantime they would have to be unloaded and kept in a warehouse anyway, so why not use the ships as floating warehouses? A landfill is just another warehouse. And today I detected no smell, even though it is July.

From the mall you can't see the mountain because there is a screen of evergreen trees on the landfill side of Richmond Avenue. But there are breaks in the screen. You can see some parked garbage trucks at a Sanitation Department building across the Avenue. Those trucks bring tribute to the Olympus of Staten Island. But it is not sacrifice. It is an act of hope that Man's ingenuity will continue to turn liabilities into assets, as it has so often in the past.

The landfill, section by section, gets covered with soil and grass, and so looks like a park. (In fact, parts of it are already open *as* a park.) While Prospect Park is a model of nature and Man's artificializing place in it, the landfills of the whole world are the reality that the parks fictionalize. They show the cycles of Man and Nature and they are the cycles themselves, and they show what happens if a cycle gets a kink at any point in the endless belt. Aren't you glad I decided not to use "constipation" as a metaphor?

The park is one of those Sermons in Stone (Toohey's architectural column title in *The Fountainhead*) and the soil and the trees and the pipes that re-cycle the water and the pump that powers the artificial spring and the sun that ultimately powers the pump are all paragraphs in that sermon. The natural and the man-made elements are there for emphasis by contrast. Counterpoint, if you prefer a musical metaphor.

Deriving joy and meaning from a cyclical activity – sounds like sex, doesn't it? That's why Juliet says to Romeo "the more I give to you the more I have, for both are infinite." By "infinite" she means cyclical – a closed, self-reinforcing, two-stroke engine. It is why Amy Farrah Fowler, on "The Big Bang Theory," says to Penny "Sheldon has a propensity for repetitive behavior that I hope to put to good use." Again, it is not sacrifice, but Rand's Trader Principle. And for that image of a two-stroke engine, read Rand's friend Isabel Paterson's book *The God of the Machine*. After reading half the book, with Paterson's endless mechanical metaphors, I had to wonder how many of those machine and energy images were metaphors and how many were literally true. Her "long circuit of energy" is not just a metaphor. Aren't you a part of a long circuit of energy, humans, Nature, machines, all making life possible?

And Stephen Cox's title for his biography of Paterson, *The Woman and the Dynamo* – we will come back to that in Chapter 26, below.

Now, if you want to see a dynamo, and a whole parade of dynamos all lined up in a row, take the tour inside the Art Deco Hoover Dam, near Las Vegas. Wow. You can see the line of giant drum-shaped machines of Hoover Dam stylized in Art Deco art books, but they hardly need stylization – they are a row of copies of the same object. Same size, same shape, same color, same function. Repetition of the same thing implies purpose, and so is high on the list of Art Deco's priorities and favorite themes. See the chapter THE ART DECO PHILOSOPHER in *The Age of Rand*. Art Deco is all about the celebration of Modern Man, the Machine Builder. And especially as the product being produced by a dynamo is energy. Rand had a good reason for making her hero John Galt an inventor of a machine that pulled static electricity from the air and turned it to Man's use. An aspect of that that Rand never mentioned is that such a machine, in addition to producing electricity, would also be removing the static in the air that produces lightning. Galt, like Franklin, would be saving lives and property from a fire hazard. And a third level of meaning is hit only with a glancing blow in Galt's speech: The taming of lightning is made possible by Galt's, and Franklin's, and others', learning the true nature of lightning – the coup of pure science that makes the coup of applied science possible. Thus do the scientists steal the thunder (literally) of the priests and prophets who exploited Man's fears of Nature for millennia. Here, Galt and Franklin are removing a far more dangerous fire hazard – ask Giordano Bruno what kind of fire I mean. Or Joan of Arc.

"Arc"?

BASE INDUSTRIES

Every city, no matter how old and no matter how big and how rich, had to have an original base industry – a reason why people settled there in the first place.

Jericho is probably the oldest city on Earth. A tower thirty feet tall was built there eight thousand years ago. Why did people settle there, after the ice had retreated and nomads began to settle down to agriculture? Because there is a spring there. Fitting – civilization began with a fountainhead. And look at all the "Springfields" – the most common American town name – and all the Cold Springs, Hot Springs, and all the other towns named for springs. Every living thing needs water. A whole crop of new coastal towns in this century will have names like "Desalville" and "Desaliton" for the same reason. The reason for Las Vegas ("The Meadows") was also a spring. The first settlers were Mormons! On my tours I will show you the Collect Pond site, and the Tea Water spring, the Broad Street spring, the Spuyten Duyvil spring and the Maiden Lane spring. You can still see, in the basement of a bar at Spring Street and Broadway, the well, owned at the time by Aaron Burr, where Gulielma Sands's body was found in 1800. Burr and Hamilton worked together, for once, defending the accused murderer. How did it turn out? See *Ghosts of Manhattan*, by Dr. Philip Schoenberg.

Springs were important to our ancestors. Lots of history, lots of legends.

A ford means a place in a river where it is shallow enough to wade across. When you saw the word "ford" just now, you probably thought of a car. But the first wealthy Detroit family by that name was in the salt mining business and were not related to Henry of the Model T. It is a very common name. In German it is *Furth* – the name of the Bavarian city that Henry Kissinger was born in. Schweinfurt must have begun as a ford for hogs on their way to the slaughter. London began as a ford. For the pre-Roman Celts, and for the Beaker People or whoever else inhabited Britannia before the Celts, the London ford was the farthest downriver ford on the Thames. Any farther downstream and you had to swim or build a boat. Utica, New York also began as a ford, on the Mohawk River, for the Mohawk Nation and whoever preceded them.

Other cities, or buildings, are named for the mineral or vegetable resource that gave them their local base industry. Tin City, Alaska. Uranium

City, Saskatchewan. Port Radium, Northwest Territories. St. Lawrence County, New York has a village called Pyrites and another called Talcville, Jefferson County has Calcium, and Clinton County has Irona, in an iron-mining region. Olean, New York, and nearby Oil City, Pennsylvania proclaim America's first petroleum-drilling region. We mentioned Petrolia, Ontario. Mitchell, South Dakota has its Corn Palace (Moorish Revival; available for conventions, weddings, bar mitzvahs) and San Francisco has the Cow Palace, where Senator Barry Goldwater was nominated for president in 1964. Edgar Rice Burroughs has his hero John Carter marry Dejah Thoris, princess of Mars's City of Helium. (Burroughs sold his ranch near Los Angeles to a developer, who built a subdivision there and called it "Tarzana.") Salina is the town next to Syracuse where settlers evaporated salt from the nearby salt lake and salt springs.

The whole nation of Argentina is named for its silver, as is its main river, the Rio de la Plata. "Cyprus" means copper. Some of the earliest copper mining was done there.

Know why there is gold in the German tricolor? And why there is a Wagner opera and a beer called Rheingold? Because there really is gold in the river Rhine. It may be all gone by now, but in Roman and medieval times you could still pan for it. Australia had a gold rush, and Melbourne, being the nearest ocean port, was Australia's San Francisco, while Ballarat, right in the goldfields, was like Sacramento, or Virginia City, Nevada. Same with Capetown and Johannesburg, South Africa, and Skagway, Alaska – gateway to the Klondike River goldfields in Canada's Yukon Territory.

Batavia was the Roman name for the Netherlands. Batavia, New York was the headquarters of the Holland Land Company, a group of Dutch investors who bought much of western New York State, with its Genesee River, from Congress after independence. Settlers rushed into the Genesee River Valley for the cheap and fertile land. New York City, watching the canal boats start up the Hudson full of land seekers, spoke of "Genesee Fever." The Holland Land Company office in Batavia did a brisk business, and it was there that "doing a land office business" became part of the American language. It was used at least as recently as 1960, in a Bob Newhart comedy routine.

Gold rushes, silver rushes, diamond rushes, land rushes, any kind of rushes, are good things. They spell opportunity. Never mind the movies about everybody shooting each other in saloons. Never mind the fashionable Altruist name-calling about "the White Man's greed for gold." The point is: human beings opening up new territories for creative, productive work and naming things after that work, instead of naming things after kings and queens and generals and battles. The older, bigger cities are downstream. They are old river ports, fords, and ocean ports and center in farming regions thousands of years old, and have names as old. Paris is named for a Celtic tribe, Rome after a king, New York after medieval York, the Roman Eboracum, another Celtic tribal name, and as for London, no one knows for sure. Perhaps for the "dun," or fort, of a Celtic god named Lud. The Battle of Hastings was fought near the city of Hastings, but today, on the exact battleground, there has developed a village called Battle. But even if Ayn Rand is forgotten today, map gazers like me will notice that settlers do name places after the local resource that created the opportunity that attracted them there. And in new settlements, people have always improvised new institutions of not only government, but in the profit- and non-profit sectors, too. Look at new settlements and see Man's ingenuity in every part of individual and community life.

Cities are even named for principles and moral aspirations, like Providence, Rhode Island and Santa Fe (Holy Faith), New Mexico. The City of Brotherly Love might someday be joined by the City of Mind Your Own Business and Do Good Work.

Harrison Ford (I told you it was a common name), in "Mosquito Coast," leads his family up a river in Central America, seeking opportunities and escape from the big city and its suburbs and advertising. When he gets deathly ill, he insists that they continue upstream, into denser jungle. "Dead things go downstream," he avers. Rushes help balance, with centrifugal force, the lure of the big city, with its centripetal force.

As cherubs celebrate the possible and beams celebrate what makes the cherubs possible, so the upstream lands celebrate the natural resources that make the downstream cities possible. See "The Farmer's Daughter" and other movies from the 1940s or before about class difference in America. This is the psychological side of Beams and Cherubs: not wanting to admit that your beginnings were humble. American and Australian culture is about glorying in your humble beginnings. This is why Rand's *The Virtue of Selfishness* is subtitled *A New Concept of Egoism*. This is not Percy's pride in the oldness of his money. This is not Stirner's Egoism or Nietzsche's. And Egoism is not Egotism, as Rand explains in the Introduction to the 25th Anniversary Edition of *The Fountainhead*. The boast that "my money is older than yours" is for the Peter Keatings of the world. Naming a new city Tin or Uranium, and glorying in *new* money, means taking pride in making something out of raw materials – the rawer the better. This is pride in the *process* of creative, productive work.

The George Washington Bridge opened in 1931. It was supposed to open in 1932, but the chief engineer, Othmar Amann, decided to dispense with the stone cladding. The opening was to be in the bicentennial year of Washington's birth, but a year was saved by leaving the steel structure unclad. Lewis Mumford might have called this "architectural nudism," as he did when a Central Park South hotel put its restaurant diners in the first floor window for passersby to watch eating. The cladding had already been designed by Cass Gilbert. You can see his sketches for the cladding in Robert A. M. Stern's *New York 1930*, but when you drive to New Jersey, all you see are the steel beams – just like what we discussed above in BEAMS VERSUS CHERUBS. No cherubs here – the GWB is nothing but beams. But the critics didn't mind. The critics and the public both liked, or maybe the word is *respected*, that look – a new "steel esthetic," the effect has been called. The two towers of the George Washington Bridge are New York's Eiffel Tower. An Army combat lieutenant was once asked whether his men liked him. "They don't have to like me," he explained. "They have to respect me. They have to have trust and confidence in me." Isn't that what you feel when you see those giant beams that *make possible* your flight over the Hudson River, 213 feet in the air, in your car?

Now, where are you going, as you ride your steel-borne magic carpet over the Hudson River? You are on Interstate Highway 95. That highway, like all odd-numbered Interstates, goes north and south. Ninety-five runs from Florida to Maine. This short stretch, though, goes east-west over the river. Soon you are past the city of Fort Lee, New Jersey and on to Hackensack, where you interchange onto one end of Interstate 80. The other end is in San Francisco. It will take you past six state capitals: Des Moines, Lincoln, Cheyenne, Salt Lake City, Carson City, and Sacramento, plus Scranton, Cleveland, Toledo, Chicago, Omaha, Reno and Oakland. *A Mare Usque Ad Mare*. From Sea Even Unto Sea (the motto of Canada). From Ocean To Ocean (the motto of Taggart Transcontinental). Interstate 80 can truly be called the Main Street of the USA.

"Continent" was a favorite word of Rand's. She uses it several times in Atlas. She wrote of "building a continent." Why not a "nation," or, as most people say when they mean "nation," "country?" Perhaps she just forgot about Canada and Mexico; Americans sometimes do that. Or maybe she was putting deliberate (she was usually very deliberate) emphasis on the continent as an economic unit, regardless of borders. Coming from Europe as she did, she may have seen Europe as Tom Paine did – "thickly planted with kingdoms." The free market leaps over borders and builds continents. And continents are made of rock. A continent is a big pile of natural resources; raw materials waiting for the hand of Man to turn them into products; waiting for "value added through manufacturing."

New York and Los Angeles, America's biggest cities, are just the exclamation marks at either end of the continent. Los Angeles, being Spanish, is the upside down one.

CHAPTER 18
THE VIEW FROM THE BRIDGE

When I was about 14, my friend and I were camping out in the woods behind his house. We had found ourselves unable to sleep and unable to escape curiosity about the larger world. Since the "larger world" for us was Syracuse, we started walking there. It was about five miles away, but for a night walk before returning to the tent, a mile or three Syracuseward would have to do. The thing was to approach the colored lights in the distance – Thruway Exit 35, the motels around it, the Carrier Air Conditioning main plant – something to look at besides the fields and farm houses and our rural/suburban school.

We walked down Fremont Road to its bridge over the Thruway. Atop the bridge, we stopped and looked west, toward Syracuse, and east, down the Thruway, toward Utica, Albany, the Hudson River Valley, and down to the root, the Prime Mover, the source of all energy in our world, the place of the gods, the bigshots, the movers and shakers – New York City.

And something inside me said "I've got to get there someday."

But why?

Because, even if I did not know what lay at Exit Number One of the Thruway, the mere fact that I was seeing so many cars coming and going from that direction couldn't help but make me curious: What goes on down there at Exit Number One? It must be an entrance, not an exit. An awful lot of cars and hence people must be entering the Thruway close to the eastern edge of this continent. (There's that word again. Rand, throughout Atlas, was thinking of Atlantis, the lost continent. That's at least part of her meaning.) There must be a reason why they numbered the exits starting at the ocean and going inland and not the other way around.

Many years have passed – years passed mostly in New York City. I did make it there. I have looked, from the Empire State Building, from the first World Trade Center, from the George Washington Bridge, and from the Hudson River line of the former New York Central Railroad, up the Hudson, back up to where I started. There was a TV episode where Steve Allen plays a man checking into a hospital in Manhattan. He is dying and he knows it. He is put in a room facing north, toward The Bronx. He came from The Bronx. He hates the memory of his humble beginnings there, so he angrily demands a room with a southern exposure. At the end of the movie "Genghis Khan," Omar Sharif, playing the Khan, is dying and is sitting up in a chair. He asks to be turned to face west. "I want to look the gods in the face," he explains. The gods live on the Tien Shan Mountains (the Mountains of Heaven), west of Mongolia and China.

We invest a city, or a state, or a nation, or a continent, or a planet, with meaning – and the meaning, in cases like these, is our own life. In "Return to Earth," Cliff Robertson, as the depression-crippled Buzz Aldrin, looks up at the moon, many painful years after Apollo 11, and says with quiet pride, "We were the first."

President Kennedy, speaking at a university, said that if we (meaning government, of course) don't subsidize the arts, we invite the fate of Robert Frost's Hired Man, who dies with nothing to look back on with pride, and nothing to look forward to with hope.

CHAPTER 19
THE FIELD AND THE TOWER

Here is the "secular spiritual" for you: Every day, on the Number 7 train, I pass the Liberty Brass Turning Company on Queens Boulevard. A small company, still surviving. In manufacturing. Still in the USA. Still in New York City, not in the Sunbelt. Not bad.

On the History Channel there is a show just about how things are made. How a tire is made, how a motorboat is made, how the Burj Khalifa, the world's tallest building, was made, etc. Or, as Johnny Carson used to say, "How dey do dat?" I could watch it all day.

There is a French-US movie, made in 2009, called "La Dance: Le Ballet de l'Opera de Paris." It shows rehearsals, meetings, backstage preparations for performances. Endlessly fascinating.

"Ladder 49", 2004, is about the lives of firefighters. In "Casino," Robert DeNiro does a lot of voice overs, explaining how a Las Vegas casino works. I enjoyed that part much more than the gangland rub out scenes.

Want to learn how to make a copper etching? See a movie called "Goya's Ghosts."

There is a Canadian movie from 1996 called "Kissed," in which you will learn the art and business of embalming. Don't laugh – the high school kid who went on to run a funeral home is coming to the class reunion in a bigger car than yours.

These are not meant as documentaries or instructional films. These are dramas and comedies. They are meant to entertain. But for drama and comedy, you have to have characters; persons; humans. And what do humans do? They think. They solve problems. They create and produce. And watching them do some clever bit of thinking is both entertaining and uplifting.

My "worship machine" – my computer – is showing me Charon orbiting round and round Pluto. Those alive this year, 2015, were the first to see this. Wow! We were all Columbus.

The past five or ten years have seen some fashionable overuse of the word "iconic." Guys, when you start seeing a certain word in *every* advertisement, and you are seeing it or hearing it a dozen times a day, find a different word! But also, ask yourself (in this case) which things are like icons to you, and why.

Nietzsche's Zarathustra, perhaps in a parody of Christ's "Blessed are the ..." list, lists people he loves. "What is great in Man is that he is a bridge and not an end: what can be loved in Man is that he is a *going over* and a *going under*." The pun works in German (*Übergang und Untergang*) but not so well in English: he means that Man's achievements are not meant to be final records never to be surpassed, but are meant to make possible even greater achievements in the future. Any record you set will someday go under, and will be remembered, not as the only such achievement, but as the first. The overture will go under. Rand told her readers that *The Fountainhead* was only an overture to *Atlas Shrugged*. Zarathustra goes on: "I love those who do not know how to live, except by going under, for they are those who cross over. I love the great despisers because they are the great reverers and arrows of longing for the other shore. I love him who loves his virtue, for virtue is the will to go under and an arrow of longing." (*Also Sprach Zarathustra*)

(For some reason, Webster thinks that one who reveres is not a reverer, but a reverencer.)

The Founders were pretty clever fellers – don't you think they knew, perfectly well, that their revolution would go on after them, surpassing them? They were starting over a bridge of which they couldn't even see the far end. They knew that, by going over, they would go under. Likewise Andrew Stockton, in Galt's Gulch, by saying that the employee who might put him out of business someday is the only kind worth hiring. (Page 725)

One New York Objectivist is currently compiling, and sending out as emails, a collection of what he calls "Beautiful Things." Google "St. Crispin's Day Speech, Kenneth Branagh" and you will see a candidate that I sent him for that list. I know another man who has his own "Museum of Interesting Things." You can Google that, too.

The best icons – things we keep around because we love them – are ones that continue to serve a practical purpose even after you have decided to keep them with or without a practical purpose. One such is my map of the Battle of Fort Washington. I refer to it, and on my tours of that battleground I show parts of the map that I have copied and blown up to show the map's incredible detail. The mapmaker not only shows the movements of the infantry regiments, he even shows, in dotted lines, the trajectories of the cannonballs. I bought this map years ago at a Rockefeller Center bookshop, now long gone, called New York Bound: a whole shop just of books about New York City. Remember bookshops? Remember books?

When I worked at the Strand used bookstore in the 1980s, I found a book about future technology, profusely illustrated. One picture showed a farm of the future. There were fields, absolutely flat, straight rows of green crops stretching to the distant horizon. But next to the fields was a range of mountains of bare red rock, so this apparently represented irrigated fields in the intermontane basins of Arizona.

I have so far been unsuccessful in finding that exact picture online, but if you google "future farm," you will find several artists' concept pictures that come pretty close to what I remember.

I first saw that word – "intermontane" – in tourist literature on my first trip west, in 1974. I just loved that word. It reminds us that even in the mountain states not all the land is tilted at a 45 degree angle. "Broad intermontane basins," the magazine promised, and the west was as good as its word. Sure enough, out the bus window were flats stretching away to distant mountains. I thought "My god – there is enough land here, not only empty but flat, to plunk down a New York here, a Chicago there, with room to spare." I had not realized before how much flat land there was between those ranges of mountains. I could see no reason why Ellis Wyatt's dream of a Second Renaissance could not come true in the basins of the west, given a supply of fresh water, of course.

Now, I don't know what turns you on, but I had by this time internalized enough of Rand to have a visceral feeling of joy and optimism ("getting all Ayn Rand about it") at the thought of a future of deserts turned to productive use. Part of the reason for this feeling in the 1980s was the preoccupation of the 1950s, 1960s, and 1970s with a future of nuclear war. A short future, and not merry. Whether it was this artist's conception of the industrial farm of the future, or the icon of the Enterprise plying the trade routes of space between star bases, we of that era were always brought up short by any vision of a future long and prosperous for Man, and we thought "Oh! You mean we might make it to the year 2000 without dying of radiation sickness among the rubble?"

In the future farm picture, there is a tower, and there, behind vast windows, a man stands working the controls of the huge machines that roll along the crop rows, planting or weeding or harvesting or whatever they are doing, faster than any ten men. (Remember the story of John Henry?) Just as the broad intermontane basins promise room for civilization to grow and make fresh starts and correct the mistakes of the past, so the image of the tower above the field holds a promise for me personally. That tower means the direction by Man's mind of productive operations across the flat fields. The tower becomes, then, Man's mind and brain, looking down from the top of his body to the work of his hands, and to the land that his hands work on.

Throughout this book, we are focusing only on the spiritual – on certain experiences common to all sapient beings – experiences that carry certain meanings that our lives are richer for keeping in mind every day.

The "Tower and Field" experience is one of these. It means the feeling of looking down on a field (literal or figurative) that you have just finished a day's work on. It is Hank Rearden watching the pouring of the first heat of Rearden Metal – one thing the "Atlas Shrugged Part One" movie did manage to get right. Grant Bowler caught Rearden's look of pride and joy perfectly. It is two experiences, really – the feeling of looking down on the field, or the factory floor, while you are working, although you usually can't take the time just then to savor the feeling, but it is in the back of your mind, and the feeling after quittin' time, when you do have time to enjoy it. The experience of looking down while you are still absorbed in your work might not be your experience. It might be the experience of the person standing next to you, admiring you in the intensity of your concentration on that field below. Another movie that shows this moment is "Patton." George C. Scott is shown with his staff on a ridge looking down on Rommel's advancing Panzers at El Guettar, Tunisia. With the battle successfully concluded, Patton puts down his binoculars, puts his hands on his hips, and smiles.

I had to mow the lawn growing up. We had an acre of lawn, and it was wet ground. The grass grew luxuriantly. The lawn mower sometimes took half the day to start. It took two fillings of the gas tank to do the whole lawn. At the end of a long day I was hot, sweaty, tired, and dirty, and the sun was low in the western sky over our west lawn. I would have a tall iced tea and sit on the porch and look over the rows of cut grass. The porch was my tower. The job was done. Best of all was the smell of the cut grass.

205

Google "Poul Anderson," go to his Wikipedia entry, and you will see the cover of the April 1951 issue of *Galaxy Science Fiction Magazine.* The illustration is for Anderson's novelette "Inside Earth." It shows several people in a small glass room, held up by several arm-thin vertical poles, and so high up that it looks down not only on a city square and blocks of surrounding buildings, but also on farm fields beyond the city's edge. Then you notice that the scene has a rocky ceiling arching over everything, instead of a sky. Hence the title "Inside Earth." You will often see panoramic scenes like that in science fiction illustration, since a large part of the attraction of science fiction is speculation on the look of future cities. If the future turns out to be agricultural, it might not look all that different from today's farm. That might be pleasant for a real future, but not good for fiction. For fiction to be science fiction, the world has to change. But there will still be towers and fields of some kind.

My first tour guiding job was with a downtown nonprofit called Heritage Trails. The office was at 65 Broadway, and had windows facing west over Battery Park, the Hudson and the Statue of Liberty. We had many maps of downtown in the office, and we collected historical information and planned ways of using it. We did a tour called "George and Martha Washington Walk the Heritage Trails." We hired actors for George and Martha, I wrote a script, and I would give the tour with additional comments by George and Martha, in their costumes. After a tour, we would be back up in our 19th floor office, giving the tour a post mortem. In my mind was the tour route: Broadway, Wall Street, Pearl Street, Fraunces Tavern, Whitehall Street, the Bowling Green. The tours were all to the east of our office, so I could not look down on a good day's work, but in my mind I was.

After a big tour, like the exhausting Ely Jacques Kahn tour I gave to the Congress of Art Deco Societies, I like to walk back over the route as the sun goes down. I have finished a three and a half hour tour for twenty people, I have lunched and talked architecture with them, and now they have gone and I am alone, the pressure to remember my tour

206

points and to be Mr. Charm is off now, I am looking forward to making out my invoice and getting paid, I have gotten some tips, and I am tired. You have to suffer from chronic depression to really enjoy being tired. When I am tired because of working hard, I think: how wonderful to feel tired, for once, for a reason and not feel tired even though I just got out of bed, because of my depression. I remember Dagny, after having her first sex with Francisco, going to bed but not wanting to "fall asleep and lose the most wonderful tiredness she had ever known." That's how I feel after putting in a good day's work … perhaps not quite so intensely as Dagny, and for somewhat different reasons.

Looking west from 65 Broadway, 19th floor, I could see across the river to Jersey City, Newark and surrounding industrial areas. I thought of Dagny realizing with concern that this city is fed by a continent three thousand miles long, with only the Taggart Bridge over the Mississippi to hold it together. For Dagny, the tower would be the New York Central Railroad Building, which straddles Park Avenue between E. 45th and E. 46th Streets. Rand interviewed the NYCRR Vice President in Charge of Operations there. On the first page of Atlas Rand describes the Taggart Transcontinental Building as "standing over the street, as its tallest and proudest structure." It does exactly that – it stands *over* Park Avenue. The avenue goes through the building. It is not right behind the Terminal – the Pan Am Building (now Met Life) stands between them, where the train shed used to be. The train tracks and platforms are deep in the ground underneath the Pan Am Building, and continue north under Park Avenue, emerging only at 96th Street. Rand compares the train tunnels under Park Avenue to the hollow roots of a tree – the tree being the tall Taggart Building. The roots suck in nourishment from the farms and factories of a three million square mile country. Dagny, from her office, would not be able to see much of her empire – her Field – because it is all underground, or stretched out across the continent, from ocean to ocean. But she can look down on the roof of the Taggart Terminal (the Pan Am Building was not built until 1963, six years after Atlas was published), provided her office faces south.

I am having a particularly productive writing day today, so when Belen comes home I will feel justified in knocking off for the day and watching TV. I will sneak an occasional glance from the TV in the living room into my study, knowing that there are more pages of this book on my hard disc than there were this morning. Though on the same plane, my living room armchair will be my tower, and my study my field.

Do you know why a farmer will often leave one tree unfelled, right in the middle of his field? So he can have some shade to sit under midday, when he takes his lunch break. He can sit facing what he has plowed in the morning, or face what he still has to plow in the afternoon.

Well, those are some of my fields and towers and some of Dagny's. What are yours? What icons, what memories of plowed fields, hang in the temple of you?

The purpose of a tower, in this case, is observation. You can see The Big Picture if you get up in a tower. That's why the end of the day is tower time. It is at the end of the day that you want to sum up you progress and put it in context: the context of "how much did I do today, out of the whole project that will take weeks, or months, or years?" Another reason for a tower is broadcasting, and yet another is taking full advantage of very expensive land – that is what a skyscraper is for.

But in any case, getting up higher – defying gravity – always implies purpose. Howard Bloom, Renaissance Man, Chronic Fatigue victim, outside-boxes-thinker, and recent speaker to the Queens County Libertarian Party Chapter, wrote a book in 1995 called *The Lucifer Principle*. This is also what he spoke about in Queens. Living things strive against gravity. Plants grow taller. Giraffes evolve. Lobefin fish crawl up on land and turn into dinosaurs. Monkeys climb trees. Men build aircraft and spacecraft. Arthur C. Clarke pointed out that a communications satellite 22,300 miles above the equator would remain over the same spot on Earth. There must be some compelling reason to bother getting up out of our accustomed horizontal plane. It must be important to do so. It costs money to build up, and money is time and life. It must have been worth the time of someone's life to build a taller building, or build bridges over bridges to carry Interstate highways over city streets. That implication of importance is what draws tourists to New York and the more recent skyscraper cities, even if they have not yet put that lure into words.

Here is another New York City movie image, and a very vivid sense of the worker in his field and in his tower. Truman Capote was a literary prodigy. Some short stories of his were recently discovered, and the *Times* reviewer said that these were already mature works – even though Capote was only fifteen when he wrote them. He wrote for *The New Yorker* – the very arbiter of literary somebodyness – the epitome of the Establishment organ, that has never mentioned Ayn Rand but to sneer at her. (Did you know that there is some right wing nut who actually gives Ayn Rand walking tours?! Smirk, smirk. It is just too, too *risible*.) Capote was like Howard Roark, in reaching professional success, but reached meteorically, not after any eighteen-year struggle with rejection. An Ayn Rand hero, in ability, but one who played the establishment game and never questioned it, and so was never questioned.

He was an incorrigible gossip and society lion. He liked nothing better than to lunch at the top restaurants of 1960 mid-Manhattan and gossip with his "swans," his rich lady friends, about … his other swans. Whichever ones were not present. He was supremely confident about his writing ability. Like the young Ayn Rand, he never spoke about what he might do *if* he got the breaks. He spoke endlessly about what he *would* do, period. And he did. One project he talked about for years was writing a "non-fiction novel." He made good on this boast with *In Cold Blood* in 1965. (Sort of: scholars now say he made some of it up. After all, he dialogued, at one point in the book, a conversation between members of the family who would all be murdered a few hours later. How could he know what they said amongst themselves in their last hours?) He wrote a non-fiction book, he claimed, in the *style* of a novel, with dialogue, narrative passages, and the other techniques of fiction.

Two movies were made about Capote, "Capote," in 2005, with Philip Seymour Hoffman, and "Infamous," 2006, with Toby Jones. The two films cover exactly the same ground: he decides to write about the murder of the Clutter family in Holcomb, Kansas, he goes out there with his lifelong friend Harper Lee (who published her own famous novel *To Kill a Mockingbird*, in 1960, while helping Capote with his research), he does his research, he waits till the two murderers have been hanged, he publishes his book to great acclaim in January of 1966, after its serialization in September, 1965 in *The New Yorker*, then spends the next eighteen years drinking himself to death and never finishes another book. He sounds like the composer Richard Halley in Atlas: "Fame hit him in middle age and knocked him out."

His pinnacle, his tower, came in November of 1966, when he threw his Black and White Ball, at the Plaza Hotel. All summer and fall, the high society of New York and the world pulled all the strings they could to get invited, or at least to fool their friends into thinking they had been invited but had a cold and couldn't go. Capote had so many famous friends already that the long drawn-out drama of who is on the A list, on top of the huge success of his book, made this "the party of the century." Hundreds came. The media camped outside.

The two movies cut back and forth between New York and Holcomb, a very small railroad town in southwest Kansas. We see Capote telling his rich and powerful New York friends (including his publisher, Bennett Cerf, of Random House, eight years after Cerf published Atlas) about the murdered family, about the killers and their trials, and about those funny people who live out there in not-New-York-land. The director and screenwriter of "Infamous," Douglas McGrath, in his commentary, says that his favorite shot in the movie is of the train pulling away to reveal Capote and Lee standing on the windswept, deserted Holcomb platform. The shot, and many to follow, look like David Lean's "Lawrence of Arabia" scenes: desolate flatness as far as the eye can see. Then it's back to swank parties in New York, where Capote is always the star of the evening, telling stories about his friends Bogey and Frank and Mia.

Capote appears at El Morocco without reservations, and they roll out another table just for him. He truly is Percy. Then it's back to the land of wheat fields and covered dish church suppers. You see vividly how Capote saw the world. Kansas was the field. It was where he worked, gathering facts. New York was the tower. It was where he took his bows.

You see the field-and-tower experience in both its good and bad aspects. You see a talented, disciplined creative person working hard and getting the applause he deserves. But you see the snobbery and the out-of-touchness of the upper crust. Which will win? Happy ending: Capote made lifelong friends in Kansas. He was vastly kind and warm to them and never forgot them. And he invited eleven of them to his ball.

You have been staring at one tree all day; now it is time to step back and see the whole forest. Put it all in perspective. Measure how far you got from this morning until this evening. If you come to New York for the first time, the time to go to the Observation Deck of the Empire State Building is at the end of the week. You can look down and recognize the Flatiron building. You had, before coming to New York, never heard of the Flatiron or knew very little about it, but now, having seen it up close and learned something about it, you can see how small it is next to where you are now, on the 86th floor of the Empire State. You look down the length of the Bowery – the ancient Weequaesgeek Trail. You can see how the Weequaesgeeks and whoever was here before them walked around hills and swamps, resulting in the curves in their trail. You can picture Governor Peter Stuyvesant in his coach, disgustedly glaring out at the passing *bouweries* – farms – as he rode home up the Bowery Lane after surrendering his colony to the British. All this from a thousand feet up.

One Christmas, when I was about twelve, I got a model ship, the U.S.S. *Pennsylvania*. It was one of the battleships sunk at Pearl Harbor, repaired, and used throughout the war. I had never had the patience, thanks to chronic depression, to put together a model before, but I decided to be methodical and careful and read the instructions this time and follow them. I did it. Hours later, I glued in the last piece and took a break. I went to the living room and watched "Scrooge," with Alistair Sim, and returned to the playroom to admire my handiwork. I entered the room and looked around. For a few seconds I could not locate the model ship in the room. Then I spotted it on a table. I exclaimed "Is that all the bigger it is?!" It looked as though it had shrunk. It was only a foot long. I had the idea that I would come back to the room where I had just spent hours laboring on this model, staring at each tiny plastic piece till my eyes crossed, to find the *Pennsylvania* filling and dominating the room. But the ship had grown only in my mind, because of my staring at it so minutely for hours. Funny how perspective works.

And finally, to return to our "night" theme, and our "night time skyline" theme, evening – the time of the Blue Place – is Reward Time. Miller Time! It means you are entitled to go up to your tower and look down and see the totality of what you have accomplished during your workday.

Tower Time.

CHAPTER 20
SLAVERY

The African Burial Ground was buried, all right – forgotten from about 1800, when it closed, until 1990, when it was re-discovered. Today there is a fountain and sculpture in the center of Foley Square, north of City Hall, downtown, and a quiet, grassy area with a walk-in monument, and bronze plaques in the sidewalks telling of the Burial Ground, and a site marker with a few paragraphs and a map of the area, and finally there is a whole museum on slavery in New York nearby, on Broadway at Duane Street. New York's past, warts and all, has been turned from a dirty secret into a chance to teach the young and to honor the dead.

Just this year there has appeared a sign at Wall and Water Streets, northeast corner, marking the site of New York's slave market.

I can't see the African Burial Ground, or the site of New York's slave market, without hearing Gary Cooper say these words in the movie "The Fountainhead": "Look at history. Everything we have, every great achievement, has come from the independent work of some independent mind. Every horror and destruction came from attempts to force men into a herd of brainless, soulless robots, without personal rights, without personal ambition. Without will, hope or dignity." (Don't look for those words in the book. Rand wrote them just for the movie speech.)

Rand's friend Cecil B. DeMille may have had those words in mind and passed them on to his writers on "The Ten Commandments." When Pharaoh Seti finds out that Moses is plotting to free Seti's slaves, he demands "What evil has done this to you?" Moses replies "The evil that men should turn their brothers into beasts of burden. To slave and suffer in dumb anguish. To be stripped of spirit, and hope, and faith – only because they are of another race – another creed. If there *is* a god, he did not mean this to be so."

Rand wrote those Fountainhead movie lines in 1948, and DeMille's writers wrote theirs in 1956, so they were thinking of World War II and the German and Japanese forced labor camps, and of the Soviet GULAG when they said "slavery." They may have given some thought to antebellum slavery, unless "Gone With The Wind" had sanitized the subject too much in their Hollywoodized minds. They knew a little about ancient Greek and Roman slavery, for instance through reading Henrik Sienkiewicz's *Quo Vadis*, one of Rand's favorite novels, but they were not experts on slavery. Rand's description is apt, though, in all those cases.

Slavery goes back perhaps to the cavemen. It appears in primitive societies as a byproduct of war.

When one primitive band attacks another, they slaughter the lot, because the other band is a competitor for food. But sooner or later, someone would discover that a baby, if taken alive, can be brought up as one's own, to increase the tribe, and will not slit your throat in the night as he would have if he had been 10 or 20 and had seen you kill his family. So the rule became: just kill the men, and take the women and children. Then some brave, in the heat of battle, happened to get the drop on one opponent. The victim might plead for mercy. The victor had an idea: I'll drag him back to my village alive, and the home folks will laud me as even braver than if I had killed him immediately. Then I will entertain my village all day by torturing him to death.

Our primitive ancestors would do that. See *The Death and Rebirth of the Seneca*, by Anthony F. C. Wallace. Then he had another idea. I'll keep him alive for two days, and tell him to fetch water. The victim himself may have had this idea. He might have said "I'll make you a deal. Let me live and I will do things for you." With that, slavery was born.

Does that story sound familiar? It's Scheherazade. The sultan hated women, so he would marry one and then have her beheaded. But Scheherazade was clever, and beautiful. She told the sultan a story, but then she said she couldn't think of a good ending. So he kept her alive one more day. The next night she finished the first story and started a second. She kept this up for One Thousand and One (Arabian) Nights. By then the sultan had fallen in love with her, and apparently gotten over his misogyny.

This ancient story probably reflects how slavery really started. Slaves are more useful alive than dead. But only if they stay docile, and terrified.

But they don't, you see. And sometimes they murder Master in his bed, and all his family, and run. And so the slave owners get more paranoid about their slaves as time goes on. That's why Thomas Jefferson said "Owning slaves is like having a wolf by the ears. You're afraid to hold on, but you're more afraid to let go."

In the 18th Century, the slave owners in America were having trouble answering their growing legions of critics. Many Christians were coming out against the "Peculiar Institution." In the Middle Ages, the rule had been that it is okay to own a slave, but not if he professes your own religion. Muslims could own Christians and Christians could own Muslims. If your ship was captured by Barbary pirates and you were sold into slavery in Algiers, you could get out of it by converting. But in colonial times, as the clergy converted more and more slaves, here in New York and throughout the British Empire, the owners came under pressure to free these now-Christianized slaves. And then the slaveowners got it from the other side, too: the Enlightenment thinkers, and those they enlightened, argued for Natural Rights theory, and said that slaves are human and have the same rights as the slaveowners. So to mollify their religious critics, the slavers said that blackness is the

Mark of Cain in the Book of Genesis. Your black skin marks you as a descendant of Cain, who slew Abel, and you are fit only to serve the white folks. To their Enlightenment critics the slavers said that it was a scientific fact that blacks were not smart enough to do anything but pick cotton.

This is where Roark's comment comes in. The slavers' attempt to justify slavery on scientific grounds just did not hold water. Washington and Franklin did not agree with Jefferson's claim that blacks are less intelligent than whites. They believed that some blacks might become doctors, lawyers and professors if given the chance and the training. The slavers, by trying to make the slaves appear as farm animals, succeeded only in showing how hard they had to try. The fact is that a human is not a farm animal. Here's how the slavers tried to make their non-fact appear fact:

They took from each captive his clothes. They took from him any possessions.

They took from him his language – he had to learn English.

They took from him his religion – he had to, for example, eat pork, even if he was a Muslim.

They took from him his name, and gave him a slave name.

In short, they took from him everything that makes a human human. Everything that *could* be taken away, that is. But it didn't work. It may have fooled Jefferson, but not Washington or Franklin. And eventually the truth came out. The slavers had tried to de-nature the slave. They tried to turn the slaves into Roark's herd of brainless, soulless robots. But you can't make Man something he is not. A is A.

CHAPTER 21
WAS AYN RAND A PERFECT BEING?

When Ayn Rand appeared on the Phil Donahue Show in 1979, a woman in the audience asked Rand whether she was a perfect being.

That woman would have known how Rand would answer if she had read Rand extensively. Rand was fond of throwing challenges back in the challenger's face. She was fond of paradox. On the first page of *The Fountainhead*, she writes "The water appeared immobile, the stone – flowing." When a questioner at the Ford Hall Forum asked why she took no fee for speaking there, and wasn't this altruistic, Rand replied that there isn't much money in lecturing, and so to try to make a fortune that way would be to rate your monetary self-interest terribly low; terribly cheap. She was making her fortune by writing, she explained, and she considered speaking out publicly on current issues more important (to her own self-interest) than the money she would make from a fee – especially since speakers' bureaus like the Ford Hall Forum were rare and struggling. And her favorite political quote was "If this be treason, make the most of it!"

So the questioner on the Donahue Show would have known, after a little research, that Rand could only answer "yes." She was a perfect being. And she looked the questioner right in the eye, as if to thumb her nose at her. Bidding defiance, just like her hero Patrick Henry.

Actually, though, Rand's answer to this question was not so bad. She replied "I never judge myself that way." If you believe that you have absorbed and practiced the principles of your philosophy, then you have behaved as perfectly as morality requires.

Rand always hoped to unite the moral and the practical, but the two are distinct things and there are some differences between them. For one thing, moral perfection is easier than practical perfection. If you do your best, no one can fault you morally. But sometimes your best just isn't good enough to answer the practical need at hand. If you try to be hard working and pursue a career, you get an A for effort. But you may simply not have good enough grades, try as you might, to get into Harvard.

So although moralists seem stern and demanding, moral judgment is actually more forgiving than practical judgment. That means that however mediocre your efficacy, if you do your damnedest, you are (morally) a perfect being.

CHAPTER 22
WHO'S AFRAID OF AYN RAND?

The conductor of the New York Philharmonic was just on TV saying something about asking his musicians to do things like dancing and acting onstage and clowning, and getting out of their comfort zone. That term "comfort zone" flipped a switch for me. Comfort zone … yes … Ayn Rand took people out of their comfort zone, challenged their assumptions, clichés, nostrums, and her favorite word, bromides (which actually means a sleeping pill). How come other philosophers fail to make people bristle with anger and outrage at the mere mention of their names, as Rand did? Say the name John Rawls and what happens? Nothing. Stand outside Grand Central holding up a sign that reads JOHN RAWLS' PARK AVENUE WALKING TOUR and … nothing. He left people in their comfort zone. Philosophy deals with fundamentals. If it does *not* scare the bejeesus out of you it is not doing its job.

But she scared you by showing you why your failure to be moral is also a failure to be practical. The Altruists scare you into choosing the moral *over* the practical, or vice versa, because they teach you that the two are irreconcilable enemies. Rand taught that they are not.

Rand brings freedom from fear of morality and the moralist. Rand's moral principle of Egoism means that morality and the moralist are your friends, not your enemies.

Fear of the moralist is yet another bad effect of the Age of Altruism. Naturally, people don't like the enforcer of Altruism – the Church Lady. (Look to the RCA Building at Rockefeller Center as the source of "Saturday Night Live" and Dana Carvey's Church Lady character.) The Church Lady makes you feel guilty for failing to follow a moral principle that cannot be followed. Rand's insight was that Altruist morality was not even *meant* to be followed. If you could follow it, you could escape feeling guilt, and Church and State don't want you to escape their guilt – ever. As long as they can keep you feeling guilty, they can keep you coming back to them every week for confession, penance and absolution, and the payment of taxes.

Rand's painter friend, Joan Mitchell Blumenthal, created a painting called "Not Guilty." It shows a nude woman contemplating the New York skyline. Her back is to us, and her hands are clasped behind her. Is she trying to seduce us with her nudity? Hell, no – she isn't even looking at us. She isn't striking a pose. She is just enjoying the view. The meaning of her nudity is that it has no meaning. Her clasped hands mean that she is relaxed. This isn't about her. Or, it is about her being relaxed and unconscious of herself and who might be watching her. She does not care. She has nothing to hide. She is not guilty. Neither are the skyscrapers she contemplates.

Why is it so important to Church and State to keep us nervous about being found out in our guilty deeds? Because, as Toohey points out, "Innocent men can't be ruled."

The KGB, in their usual unsubtle way, once tried to blackmail President Sukarno of Indonesia. He was notorious for his sexual appetites, and so they presented him with many photos of himself *in flagrante delicto*. He looked them over with no look of worry, and said "I'll take a dozen of each." Moral: You can't blackmail a man who has no shame – who either does not think others will condemn him, or he does not care if they do. Since he was a dictator or nearly so, he probably thought he could control his national press and keep the pictures under wraps. But maybe he thought his people would not hold the photos against him even if they did see them. Let's take this principle out of the hands of a potentate and apply it to citizens like you and me. In "Night of Jan. 16," when the Prosecutor impugns Karen Andre's morals, and her Defense Attorney objects, Rand has Karen say "No, Stevens – maybe it will bias the jury in my *favor*." The line gets a laugh from the audience. Likewise, Rearden makes monkeys out of the panel of judges at his trial by refusing to plead, or even admit that his action is a crime, or help them pretend that this trial is anything but a railroading.

There were some NBI students in the 1960s who wallowed in guilt as they learned Rand's moral system – scared to death of straying from Rand's straight and narrow as they had the old Altruist one. Some people just won't take Yes for an answer. People have always done that. See *The Barbarian Conversion*, mentioned earlier. Meet the new god; same as the old god. ("Won't Get Fooled Again," by The Who. A libertarian anthem.)

The night I met Ayn Rand, at the Hotel Pennsylvania in 1978, everyone entering the room was handed a printed notice that photos and tape recorders were *streng verboten*. As Rand stood talking with people at the end of the autograph session, she, and the whole crowd, saw a flash. Rand looked around and spotted a man with a camera. "GIVE ME THAT FILM!" she brayed. "I CAN'T STAND PEOPLE WHO ARE DISHONEST!" She stamped with rage on the word "stand." But unlike everyone else in the whole world, she did not say the man was selfish or greedy. That was not the problem. The problem was his dishonesty. His time would have been better spent – more self-interestedly spent – working on real, creative accomplishment than looking for ways to cut corners. Every time you hear a victim say that his victimizer is selfish, you are hearing centuries of Church and State – the Church Lady and her Marxist sister, Comrade Sonia from *We The Living* – teaching children to misidentify the nature of evil. An act is evil because it is evil, regardless of whose benefit it is done for, self or others.

Reputation is the big reason why I don't fear an approaching moralist. Reputation is money in the Temple of Savings that you get by being moral and letting people know it. Think of those domed bank buildings: temples of savings. Think of the need for reputation between depositors and banks and borrowers. Virtue leads to money – even Plato admitted that! – and here the metaphor of reputation as money in the bank becomes literal money in literal banks. Reputation thus ties morality to self-interest. Morality should not be a sacrifice of your self-interest. You should be looking for people of good reputation and they should be looking for you. Only in the upside-down Altruist world is Utopia thought to be boring and moral people seen as boring prigs, and immorality seen as exciting.

And that leads to another idea I got from Rand. To get out of the Altruist mentality and into a happy one, you must drop the habit of thinking of morality as a list of don'ts and think of it as a list of do's. This is where the city-as-temple comes in. Walk down any street and say "This is the tallest building – the first of something – the greatest of something – a landmark – a turning point in history, architectural, economic, political, or something! This is something! Here is a site important enough for mention in a walking tour or in a guidebook. Here, somebody did something great. Some person could have just gone to work, watched the clock and come home and watched TV. But he didn't! He had a vision and he made it come true! He wrote a book because he had something to say and a burning need to say it. He spent years experimenting, and facing failure time and again, until he came up with a light bulb. That's morality! Indeed it is moral acrobatics: going above and beyond, even if others don't follow you."

Check out the plaque on Fulton Street, between Pearl and Cliff, marking the site of Thomas Edison's first commercial power plant. Sit down on a park bench nearby and read *Anthem*.

And not just big buildings. We mentioned pipes in Chapter 7, and the factory icon on Rand's wall instead of a saint. Rand said that buildings, especially factories, are a code of morality made visible. Every nut and bolt in a factory is there for a purpose. Hers was the Morality of Purpose.

Walking from the RCA Building, home of the Church Lady, to 36 E. 36th Street and 120 E. 34th Street, Rand's homes in the Atlas and NBI years, I am thinking about the many people who think that Rand *was* the Church Lady. "Didn't she take an attitude of 'my way or the highway'?" people have asked me on my tours. I explain that Rand had her share of purely social friends and she did not try to make them into "movement" people. One such was Deems Taylor, narrator of the Disney movie "Fantasia," musicologist, fellow resident, today, of Kensico Cemetery with Rand, and father of Rand's friend, Inner Circle member Joan Kennedy Taylor. (A biography of Joan came out in 2014, *Persuaded By Reason*, by Jeff Riggenbach.) Rand cautioned Joan not to try to "convert" her father. He was old and set in his ways by that time, and Rand probably did not want to annoy him and drive him away as a social friend. But the Inner Circle itself, and the NBI students, were people who were representing themselves to Rand as her heirs; they would carry on her work and represent her philosophy to the world. So of course she was concerned that they understand the message and stay on it.

Rand's lifelong project, or the biggest part of it, was to explore the concept of aristocracy. She saw the class system of Imperial Russia up close in childhood, and also those who promised a classless society. She asked, Why are some people more important than others? In whose eyes? In what sense? Is there any validity at all to ideas of class, rank, quality, equality, inequality? Are differences in importance merely unavoidable, or undesirable? Or desirable?

Here is a line, in *Anthem*, that might still scare some people. "Many words have been granted me. Some are wise and some are foolish. But only three are holy: I will it!" In the decades following the Nazis, I can well imagine someone taking those words the wrong way. Look up "Ayn Rand, William Hickman" online and see the spin that some have put on that reference in *Journals of Ayn Rand*. (Someone needs to collect all the crap that has been written against Rand over the years, but especially since 2008's recession, and refute it, in one big volume. Maybe Greenspan should do that – he had something to do with that recession, they say.)

"I will it!" That means a baby learning that he has a will, and learning that he can will the muscles in his arms and legs to move. It means a man in his sixties who has had a stroke finding that his will *no longer* makes his arms and legs move. But he summons up the will to endure months in a nursing home until he recovers the connection between his will and his muscles. Will is the beginning of accomplishment. Will is what comes after dissatisfaction with the way things are now. Will comes after imagining things being better.

In *2001: A Space Odyssey*, Arthur C. Clarke has the Monolith awaken the Man-Ape's problem-solving ability by showing him images of himself and his band eating flesh, fat and replete and burping and relaxing in their cave, instead of emaciated, starving and grubbing for roots and leaves to eat. That's what Nietzsche meant by the Hour of the Great Disgust, when you grow dissatisfied with things that used to be enough for you, just because you had never imagined anything better.

Doesn't the sound of an approaching moralist lose its terror if you know that she is going to tell you "You have a great future ahead of you doing creative, productive things and getting rewards of all kinds, material and spiritual, as a result. You will be greeted with smiles on all sides from fellow human beings who are benefitting from what you produce." *"All work is creative work if done by a creative mind"* (Rand). That's because even the simplest repetitive work involves problem solving, which is what you as a human being do. And being dissatisfied with your erstwhile life begins with being satisfied with yourself – satisfied that it is okay for you to want more out of life. *"You are enough. And more: You are much more than enough"* (Branden). *"The world you desired can be won. It is real. It exists. It is possible. It's yours"* (Rand, Galt's Speech). (Mentioned above. Often quoted by fans. Bears repeating.)

CHAPTER 23
EUPHOBIA

"Euphobia," I understand, means fear of good news. The Greek word "eu" means "good," though, so it looks to me as though euphobia means simply fear of the good. I can understand that. If you are invested heavily, psychologically, in bad news, or in some particular piece of bad news, then you might well fear good news. If you just can't believe that things can go right for you, you might have a case of euphobia, but Rand would call it low self-esteem. Nathaniel Branden, in a TV interview, said that some people just can't bring themselves to believe that they even have a *right* to take proper care of themselves. I've seen that happen to many people, in one form or another.

Rand called the 20th Century the Age of Envy. By envy, she meant "hatred of the good for being the good." That analogy is what makes the concept of euphobia make perfect sense. If you can hate the good, you can fear the good. I don't know that Rand's era was any more an Age of Envy than previous ages were, but there is less excuse for it today. Talent will out.

In *The Fountainhead*, Ellsworth Toohey says "A man abler than his brothers insults them by implication." When you outperform others, you put pressure on them to do better. Some people feel threatened by superior performance by others. The solution to this problem is courage. You have to do your best, even though you can't always expect to be the best at everything. You have to honestly assess your potential and plan accordingly. Okay, maybe you won't make partner at the first law firm you work for. Maybe it will be a better strategy to be a partner at a less impressive firm than continue as an associate at a more impressive one. (They won't let you do that anyway.)

Branden was annoyed, by the 1990's, that self-esteem had suddenly become the word of the day and people were using it in ways different from his. But as I read his books on the subject, his sense of self-esteem boils down to simply *courage*. You have to give your purposes the old college try, even in the face of the possibility of failure.

Part of being a Great Soul (a *Mahatma*) is rejoicing in the success of others. The guy who starts a successful business may have put you to shame when you competed with him for the prestige of being Big Man on Campus, but later he may be the one to give you a job when you need it. That's on the practical level. Meanwhile, on the psychological level, let him be your proof that you *can* succeed. He did it, so I can too. The obverse of that lesson is: Don't hide your light under a bushel. (That, note well, is a Biblical quote.) Let yourself be the inspiration that challenges those around you. Look eagerly for good news – both coming in and going out. I know that's not easy – not when you are used to the comfortable old routine of crying in your beer.

Let this be the lesson you take as you pass the green-roofed red brick old Queens County Courthouse in Long Island City, Queens on the 7 train. That is where Roark's trial would have been held, since his crime of blowing up Cortlandt Homes took place in Astoria, County of Queens. By being acquitted, he forces Keating, Dominique, Toohey and Wynand to face the bad good news they have all been dreading: that a man of integrity is possible.

Branden had a good, helpful hint for teens reading *The Fountainhead* for the first time. This was on his "Seminar" series of vinyl records. He was asked why Toohey would knowingly choose the evil over the good, as he seems to have done. Branden explained that Toohey does not in fact understand the nature of good and evil. He could not have given Roark's speech. He does not have that kind of conceptual understanding of what Roark is all about. He knows that Roark is the man he cannot manipulate, and therefore Roark is the man he must destroy, but he knows that only because of the fear he feels seeing Roark across the room at the party at the Enright House. Toohey is not a brilliant person. He is a shrewd and cunning person, which Branden says is a different thing entirely. In the 1990s I sent Branden an email asking him to write more of this kind of explanation of similar points of confusion among Rand's readers, but he replied that he did not want to start another Rand-related project at this time. Too bad, because I found that comment very useful.

In the movie, Roark's Enright House – a luxury apartment high rise – becomes an ethereal, all glass and light, very tall and skinny building that looks like it stands at Madison Square. We mentioned this in Chapter 13. One Madison Avenue has recently been built on that very spot. Rupert Murdoch has bought the $50 million four-story penthouse. The stairways in the movie's party scene are very similar to Murdoch's. Edward Carrere, the Warner Bros. art director, would be proud. But not if he hated or feared the good or the vertical. There's a movie title for you: "The Good and the Vertical." But you would probably cast Rupert Murdoch as Gail Wynand, not as Howard Roark.

Poor me! I should leave this land of opportunity and sail into the port of Latakia, Syria, past the statue of "Tyranny Darkening the World," and heave a sigh of relief that no one can blame me now for my miserable life of failure.

CHAPTER 24
YENTL

I know of no reason to believe that Alan and Marilyn Bergman are or ever have been Objectivists. But in their song lyrics for the 1983 Barbra Streisand movie "Yentl" they set some Objectivist ideas to music that I can't hear without getting *verklemt*.

Remember the sculpture "The Immigrants" in Battery Park, mentioned in Chapter 11 above? Keep it in mind here. (Cue "Coming to America," by Neil Diamond. Again.)

The Bergmans have been a husband and wife tune and lyrics team since the 1950s. They wrote the Yentl lyrics and Michel Legrand wrote the music.

Yentl is a very smart girl. She is a 28-year old spinster in the movie, but eighteen in Isaac Bashevis Singer's original story. She lives in Poland in 1904. Her father, a widower, is a rabbi. Yentl loves knowledge and dreams of studying at a yeshiva, but women are forbidden to study in her time and place. She sings of the thousand questions a day that she wonders about, "searching for the reason and the logic in the world that God designed." Why does a woman like herself have a relentlessly searching mind, and a need, a thirst, for knowledge and work – only to be condemned to the single role of housewife and mother? "Where is it written that I can't have my share of every sweet imagined possibility?" Here she echoes Kira, in the very last line of *We The Living*: "She smiled – her last smile – at so much that had been possible." And elsewhere, Kira thinks of St. Petersburg, the city where anything is possible. (See Chapter 14 above: WHAT MAKES IT POSSIBLE ...)

Yentl, by disguising herself as a boy, does manage to get admitted to a yeshiva. Here she sings "There are moments you remember all your life. This is one of those moments. I will always remember this chair, that window – the way the light streams in ..." The movie's cinematography is gorgeous: here we see the sunlight streaming in the high windows of the yeshiva. Remember, in Chapter 16 above, Wynand's "typing exercise" moments? This song is about those moments.

But the most intriguing turn of phrase in Yentl is in the song "No Matter What Happens." Yentl is disguised as a boy, but he – she – has fallen in love with a young man, Avigdor, another yeshiva student. Yentl realizes that her deception can't go on indefinitely, and decides to out herself to him. Even though she will probably lose him, she can't *not* tell him that she is a woman and that she loves him. She can't stand denying her nature any more. (See Chapter 20 above on slavery.) She sings of darkness and light (see Chapter 6 on *New York Night*): "I've run from the sunlight, afraid it saw too much ... I wanted the shadows, I don't any more ..." She sings of her heart "that tells me to *free* myself, to *see* myself, to *be* myself at last." Notice how those three rhyming words descend from the political and the moral to the epistemological to the metaphysical (ontological) – the four main branches of philosophy. It sounds as though Yentl is seeing her immediate problem, and then seeing deeper and deeper meanings underlying it.

In saying "free myself," Yentl is using a word – "free" – that people usually use in a political context, but Yentl is referring to a corner that she has painted herself into. A prison of lies of her own making. If morality asks "What should I do?" and politics asks "What should we do?" then Yentl has to convene herself as a committee of the whole and reverse a bad policy. The real Yentl must be freed from the masquerade. If metaphysics asks "What is?" and epistemology asks "How do we know what is?" – then Yentl realizes that she has not known herself – has not seen herself – fully until now. She had seen herself as an ambitious student up to now, but now she realizes that she is also a woman. So she must act like a woman. Everything has a nature, and must act according to its nature. Nature, to be commanded, must be obeyed. To be is to be some*thing* and not anything else. Existence is Identity. A is A.

And then, having lost Avigdor, and unable to continue in this yeshiva or even in this town, and, she realizes, in the Jewish culture of the Old World, Yentl gets on a ship "to a place where *I hear* things are different."

America.

CHAPTER 25
EQUALITY

Nature forces a lot of inequalities on Man. There is no need for us to make up artificial ones. But our primitive ancestors thought there was such a need. They believed, until the American Revolution, and many around the world still believe, that society would fall apart and we would all kill each other immediately if there was not an elaborate system of hereditary classes, offices, ranks and titles. Placemen. Sinecurists. Watch PBS and what do you see? Endless re-makes of *Pride and Prejudice* and other British stories about people wailing "Oh, alas and a lack a day! I've fallen in love with someone above my station!" That worry is going away in our time. It is being replaced by a more subtle and sophisticated view of society, in which self-interest is the glue that holds society together. You do what you do because life is not about war, it is about trade, and others represent, not potential enemies, but potential buyers of what you sell and sellers of what you buy. The Internet, much more than any influence of Ayn Rand, is doing this (along with all other modern technology). It allows us to talk to people all over the world over the heads of the governments that would divide us.

On East 20th Street is the birthplace of Teddy Roosevelt, preserved as a historic site. Among the items mounted on the walls there are many cartoons of TR. Some of them show him battling the "malefactors of great wealth." Those malefactors are identified by dollar signs somewhere on their persons. This is the way the Altruist world identifies the enemy: it's how much money you have, not how you got it. Thus do Church and State ignite your fear and hatred of the rich, and teach you never to distinguish between the good and the bad deeds that went into how they got rich. In Atlas, Owen Kellogg tells Dagny what the dollar sign stands for. He mentions that it is stamped on the forehead of fat, piglike cartoon characters. I have begun collecting examples of the uses of the dollar sign in art and commercial illustration.

I find meaning in the small business buildings in the suburbs. A freestanding McDonald's will do. There is the front, where the counter staff interfaces with the customers and where the office staff work, and there is the back of the building, where the cooks make the burgers. Let's say it's a print shop. The boss and the counter staff are in the front of the building and the presses are in back. Brain and bowls. Mind and body – and for once with no dichotomy between them! Man and Machine, Management and Labor, White Collar and Blue collar. Head and hand.

What this means is the division of labor, not "class." There have been, for centuries, and there continue to be, millions of people working in "front" and "back" arrangements, but trying hard every day to not fall into ideas of "class." The only people who need class are the professors – they need to classify things in order to have topics to write books about, and they need to divide their books into chapters, so they have to sub-classify everything. But Herr Professor Doktor sometimes falls in love with his system of classification, like Pygmalion, and then he tries to make his class system do tricks it is not really up to.

Class is not inevitable. Class is a game that some individuals choose to play. But you don't have to. The new game, born in the Enlightenment and the American Revolution, is: get better off, by living in a community of people who are also trying to get better off. And the better your neighbors do, the better you do. A plus-sum game, not a zero-sum game. The United States was the first nation to proclaim this as a new way of life. Not the only; the first.

MORE OF A CLOUD AND LESS OF A NAVE

"Cloudsourcing" means a lot of people, perhaps spread all over the world, investing in something. We don't all need to go to one big kahuna anymore. In *The Age of Rand* I enthused over microcredit. Got some number crunching to do? You don't need to go to one building-sized computer as in "Colossus: The Forbin Project," (which starred Rand's idol, Eric Braden). You can farm out bits of the job to a million home computers.

The part of a church with the pews is called the "nave." In the 19th Century, clergymen were always complaining about churches that had been converted to the sinful, decadent use of theaters. But buildings sometimes went the other way – from theater to church – and the reason is clear. Both types of building serve the same purpose: to accommodate a bunch of people who all want to sit facing the same way, to watch and listen to either a sermon or a show. (Google and take a video tour of St. Sebastian's RC Church in Woodside, Queens – a former movie palace, beautifully adapted.) This is one of those natural inequalities that can't ever be entirely avoided. Sometimes you are a kid sitting in the pew or the theater seat, watching one person who is the center of attention of a hundred or a thousand, or if the performance is televised, a million, and wishing you could be up there in the limelight. That is exactly what happened to Jackie Gleason. As a boy, he was at a show of some kind and he later remembered thinking, "I'm looking the wrong way! I should be up there on the stage!"

While the overall trend in this century may be from Nave to Cloud – from "*Führer Befehl, Wir Folgen!*" (Leader Command, We Follow!") to "Do your own thing!" – there will be little naves floating around in the cloud all the time. But they will be ephemeral, and so will your role in them. Sometimes you will be on stage, and sometimes dealing with others equally, and sometimes in the nave, silently listening with others to the star of the moment. But you will shake your head in pity for the generations who *always* had to be in the nave, who all had to bow as one when the monarch rode by. And you will even pity the poor monarch, who sometimes was born into a role he just wasn't up for. See the movie "The King's Speech."

You Tube is an example of Man's move from Nave to Cloud. Anyone can upload, and who knows what will go viral for a day – instead of everyone looking at one movie star or politician or god. There is equality for you – seven billion people looking at each other, not for everything, but just for the one thing you need from that one person you are looking at this minute.

In 1790, Thomas Jefferson was in New York as Secretary of State and Alexander Hamilton, a New Yorker already, was Secretary of the Treasury. TJ and the other Virginians rented a house on Maiden lane. Hamilton lived at 57 Wall Street. Jefferson told this story in a letter to Lafayette: As he was walking from Maiden Lane down Broadway to the President's house at Number 39, to confer with him about something, Hamilton came out of the mouth of Wall Street and hailed him. Hamilton was agitated and worried about the violent opposition of the south in Congress (at Federal Hall, which he had just passed on Wall Street) to his financial plan for the new nation. Jefferson says that Hamilton walked him up and down for half an hour, on the sidewalk in front of Number 39, talking about this, until Jefferson said, you bring the key northern congressmen to dinner at my quarters tonight, and I'll bring the key southerners, and we will work out a deal over dinner.

The Compromise of Maiden Lane was this: Hamilton would get his financial plan, even though it had some disadvantages for the south, but in return the south would get the new capital city.

Removing the Federal Government two hundred miles from New York meant the separating of the money men from the congressmen. It meant that New York would not be like London, Paris, or any other European capital, with all the money and all the power and all the top people in every field all in one incestuous city. It meant decentralization. It meant a balance of power. It meant power distributed around more of a cloud, and not all concentrated in one place, for all the other cities to gaze at in helpless awe. You see, while the present volume celebrates the things that make New York City special, be reminded: it is not desirable to make one city artificially great and all the other cities into sleepy provincial towns. It is not desirable that anyone say of New York or Washington or Moscow or Beijing "Rome! There is no other city like you! And none even comes close!" Make the ambitious cities, like the ambitious individuals, have to work for it. That way we all get more greatness out of the great. Greatness is as greatness does – for the audience in the nave.

Secular spirituality, the whole subject of the present volume, is us looking at us. Man looking across at other members of the same species. Levelly. Not all of us looking up like so many sheep at the sheepherder. Some king or god, or some king who tells you he is a god. We congratulate ourselves: Even if I haven't done much, I am a member of a species that sometimes rises to great achievement. Of course, that can work both ways. We are also the species of Auschwitz. So our spiritual renewal must take a cyclical form, like Jews reading the Torah over the course of a year and then starting over: We need to alternate between looking up and looking down, and in both cases we look across and remind each other that we have found both the hope and the enemy, and both are us. Rand used to say that she could stand to look around her levelly, but she hated to look down. She preferred to look up. Too bad – ya gotta do both. But I'd say about 90% up and 10% down.

The VIPs are on TV. The Nave means those of us who *watch* TV. The main character of the movie "Network" says to his TV audience "*You* are the real people! *We* are the illusion!" But sadly, it ain't so. After all, that character is himself a TV news anchor. Everyone in the TV Nave – suckers on the Glass Teat (Harlan Ellison's phrase) is listening to him say that – precisely because he is on TV and they are not. Millions of us are nearly unreal because we are nobodies, while the VIPs are on TV for a reason: they are important (in the eyes of the TV news editors). They matter. We don't.

235

This is where the historian is the bringer of hope. The historian will, in the 21ˢᵗ Century, explain to students that this all used to be much worse than it is today. In the 1960s, there were only three TV networks. Now there is the Internet. It is getting less Navy and more Cloudy.

Today Belen and I went shopping at the Ikea store at the Erie Basin in Brooklyn. We took the 7 into Manhattan and the 2 downtown, to the foot of Wall Street, then took the Water Taxi across the East river, through Buttermilk Channel, and into the Erie Basin. We came back the same way, but we were delayed. President Obama was in town – and a presidential visit gums up the whole transportation system of Down- or Midtown Manhattan every time. We saw his helicopter – nay, his fleet of helicopters – flying from JFK to the Midtown heliport and back a few minutes later. Or maybe they were police helicopters. The captain of the Water Taxi explained and apologized. The whole harbor was shut down for as long as it took for His Nibs' air flotilla to pass over. Everyone looked in the same direction, as the Great Man flew overhead, like Wotan on his eight-legged steed, dropping presents for children on the winter solstice. Our Water Taxi was a truly naval nave. Why do you think the Greek "naus" and the Latin "navis" – meaning "ship" – became the English "nave," as in the pews of a church? Because of the rows of rowers. Ever see "Ben-Hur"?

Temple Emanu-El, on Fifth Avenue at 65ᵗʰ Street, is the leading Reform synagogue in the world. It reflects a lot of big contributions from a lot of rich members over a number of lifetimes. I took a tour inside it once. Very impressive. But I was surprised that the tour guide did not mention what seemed to me like the most meaningful touch in the whole ornate design. The group sat in the front row of the nave and heard about the history of the congregation and the building. I leaned my head back against the back of the pew, and looked up.

The ceiling was peaked. It had a ridgepole running from the nave's back to its front. Rafters slanted down from the ridgepole on either side. The ceiling looked like wooden shingles overlapping down from the ridgepole, between the rafters.

Don't get it? Didn't the Church Lady, in Sunday School, ever show you a book of Bible Stories? On the next page after the Garden of Eden illustration, with its foliage artfully covering Eve's breasts, is a picture of Noah's Ark.

The ceiling of Temple Emanu-El is telling you "I am Noah's Ark. I will safely carry the Jewish people through the Diaspora, no matter how long it takes." A rather different meaning for a nave. There is some real power in architecture.

But if we are in an epic battle between the Nave and the Cloud, who will win? When your computer does not do what you want it to, you call the Help Desk. The Help Desk geek comes and fixes the problem, you hope, and you are relieved, but you also feel helpless and dependent on him. But you take heart from the fact that there are times when *you* are the geek – you have some specialty that other people need. Some days you are the priest and some days you are the helpless, dependent, frightened parishioner in the Nave. On the streets and on the subways, though, you are a helpless pawn inside the infrastructure owned and run by federal, state, and local government. Then you just have to trust the Democratic Party. They are nice people. They care about us. They say.

SHE DOESN'T TAKE DICTATION

My favorite scene in Atlas has changed over the years. Currently it is a tiny passage on page 206, in the chapter "The Exploiters and the Exploited." It is about Gwen Ives, Rearden's secretary. She is in her late twenties. Rand describes her as ruthlessly efficient, and, in a sudden crisis, Gwen is Rearden's calmest lieutenant. When the crisis is over, Gwen says "Mr. Rearden, I think we should ask all our suppliers to ship via Taggart Transcontinental." Rearden replies "I'm thinking that, too."

Notice what does *not* happen here. Gwen speaks right up, not about her duties as secretary, but about a major company policy. And Rearden does not laugh at her presumption or tell her to mind her own business or not worry her pretty little head about things that are way above her pay scale. He says that he is thinking the same thing. He does not say "I thought of it before you did," but simply that he agrees with her. These are two people, one much more unequal than the other, but relating to each other as colleagues, not as servile servant and Grand Poobah. One says "I think" and the other replies "I'm thinking," and that is what they are both there to do. No office politics, but both pulling on the same oar. Gwen is not joining in a congregational Amen to the man in the pulpit. She knows her boss well enough to know that her thoughts are welcome. If Rearden had not thought Gwen's idea a good one, she knows that he would just say "No, that would cause such-and-such a bad consequence. Better we should do such-and-such." He would turn it into a teaching and learning moment, knowing that he profits from a secretary who is learning the business.

This is another example of what Branden meant when he said that *respect for others* is one of the striking character traits of Rand's striking heroes.

CHAPTER 26
WELCOME TO UTOPIA!

Yup. That's right. This is Utopia. Right where you are sitting now. No more waiting. We have heard about Thomas More and his Utopia, his perfect world of socialism. All we have to do is outlaw greed and everyone will be happy. Bureaucratic bliss. Good luck with that. We have heard from the religious folks: all we have to do is outlaw greed and everyone will be happy. Imagine no possessions, says John Lennon. After the IRS is through with you, it won't be hard to do.

All we have to do is outlaw greed. Make everybody turn in his money, and it will be paradise … for the guys doing the collecting. Until they are overthrown by the next gang of collectors.

But this really is Utopia. The 21ˢᵗ Century world. You can tell we are living in Utopia from how hard the intellectuals need to try to tell us it isn't, in order to manufacture crises and anguish, so they can sell their latest doom-crying book. Rand did this, too. Her favorite theme is "This is what will happen if the world continues following certain premises."

Here is one of those paradoxes that aren't:

People don't complain about bad things if those things have always been bad. If something has never changed, you don't complain about it because you have never had anything better against which to compare it. James Chowning Davies wrote an influential article in 1962 called

"Toward a Theory of Revolution." In it he proposed his famous theory of "a revolution of rising expectations and relative deprivation" to explain why people rebel, not when things have always been bad, but when things have been getting better until suddenly they fail to keep getting better. It is not deprivation that infuriates the mob. It is *relative* deprivation – deprivation of what you expected for tomorrow, based on improvements yesterday. Also, if complaining seemed to get results yesterday, then you will complain more tomorrow. And if Charlie complained yesterday and got Utopia, and got fame for getting Utopia, then my game will be to complain tomorrow even more bitterly than Charlie did yesterday, even though I am living in Utopia today. Then I will get the Nobel or the Pulitzer or the MacArthur for giving the world a NEW, IMPROVED UTOPIA! It's kind of like the Chinese and Roman empires paying the barbarians not to attack them. The barbarians weren't stupid – they knew that the money would keep flowing from Rome only as long as the Romans feared further attacks. So we have to keep attacking them!

And here's another:

Ayn Rand was the only thinker who was *not* a Utopian, and the relatively Utopian 21st Century is the first century to *not* be Utopian – that is, not ridden with Utopian plans being foisted on the public from all quarters. The 20th Century was outstandingly Utopian and soaked with blood shed by Utopians who tried to force their Utopias on the world. Rand was not proposing a Utopia by force. Her message was "Just be normal. Go about your peaceable business. Cultivate your own garden and leave your neighbor alone to cultivate his." See the NORMALCY chapter in *The Age of Rand*.

Some commentator recently said that Americans are turning into a whole nation of realtors, selling each other real estate. Is that so bad? Land here, for residences, is in demand by both rich and poor immigrants from all lands because there is freedom and political stability here. And the rest of the world is slowly coming to understand that they can have what we have only by offering what we offer. America will be, not the world's *only* Utopia, but the *first*.

You know you are in Utopia when parody and satire become difficult, and they have. By the time the satirist writes his satire, the laughable exaggeration he describes has already been accomplished in fact, and these days, frequently outdone already! In Utopia, we make everything happen in reality, not just in fiction, for good and ill. Reality itself becomes our work of art, and it is always a work in progress, never dull for a moment, always changing, kaleidoscopic.

And never passive. Sure climate change is real and man-made, but isn't it better to live in the age when Man debates how to control the weather, than to live in the ages when the weather debated how best to kill helpless Man?

The politician naturally wants you to believe that nobody ever did, or could do, anything about any problem except through government. But people around the world, but especially in America, have been coming up with thousands of schemes for the improvement of the human condition for centuries. And, since these schemes are undertaken outside of government, you are not forced to join any one of them. We not only have Utopias all over the place here, we have competing Utopias. Utopia too has to prove itself in a competitive market or go out of business. Here is just one example:

Alfred T. White built the Riverside Buildings in Brooklyn Heights in 1890. He announced that he was building good, low-cost housing for poor immigrants, and that he would make a profit doing it. A small profit. He called his strategy "Philanthropy plus 5%. And for a hundred years, that is what the project has made. The surviving buildings of the White project can be found on the southwest corner of Joralemon and Columbia Street. The rest were condemned and torn down for the Brooklyn-Queens Expressway. (by Robert Moses, the poster boy for placemen; a character out of the bad guys of Atlas.)

White admired his immigrant tenants. No "Nativist" fear or hatred of foreigners for him. He took Rand's attitude toward the immigrant: You have to admire the individual who decides, as an individual, to uproot himself from his own country and move to another, usually necessitating learning a new language. The emerging 21st Century world, in which many if not most persons in every country have moved there from someplace else, is Rand's kind of world. "The man who sees with his own eyes and thinks with his own brain is my kind of man. Such men may be rare, they may be unknown, but they move the world." That Fountainhead line was a sneak preview of the "What moves the world?" theme of Atlas.

And Jacob Riis, who photographed the terrible slum dwellings of the Five Points, admired White's development.

Here's another: Jacob G. Schmidlapp was a Cincinnati developer who built low-cost housing for Black families in 1911. He charged rent on an "Ability to Pay" basis. He included a co-operative grocery store in the development.

What! Good developers? You will never read about such miracles in government history books.

Did you know that co-operative banks go back to about 1800, in the U.S., the U.K., and in Europe?

What site in New York City comes to mind when you hear words like "Utopia" and "peace on Earth" in regard to the 20th Century? The United Nations. But the 19th Century had its own United Nations – it was called Free Trade. And it was called simply the need of the leading nations, which were the nations of world trade, industry, and technology, for peaceful sea lanes and stable trade and travel relationships amongst themselves and with all nations. Which century saw fewer and smaller wars?

A movie history expert, commenting on Alfred Hitchcock's "Rear Window," said that this movie, with its path-breaking set showing a Greenwich Village courtyard surrounded with four stories of apartment windows, shows how we are all isolated in this modern life. We are all in our individual prisons. But of course the whole movie is about how *easy* it is for neighbors to snoop on each other and talk to each other across a small courtyard. And it is about how the murderer kills his wife and comes close to getting away with it simply by moving out of his apartment, his neighborhood, his city, state, and nation, just as millions are doing every day. Prison?

See how easy it is for a *great* expert to claim the exact opposite of what any viewer can see in a movie with his own eyes? And "isolated"? How many unanswered emails does that movie expert have in his inbox – from thousands of people who can reach him all too easily?

Man has never been so *un*-isolated; so *un*-imprisoned.

Utopia snuck up on us and no one noticed. They didn't want to notice, because this Utopia didn't have any of their names on it. It wasn't More's Utopia, it wasn't Marx's Utopia, it wasn't Plato's, it wasn't David Koresh's or the Reverend Jim Jones's or the Guru Maharaji's.

But you say, how can this be Utopia if it's not perfect? The world has flaws.

But can you do something about the flaws?

Yes, we can.

Then that's all the Utopia you can expect. You see, when we hear the word "Utopia," we imagine a system that is set up perfectly in the first place and so is without flaws, and so is never in need of any correcting. But the framers of the Constitution were among the few human beings who ever had it in their power to begin the world anew, and many of them were business lawyers and constitutional experts. And so they knew that the most perfect way to write a constitution is to never assume that a sufficiently clever plan in 1787 can ever pinch-hit for good government in 1887 or 1987. They knew that business contracts always provide for the possibility of their own amendment. Times change. Not every future contingency can be anticipated. So a Utopian system must be one that anticipates rolling with some unexpected punches in the future.

Nathaniel Branden was asked in the 1970s why the self-improvement movement was taking off just now, and why in the United States. He replied that self-improvement would not be a priority for people in a country where putting food on the table was the main preoccupation. The United States is the nation that more than any other has already conquered the external world of physical survival, he said, and so the next challenge, the next frontier, is the inner world of awareness. It's the next undiscovered continent.

There's that "continent" theme again, as Rand uses the image several times in Atlas and in her later non-fiction. Columbus discovering the American continent – Atlantis—the chance for a new beginning. Sir Francis Bacon kicked off the Enlightenment with *The New Atlantis*, a novel in which a European traveler happens upon an island in the Pacific west of Peru – an island where the state is not quite so important as the university and the pursuit of knowledge. Remember that Rand and Branden were both immigrants, although Branden was catching a train or a plane from Toronto to UCLA; not quite the same as Rand fleeing the Soviet Secret Police. But just spending two months in California in 1979 made me feel a little like an immigrant. I started to consider the possibility of staying out there, and I also felt the intriguing temptation to re-invent myself. There was a fashion for making up new names for themselves among Rand's circle in the 1950s and 60s. You can, if you wish, be your own undiscovered continent. Utopia does not lie in the total absence of problems, but in escaping to a place of new and different, and preferable, problems. What the German call *Luxusproblemen*—luxury problems.

By living at the dawn of the 21st Century, you not only are living in an era far better than any known before, but you are privileged to witness the birth of that era, and participate in that birth. Bliss should you recognize when you see it, in this dawn. Bliss is it in this dawn to be alive, but to be young is very heaven. (See William Wordsworth on "The French Revolution.")

In *2001: A Space Odyssey*, Arthur C. Clarke pointed out that there are enough planets – enough real estate in the sky – for every human who has ever lived to build his own world-sized Heaven, or Hell. Human means choice-making. To live for the future is to live in it today, said Rand. To get steady increments of improvements, and to also have the fun of being the one to detect the flaw and attract attention to yourself when you bitch about it. To look like an eternal rebel and idealist (with an idea list) to others by always being dissatisfied no matter how much better things are than they used to be – that were paradise enow! (*The Rubaiyat of Omar Khayyam*)

Cool! To be dissatisfied in Heaven – to be, in short, Lucifer.

DYNAMO VIRGINS

In 1905, the year of Rand's birth and Relativity's, Henry Adams wrote *The Education of Henry Adams* and had it printed privately in 1907. After being released generally many years later, it got to be one of the most respected books of the twentieth century. One chapter in the book was called the "Dynamo and the Virgin." Adams wrote it after writing, in France, about how wonderfully unified Europe had been in the Late Middle Ages under the Christian cult of the Virgin Mary. Adams saw Mary as a Christian version of Venus. Both of these feminine ideals of ages past had shown the power of a symbol or belief to get people to unify and achieve something. After seeing Chartres Cathedral, Adams saw the Paris Universal Exposition of 1900 as it summed up the advances of the last century and showed what promised to be the wonders of the next. The fair was powered by steam-driven dynamos in the Palace of Electricity. Sir Francis Bacon had alerted Adams to "power," in any sense of the term, as the predictor of the future and the signpost to both the good and the evil to come. These dynamos and other gadgets, and attempts, like Marx's, to explain all of history as a big gadget whose future workings can be understood and predicted – what did these newfangled developments mean? It all seemed so overwhelming and confusing, when Adams had just found such admirable order and unity in the Virgin and her cult's era. Which was worse – a coming Twentieth Century of disorder and disunity, or one of order and unity but of the wrong kind?

Adams's trap was of his own making. He was, first of all, into Jewish conspiracy theories. Being a Christian of the pre-Hitler days, too, he could say and write and publish for all to hear, unabashed, that he loathed the Jews and wanted them all dead, and all that they stood for. And what did Jews stand for, in Adams's mind? Lending money at interest. Secondly, he wanted Christian (well, Unitarian) order and unity. He was, therefore, a Dynamo Virgin. He just was not prepared for the monstrous shape of things to come, or the wonderful shape of things made possible precisely by lending at interest. It's just as well he died in 1918 and did not live to see Man walk on Luna and build Dubai and invest all over the world through Grameen and Kiva International and Kickstarter. He would not have minded the horrors of the World Wars; they would only confirm his belief in the sordid world's comeuppance. He suffered from Euphobia. He would have been upset by the good news – the dissolving of groupthink and group hatred, such as his own anti-semitism. He would have objected to the triumph of the Ego – the Twenty-first Century of human individuals encouraging each other to achieve and to live in peace. The variousness of Man, and his tolerance for people who are not straight, white, gentile, Boston Unitarian Brahmins, would have done him in. He would not have understood the principle of "Unity in Diversity" – a slogan I got from Gene Roddenberry.

Another Dynamo Virgin, a little further along in the dating process but still a virgin in 1965, was Alvin Toffler, author that year of *Future Shock*. The year before, 1964, Toffler had interviewed Rand for *Playboy* Magazine. In *Future Shock*, Toffler explained that today our stress and bewilderment comes not from this or that particular change, as Adams had felt when he looked up at those giant, spinning dynamos lighting up the Exposition. It comes not from the advent of electricity, or the advent of atomic power, or the advent of computers, or the advent of space travel, or the advent of the Internet, but just from having to learn to use and deal with a whole advent every other day! Not the particular nature of today's change, but the pace of change. The numbness that sets in when you realize that all the new stuff you had to painfully learn today will be obsolete in two years.

Stephen Cox apparently got the title for his biography of Isabel Paterson from Adams: *The Woman and the Dynamo.* But "Pat," as her friend Ayn called her, was no Virgin Dynamo. We mentioned her "long circuit of energy" idea in Chapter 17 above. What moves the world?

I shouldn't be too hard on Toffler; he was doing the best he could in 1965. It's just that 1965 seems like retiring to an Amish farming village now, in 2016. The rate of change in 1965? Are you kidding? *What* change, compared with 2016?

Some Objectivists are also Dynamo Virgins. As they age, they will have to deal with the fact that Rand was not always right … or wrong. Times change. *You* change. You grow.

TEAR IT DOWN AND START AGAIN?

Ayn Rand wrote four novels. The first two, *We The Living* and *Anthem*, were cautionary tales for the horrible age in which they were written. They showed what had happened in Russia, and what might happen in a Statist America in the future. As Scrooge quite logically points out to the Spirit of Christmas Yet to Come, it is a waste of time to warn

Scrooge if Scrooge's fate is already written and can't be changed even if he does reform. Rand had every expectation that John Dewey and all the fashionable American thinkers of her time would eventually be replaced by others. America and the world could still be saved.

But the second two novels covered two other contingencies. *The Fountainhead* was written on the assumption that you can go ahead with your career and other interests as Roark does in this best of all possible nations. *Atlas Shrugged* assumes that all is lost, and the just have both the right and the duty to stop collaborating with the unjust (see *The Age of Rand* on Gandhi and Galt), but also to seize ships, as Ragnar does, or seize the airwaves, as Galt does, to win what has now degenerated into a war. You can't just live a normal life, in the fictional universe of Atlas.

That was one of my first questions, when I first read Atlas at 13. Is this Rand person saying that things are in fact bad enough to necessitate a strike? And I was not alone. At the Ford Hall Forum in 1972, a man in the crowd asked Rand "If it is not yet time for a strike, how much worse does it have to get?" Rand, very sensibly, answered that we still have freedom of speech. As long as that is the case, everyone, of any persuasion, is obligated only to use the freedom he has, freedom of expression, to get more. If you are still free to speak, speak! One of the things many readers miss in Atlas is that the United States is sinking into fascism in the story – not Communism, but fascism. But in any case the government is starting to control the news. Cherryl believes what the government-influenced papers say about Jim Taggart, for example.

If you saw Ayn Rand writing a novel about a strike rather than actually going out on one, that means that we were, in her lifetime, still living in a Roark world and not a Galt world. This is one of those points that remind us that Atlas is only a novel; a fantasy, not a literal manual on what to do (strike) and how to do it (seize ships like a pirate or make a radio-pirate speech).

I suspect that Rand chose the name "Wynand" for the character in *The Fountainhead* because it sounds like "whining," just as "Keating" sounds like "cheating." Wynand is the swing character: He is great, but flawed. Roark mentions Wynand's integrity and adds "I'm saying that about Gail Wynand of Hell's Kitchen, who had the strength and courage to rise by his own efforts, but who made a bad mistake about the way he chose." Wynand is morally wounded at a young age. He becomes bitter and cynical. At the story's end, having closed his newspaper, and heading toward suicide, he calls Roark in to sign the contract to design the Wynand Building. "This will be the last skyscraper ever built in New York. The last achievement of Man on Earth, before Mankind destroys itself." Melodrama. Self-pity.

"Mankind will never destroy itself, Mr. Wynand," replies Roark, "not so long as he does things such as this." Roark is the unwounded. His is the face without pain or fear or guilt.

This is not Russia, 1917, or Germany, 1933. It is not the world of *Anthem* or The Place of the Gods. It's not yet time, Mr. Wynand, to pull the plug and go Galt. It is earlier than you think.

But that all means that we are in Utopia! We should be doing what Rand herself did – pursuing a career. I confess that the 14-year old me would have been very let down to hear the 62-year old me say that. I was packing my bags for Galt's Gulch!

INNER CONFLICTS

By the way, contrary to the lit crits who (I suspect) have never read Atlas, the heroes of Atlas do have inner conflicts – that is the whole story of Atlas. Galt has to persuade his heroes to abandon the work they love and the companies or careers they have built, and go to a valley in Colorado. Francisco warns Galt that Dagny will be the hardest one to persuade. The story is told mainly through Dagny's eyes. That's why Rand told Al Ruddy, the first to try to make an Atlas movie, that Atlas is just a love story. She meant that it is, among other things, the story of Dagny's search for her ideal man. But Dagny's ideal man is so ideal that he sees something about the world that she does not – the nature of the Guilt Game and the need to stop collaborating with Church (read intellectual class) and State and go on strike. When Dagny finally does this, she is in her office in the Taggart Building (read the New York Central Railroad Building, which straddles Park Avenue between 45th and 46th Streets). So that building is the site of the story's climax. The climax is Dagny's "conversion," not the two chapters in the valley, not Galt's speech, and not the rescue scene. Only by being converted to the strike can she get her man.

THE UTOPIA OF PURPOSE

What does Utopia sound like? It sounds like the opening scene of the 1950 movie "How to Marry a Millionaire." The shots are of the bustling streets of Mid-Manhattan. Cars, pedestrians, building fronts, sidewalks and curbs and taxis. The music is bustling. It suggests the honking of horns and the footsteps of hurrying city folks. Here are some of the lyrics: "You high and mighty, bright and shiny, fabulous place, New York … Where millionaires and Cinderellas rendezvous at the Stork … Glorious, glamorous, wonderland New York!" It certainly seemed a wonderland to young Alisa Rosenbaum in 1926. The Stork Club was where the Kennedys and the Rat Pack hung out in the 1950s. The second floor of the Stork Club was called the Cub Room, and in Atlas, Rand has Francisco mention a restaurant called the Cub Club. The Stork Club was the Mecca of cool in Rand's day.

Those lyrics are a perfect example of "getting all Ayn Rand about it." If New York City is the Temple of Ayn Rand, that song is one of its many hymns.

Why is this Utopian? Because, not of its perfection, but of its imperfection: People are bustling about with purpose. They are not running from the Huns or the Roman tax collector or the plague or the locusts or the Reds or the Nazis. They are rushing to their jobs and appointments. They are rushing toward goals and improvements in their lots. They are rushing because their lives, however good or bad they have been up to now, are going to get better in some way after this appointment. They are chasing something; something is not chasing them. They are right where they need to be – therein it is utopia – but they are there to rush toward the promise of a still better tomorrow.

What does Utopia look like? One of Hope and Crosby's "Road" pictures was called "The Road to Utopia." The boys go gold mining in Alaska or the Yukon. Gold for the taking. The Utopia of the frontier: easy money and freedom. That's one kind of Utopia. In a book called *The Living Arctic*, by Fritz Müller, there is a photo of shiny steel oil tanks, three or four of them, drum-shaped, all reflected in pools of water near their bases. The caption says that the photographer had captured "an impression almost of Utopia." Why Utopia? Because the tanks are shiny and smooth and featureless, like the paintings of the distant domes and towers of Utopian cities. You don't see any windows in the distant towers of the Emerald city in the Wizard of Oz movie, do you? Windows often disappear with distance. Architect Ralph Walker, in designing One Wall Street for the Irving Trust Company in 1930, wanted his limestone tower to look like one piece of stone, carved into many Art deco gem-like facets. He thought it was a shame that the building had to have windows at all; it spoiled the single-block-of-carved-stone look. But years later, in the Glass Box era, Skidmore, Owings & Merrill built the US Steel Building at Broadway and Liberty Street, and achieved what Walker wanted – a windowless building. How? By setting the windows so far back under giant girders that as your eye climbs up the side of the building, after the first few floors you can't see the windows anymore. All you see is the edge of each flange of each girder.

The greater the distance from which you see a skyline, then, the less you can see the windows. The less you can play Peeping Tom. The less you can imagine the individuals living in those buildings, and the more you think of those buildings as mere symbols of an impersonal abstraction called "civilization." Same with Utopia. The farther away you are, the better it looks.

A friend in high school, circa 1972, told me that to him skyscrapers represented death, not life. This was a Democrat in the Vietnam era, so he probably meant death by bombs dropped from B-52s, and death by pollution, because of course socialist nations have no wars or pollution or crime. Those ills are all caused by the corporations in those office skyscrapers.

But still people come here. "Some come to work and some to play ... some come to stare and some to stay," as Stephen Sondheim says, in "Company." In the 1958 movie "Indiscreet," Cary Grant asks Londoner Ingrid Bergman if she has ever been to San Francisco. She says yes, and it is a nice enough place, but it's so far from ... everything. Theater, opera, museums ...

"Do you ever go to museums?" asks Grant, incredulously.

"I go daily!" Ingrid replies, defensively, and obviously lying through her teeth. That's that "Atlanticist" bias I spoke of earlier. They've got the ocean on the wrong side in California. And New Yorkers all know exactly what Ingrid means. I wouldn't live anyplace else, because of Broadway shows, celebrities, so much stuff going on ... and opera ... and museums! Do you ever go? No, but just to know that it is all here, just in case I ever do get around to doing it all ...

And that is where practicality turns to worship; to the spiritual lift we all get just from waking up in the city that never sleeps. See? You can't think about this without bursting into song. That's what music is for, you know: that moment when words are not enough and Nessun Dorma or America The Beautiful or something just bursts out of you. Just to know that it is happening all around you. It is real, it is possible, it's mine. The Hindus call it "darshan:" the spiritual whateveritis that you get just from being close to the Guru. The frown of concentration on a smart-looking face, as the owner of the face walks purposefully around the corner of Avenue A, left onto Street B, into Building C, up Elevator Bank D, into Wing E, into Office F, where he sits at his desk and opens Drawer G, selects Divider H, pulls out File I, takes out Page J, looks down to Paragraph K, and makes some big decision.

Is it that that person has been de-humanized into a file cabinet – or is it that the minds of inventors have expanded their thoughts out into the physical world and have built filing systems that are extensions of their minds, so that you and I can find File I in Street B, in Borough AA, in City BB, in State CC, in Nation DD ...? Is the Man-made, unnatural world de-humanizing us, or are we humanizing the natural world? Isn't your life today made possible by millions who went before you who said to the natural world "I WILL IT!"? And isn't that what you see when someone frowning, not in sadness, but just in concentration, rushes past you on the street, making a big important deal on his cell phone? Do you see that that is the face of life itself, going on in front of you, for you to get a thrill out of, even if you yourself are only a bit player in the process? I'm just another face in the nave, but what a nave! And maybe someday I will get to be the soloist in the choir.

Rand "seldom took advantage of the cultural offerings that New York uniquely possessed," writes Barbara Branden, "—art galleries, theater, ballet – but to know that the great city was there, just outside her window, seemed to give fuel to her spirit."

"A spirit, too, needs fuel. It can run dry," wrote Rand.

We *are* the Ancient of Days, leaning out from our own Noumenal Worlds – our minds – and imposing measurement and finitude on the infinite possibilities that exist only in potential in the Phenomenal World. We make what is in our minds real. "We are a way for the cosmos to know itself." (Carl Sagan)

UTOPIA BEGINS WITH YOU

Here's the problem with Utopia: The false principle of "the ends justify the means" means that the guy with a Utopian plan may feel perfectly justified in killing you for "the greater good." In *The World and the 20s*, editor James Boylan includes a New York *World* story from 1920 on presidential candidate Warren G. Harding's hometown of Marion, Ohio, and a *World* interview that same year with Socialist Party presidential candidate Eugene V. Debs, in prison. Small American cities like Marion are exactly the target of socialist Sinclair Lewis's satires. Cities like Marion are small, pleasant, bland, church supper Utopias. Socialists, circa 1920, were never happy unless they were killing people, because that made them feel important, like Robespierre with his guillotine. The world will be a better place as soon as we kill enough people. If reform does not involve killing, it must not be real reform. Socialists don't want you to think that anyone ever has, or ever could, improve the human condition outside of the state. The state must be all. If you point to the voluntary good works of the Kiwanis Club, the Masons, the Lions Club, the Elks, the Boy Scouts and so on, Comrade Professor will laugh at you. Progress requires blood. The good news is that the Communists, the *really* bloodthirsty, take-no-prisoners socialists, are out of fashion right now. The bad news is: they will be back, as long as the principle of "the ends justify the means" remains unrejected. The voluntary pursuit of happiness is the enemy of the state's power to enguilt you into killing and dying for a Utopian state.

Rand's era was the last era of the big city *necessitated* by geo-economics. New York City had to be where it was because that is where the harbor was. In the future, a city will be built anywhere, because a developer is building it for people who *want* to live an urban lifestyle; they don't *have* to live in a city because that's where the base industry happens to be. Those people will not need a harbor. They will just need laptops. This will make the city as Rand knew it, and Harding and Pulitzer and Debs and Lewis, a thing of the past. This will, regrettably, destroy some of the romance of big cities: your grandchildren will take big cities for granted, as Disneyworlds built to order. The siting of cities, and every other aspect of life, will be more and more a matter of free, individual choice. The socialist dream of individuals sacrificing their wills to the needs of the state will be over, and with it, Utopian schemes. No more Dorothy Parkers stridently preaching that the day of the "I" is over – from now on, there is only the "WE". Just as Michael Moore likes to say "Horatio Alger must die!" so for the Utopian, Marion must be destroyed! *Mariono delenda est*!

EPILOGUE

Ayn Rand said once that "Frank is more of an atheist than I am." I knew exactly what she was talking about, because I know ex-Catholics, ex-Jews, ex-you name its, like that. Some grew up in Catholic countries, going to school under the nuns. They harbor to this day a smoldering anger at the Sisters' high-handed ways, and at the Catholic requirement of weekly confession. That was the case with Frank O'Connor and his Irish Catholic upbringing in Lorain, Ohio, where he was born in 1897. But Ayn's Jewish upbringing in St. Petersburg, Russia, and my Presbyterian upbringing in Syracuse, New York, were much more easygoing. My father said that the Presbyterian Church is the "least demonstrative" of the Christian sects, by which he meant the least ritualistic and intrusive. I don't think he considered the Quakers. So Ayn and I don't have that lifelong anger and resentment. With us it is more philosophical and less personal.

That quote of Ayn's also reflects her wistfulness toward religion. She always had a deep sense of reverence, and her lifelong project was to find something or someone toward whom she could direct it – something or someone who *deserved* all that reverence she was prepared to give. This is what fascinated her all her life – what do people look up to, and why? She looked at the ranks and titles of Imperial Russia, and other European nations, and she did not see individuals who deserved the reverence, not to mention the money and inherited power, that the commoners gave them. She looked at religion, and its reverence for supernatural beliefs, and she found that wanting. She had to learn the Marxist teachings of the new boss (same as the old boss) in Russia, teachings about "the people" as a group that she was told to revere, while having contempt for each and every individual *making up* the people; "groupness" for the sake of groupness, and terror and privation for the flesh and blood individuals who made up that group, and she found that wanting, too.

And then she discovered Aristotle, who asked "What is Man? What conditions does the human animal require by its nature for its survival and thriving?" And she discovered the United States, a nation whose laws and culture revolved around creating and maintaining those conditions; a nation that, as Frank Lloyd Wright put it, was "the first to make it official, for Man to be himself."

No matter how secular Rand got, she never stopped looking to religion for the *image* of that reverence she sought an object for. She said that reading the lighter fiction of Mickey Spillane or Ian Fleming gave her the feeling of hearing a band playing in a park, but reading Victor Hugo gave her the feeling of entering a cathedral. She was determined to have those peak experiences. She was going to keep looking for that altar, even if she was the only congregant in the nave.

And she put all this yearning for the "cathedral experience" into *Atlas Shrugged*, where Dagny was Ayn's own dream-self. Dagny is all the things Ayn herself could not be. Dagny has long show-girl legs, and can drive a car, fly a plane, and fire a gun. And Dagny's search for her ideal man – the man at the end of the tracks, holding them in his hand, and waiting for her – was Ayn Rand's own search for *the* Ideal Man. That's why *Atlas Shrugged* is a love story.

There is no ideal but that which makes it possible to think of such a concept as "ideal." There is no ideal but Man, and the city is his prophet; his greatest expression.

Sophocles gets the last word: "Wonders are many, but the greatest wonder is Man himself."

Here are three articles of mine that appeared on The Atlasphere website, where they were slightly edited. Here they appear as I wrote them.

AYN RAND'S UFO

I've seen some smears of Ayn Rand in my day, but this one reaches interplanetary heights.

Anne C. Heller's biography, *Ayn Rand and the World She Made*, was reviewed in the *Forbes Magazine* of April 1, 2010, by Hannah Elliott, in an article called "Booked Bio: Who Is Ayn Rand?" Elliott lists many reasons to dislike Rand. Some of them are even true, or at least reported by eyewitnesses. But she manages to give the unsuspecting reader a far darker picture of Rand than Heller intended in her biography.

Elliott writes of Rand: "She believed in UFO's." No more than those short words does she give us on the subject. So here is the rest of the story.

In the fall of 2007, Anne Heller asked me "Did you know that Rand saw a UFO?" Already we're down from Elliott's indefinite number of UFO's to just one, and the epistemology is very different: Rand did not "believe" in UFO's; she merely reported seeing something in the sky that she could not identify. I predicted to Heller that on her book tour, at every stop there would be some clown asking about that silly UFO story. So far, I have been dead wrong about that – thank goodness. I was prompted to make that prediction by a TV debate among the dozen or so Democratic presidential contenders that fall. Moderator Tim Russert asked Dennis Kucinich about a report that he had spotted a UFO hovering over the home of Shirley MacLaine ... as if there's anything unusual about THAT.

The source of Rand's UFO story is Ruth Beebe Hill, a California friend of Rand's circa 1950 and later the author of *Hanta Yo*, a novel about the Dakota Indians. Hill told Heller that Rand had pointed out her bedroom window one day and matter-of-factly said "A UFO came by there last night." Rand had seen it at night, above a line of juniper trees across the lawn. It was round and its outer edges were lighted. It made no sound. It hovered, then flew in slow motion. By the time she had awakened Frank, it had moved out of sight.

First of all, remember that Hill is recalling the incident some sixty-five years after it happened. Secondly, if you see something at night, in the dark, surrounded by rim lights, you may be seeing just the lights, and you may be merely inferring something solid in their midst.

The moral that Heller draws from this story is that Rand, true to her philosophy, was relying on the evidence of her senses. My lesson is different. Rand, like myself, was a very literal-minded person. When she first learned the expression "UFO," *if Hill is even correct in recalling that that was the term Rand used*, she probably took it to mean what I take it to mean: Unidentified Flying Object. But my wife often reminds me that other people are not so literal-minded as I am. To most people, "UFO" means only one thing: a spacecraft from another planet, filled with little green men with antennae. To me, though, and I am guessing, to Rand, if you see something in the sky and you don't know what it is, then to you it is a UFO. The guy standing next to you may know what it is, and so to him it is *not* a UFO. People who habitually gaze at the sky see UFO's all the time: pilots, air traffic controllers, birdwatchers, astronomers, meteorologists, Grand Canyon tourists and so on. If they are trained observers, they don't jump to conclusions about what they saw.

I found a big coffee-table book on the work of Richard Neutra, the architect who designed the house in Chatsworth, at the far northwestern corner of the San Fernando Valley in Los Angeles, where Ayn and Frank lived from 1944 to 1951. He had designed it in 1935 for Marlene Dietrich and Joseph von Sternberg. It was all steel, painted light blue, and was almost as long as a destroyer, and was surrounded by square miles of orange and lemon groves, so military pilot trainees used it at that time as a mock bombing and strafing target. I read that and said "Aha! That would explain Ayn's UFO!"

If a formation of planes is flying straight at you from fifty miles away, and it is dark, then in the dry, clear, desert air of southern California, you will see the lights of the planes for a long time, and those lights will not be moving *across* your field of vision, but holding steady in a formation that will appear to hover over the tree line until they either zoom over your head or veer off to one side and disappear from your window view.

I'm guessing that if Ayn had said she saw the lights come down *in front* of the line of junipers, Hill would have remembered that, because since the junipers were only twelve feet high, we would be talking about a landing, not just an aerial sighting. It would have been great for the sales of Heller's book if she could reveal an *abduction* of Ayn Rand by aliens, but alas ...

Jonathan Hirschfeld, a Paris sculptor who happens to be Nathaniel Branden's nephew, had the wisest comment on the UFO: If Ayn Rand had been abducted by aliens, then we would merely see Objectivism flowering on some other planet.

Live long and prosper. And check your premises.

2010

BLACK HISTORY MONTH – WHY IT MATTERS

Objectivist historians ought to be in the van of Black History month. Black American history is all about the very thing that makes philosophy Objectivist; indeed, that makes philosophy philosophy: the conviction that philosophy, and science, are Man's attempt to understand and gain control over his world and over himself, so that he can make the choices he needs to make to survive. Making choices is Man's way of surviving—and so freedom of the individual to make choices is what human life is all about. Slavery is the opposite of philosophy; the opposite of Man's whole nature. Slavery is what had to go, to make Man Man.

Antebellum slavery, and postbellum Jim Crow laws and racial discrimination, were an attempt to make race, and not humanness, the criterion for a system of rights—and rightlessness. The centuries-long Black American struggle was a search for the Human as a basis for a system of rights.

Black history is about Man discovering the hard way exactly what Rand and Aristotle meant by the expression "Man qua Man." In Memphis, where Martin Luther King was murdered, the striking garbage workers carried signs reading "I AM A MAN."

In the late 1960s, what had been called the Civil Rights Movement got a little derailed and became, sometimes, the Black Movement. That threw the spotlight on claims of Black exceptionalism. But during Dr. King's lifetime, the Civil Rights Movement was well-named: it was about the universal issue of Human Rights, not the particular claims or complaints of those Black leaders each trying to be the next King.

One problem faced by the Civil Rights Movement in the 50s and 60s was the ever-present threat of infiltration by the Communist Party. Many perfectly worthy causes, such as anti-fascism in the 1930s, became irreparably tainted by Communists using them as fronts. That is why Rev. Ralph Abernathy, addressing a mass meeting in a Birmingham church in 1963, had to make the following disclaimer:

"The eyes of the world are focused upon us today. Mr. Castro is looking to Birmingham. Mr. Khrushchev is looking to Birmingham. Mr. Kennedy is looking to Birmingham. But the Communists may as well not be looking here thinking that we're going to give up our democracy and turn to Communism. No, no! They'd be glad for us to give it up and turn to some foreign ideology. But we're not going to give this country up to the White Man—we've fought too hard FOR it!"

He was referring to Black Americans fighting in America's wars; in his own case, World War II, as well as fighting for equality of rights here.

Abernathy was an astute political leader. He had referred earlier in his speech to "Nervous Nellies." One of the things Nelly was nervous about was the possibility of Communists turning the movement into a front of their own, and Abernathy was explaining why it would be illogical for Black Americans to heed the Communist siren song—it would mean losing control of the movement to men who were both foreign and white—namely, the inmates of the Kremlin. It would mean losing democracy. Just as the Black American leaders of the 1820s had rejected resettlement in Liberia as a strategy, in favor of standing and fighting for the Declaration of Independence here in America, so the Civil Rights Movement was determined to stand and fight for Jefferson's promise of equal *individual* rights in the arena of democracy, rather than follow Marx into theories of collectivized rights. (See Ayn Rand's article "Collectivized 'Rights'.") Later, that very confusion over individual versus collective "rights" is exactly where academia led the movement away from the goal of Civil Rights and toward group quotas.

If there had been more free-market economists and individualist moral and political theorists in the academy in 1963, instead of fourteen shades of pink, they might have suggested slightly different wording to Rev. Abernathy, to wit:

The Civil Rights Movement has always had a few socialists in it, but the main thrust of our movement has never been to abolish the free enterprise system. On the contrary, our thrust has been to get Negroes *admitted* to the free enterprise system, confident that they can compete there as well as anybody. And if there is a systematic attempt by the Communist Party to take over our movement from within, they will fail, because we have seen their tactics before, we know how to detect and defeat them, and there are no longer as many Communists as there were in the 1930s, when they could and did infiltrate and take over other groups and movements. And if a few Communists join our movement as individuals, and put their time and effort into the cause of Civil Rights instead of putting that same time and effort into promoting Communism, then they have not subverted us—we have subverted them!

(2016 note: This is exactly what you see happening in the recent movie "Trumbo." Dalton Trumbo's daughter does not, in the movie, follow him into the Communist Party in the 50s. She gets involved in the Civil Rights movement.)

The Reverend was wrong about one thing: there is no such thing as a "foreign ideology." Ideas are right or wrong on their own merits, not on their point of origin. There you see the germ of the later trivialization of the Civil Rights Movement into a mere "my ethnic group versus yours" movement. Only a tribalist sees ideologies, i.e., philosophies, as foreign or domestic.

Anyone who sees the philosophical as the chosen, and therefore the human, and anyone who supports universal, natural rights, will appreciate African American history. Just as Brooklynites like to say that what was written in ink in Philadelphia in July 1776 was confirmed in blood in Brooklyn in August, so American historians should say that what was promised in the Declaration in 1776 was redeemed, often with blood, in the Civil Rights Movement from that day to this—as a Black man bids fair to become the next president.

2008

THALES DAY

On May 28, 585 B.C.E., there was a solar eclipse visible in Asia Minor. Aristotle tells us that this eclipse had been predicted a year before by Thales of Miletus, a scientist, a philosopher, and a hard-headed businessman. The unusual thing about this prediction is that Thales made it on the basis of observation and reasoning, rather than by consulting omens such as the entrails of an owl.

How did he do it? Well, unfortunately, he did not have any insights into astronomy, or into the building of astronomical instruments. If he had, then he would have been able to predict the day of the eclipse and not just the year. What he did instead was to travel to Babylonia. There he found the records kept of eclipses and other events by Babylonian astronomers and astrologers – at that time they made no distinction between the two – for hundreds of years. Thales realized that by studying this raw data he could find *patterns*. That is how our brains work – we look for patterns in the data provided by our senses. That's why we humans love music and puzzles of all kinds. Thales could see that there was an eclipse every N years, and 585 would be an N year, ergo, there would be an eclipse.

Ancient sources also tell us that Thales had once predicted a bumper crop of olives, and bought up all the presses he could find, which he then sold to the farmers when his crop prediction came true. Thales lived from about 624 B.C.E. to about 546 B.C.E. He was involved in politics. He may have been the first scientist to study electricity, and may have written books on astronomy, but none survives. He may have been the first to propose the spherical shape of the earth. But no one is sure. We do know that he did original work in geometry.

What Thales did with the Babylonian astronomical raw data was a tour de force of *complete* thinking: he used induction, followed by deduction. First, he *induced* from the data the generalization that eclipses occur at certain intervals, then he *deduced* that 585 would be the next year in that pattern. People tend to become overly fond of one of those operations at the expense of the other, and that does not work. The intellectual, especially, tends to be too deductive and not sufficiently inductive. He creates a theory, and then, like Pygmalion, he falls in love with his own creation. He starts predicting future events all over the place, based on his pet theory. Eventually something happens that his theory does not account for, and he gets all upset, because he is unwilling to amend his theory.

Thales' successful prediction caused a wave of enthusiasm for science in Greece, just as Newton's explanation of celestial motion caused a wave of excitement for science and reason in the western world of his day. Therein, for Aristotle, lay Thales's importance. These triumphs for reason and science raised Man's hope for a philosophy that would likewise be based on reason—a philosophy that anyone could arrive at independently. With such a philosophy, Man would be liberated from the purveyors of religious revelations of truths that only they can know and the rest of us must take on faith. Thales' eclipse meant that everyman could be his own scientist and philosopher. A distinction started to be made between religion, which tells you *what* to think, and philosophy, which teaches you *how* to think.

May 28 should, therefore, be celebrated as the birthday of reason by all mankind.

Remember crayoning and cutting out pictures in elementary school? If you are old enough, you might remember Captain Kangaroo on TV and his construction paper and safety scissors. Turkeys and pilgrims for Thanksgiving, and three ships for Columbus Day. Imagine the child of the future, in every land and tongue, learning about Thales in first grade, and drawing pictures of solar eclipses. Then, in middle or high school, he will learn about induction and deduction, and about the deeper implications of Thales's feat – the fact that anyone could make the same prediction – that we live in a universe of objective facts, open to the understanding of all – and that no priesthood has an exclusive pipeline to Truth.

2011

These last four essays have not appeared in The Atlasphere, or anyplace else, until now.

REVIEW OF *BANKER TO THE POOR: MICRO-LENDING AND THE BATTLE AGAINST WORLD POVERTY,*

BY MUHAMMAD YUNUS, with Alan Jolis

Robert Mayhew recently wrote *Ayn Rand and Song of Russia: Communism and Anti-Communism in 1940s Hollywood.* One issue relating thereto that Barbara Branden mentions in *The Passion of Ayn Rand,* but that Mayhew mentions not at all, is the fact that *Song of Russia* was not the movie Rand really wanted to testify about in the first place. What I respect Rand for, in the HUAC affair, is that she wanted to raise the level of the whole discussion, from the silly, obvious Communist sugar coating of the Soviet reality in *Song of Russia,* to a discussion of how the underlying ethical theory of Altruism leads logically to Statism on the overlying level of politico-economics. To show that, she wanted to discuss the well-regarded movie *The Best Years of Our Lives,* and especially a speech in that movie by Fredric March. But HUAC was not interested.

March plays a loan officer in a bank. A young farmer, just back from the war, asks for a loan, but has nothing for collateral; in fact, he doesn't even know what collateral is. March can see that the man is honest, hard-working and conscientious to a fault, and wants to give him the loan, but his superior at the bank forbids it. March, at a dinner and in his cups, chews out his boss for being a heartless businessman, and questions whether bank loans need always be reserved for those with collateral.

Just to show that the Altruists never change their tune, and have always dominated the world's thinking on the collateral issue, I will point to a 1970s "politically correct" one-man show on PBS starring James Whitmore as Harry Truman, *Give 'em Hell, Harry*. The show was taped before an audience that *roared* its agreement when Whitmore said "In this country, the only way you can get a bank loan is to prove you don't need it!"

Contra the cheering PBS audience, Rand would insist that it is only fair and just for a bank to require collateral, and that loans would be impossible without it. But to leave the subject at that impasse has never satisfied me. In a world of desperately poor people who have nothing for collateral, is there no way of bridging the gap between the money men and the honest worker who is willing and able to pay back loans, if only he could get them?

Professor Muhammad Yunus, a Bangladeshi teacher of economics, found a way. *Banker to the Poor* is his first-person story.

Being a reality-oriented economist, Yunus was willing to question both capitalist and socialist nostrums, and to get out of his classroom and meet the poor personally. In a village near his university, Yunus found women making various things and selling them. The women did not lack skills—they had skills that had been passed down from mother to daughter for thousands of years. They did not need government educators or government mega-projects or government welfare workers. All they needed was a loan of a piddling twenty or thirty bucks for raw materials, but without collateral required, since they had none. They also needed liberation from village monopoly money lenders, mullahs, and wife-beating husbands.

Yunus founded the Grameen ("Village" or "Rural") Bank. It is a *profit-making* lender, but it charges far less interest than the village money lenders. It is a free-market bank, filling a gap in the market that the market had not previously been free to fill, thanks to politics. It substitutes supervision for collateral: the local bank manager requires at least five borrowers per village to start. The five women submit business plans, help and encourage each other as a sort of club, and start paying back their loans immediately, in tiny weekly installments. The manager does everything he can to help these women succeed. And they do. Hundreds of thousands, in Bangladesh and a growing number of nations including the USA, have raised themselves out of poverty with these micro-loans since Yunus started in 1976.

Free-enterprise advocates will never get anywhere without selling the idea that free enterprise is not for the rich, it's for the poor. And if a political movement cannot appeal to the many who are poor, it cannot be saved by the few who are rich, and the still fewer who are rich eccentrics. That is why free-enterprise advocates need to familiarize themselves with the Grameen model—to offer the world's poor something more immediately useful to them than socialist promises, to be redeemed only after the revolution.

Objectivists will have to get past Yunus's lines, repeated several times, to the effect that "credit is a right." That line does not condemn him as a socialist—he saw through socialism early in his career—it merely means that he has yet to hear the Lockean-Randian insights on Natural Rights theory, but no more than everyone else in the world does. Declaring an economic good to be a right does not deliver the goods. Since he everywhere seems to acknowledge that fact, he may mean something different from the socialists when he says that credit is a right. Perhaps he means that the *pursuit* of credit in a free market is a right.

Objectivists will *love* this book for its villains. Yunus had to overcome corrupt officials, "well-meaning" foundations and governments, state-protected bankers with no interest but keeping their jobs, Communist

269

revolutionaries who did not *want* the poor to know of any alternatives to Communist violence and empty promises, village clerics who supported the local money lenders and tried to spread fear of Grameen as a Christian and American plot against Islam, and above all, tradition itself—in the worst sense. In a traditional village, a woman is not supposed to even speak to strangers. She is supposed to submit to a husband who sometimes steals her money for whores and drink. The courage of the women who came forward to give Grameen a try is spellbinding. Don't look for Dagny's in US corporate boardrooms alone. It takes a village—a poor, hopeless village filled with human beings longing to escape … or rebuild the joint!

2005

2015 note: Today, Kiva, Kickstarter and general cloudsourcing are making even the Grameen model obsolete. Utopia! – if you can keep it.

AYN RAND'S COMMUNIST EDITOR AND HER "YOUNG ADULT" NOVELS

The 2010 book *100 Voices*, edited by Scott McConnell, compiles 115 interviews (some heavily edited) with people who knew Ayn Rand, or at least met her. I greatly enjoyed Tania Grossinger's hilarious story of Rand impersonating her for some foreign reporters at the Playboy Club.

But the interview that made the most important point about Rand and her place in cultural history was with a man named – ironically – O'Connor. Patrick O'Connor was Rand's editor at New American Library from about 1968 to 1971. Even more ironic: he describes himself in the interview as a Trotskyite Communist. He discusses Rand's warm, compassionate side, as do many other interviewees who knew the real woman and not the fanged and horned public image you read about when you google "Ayn Rand." He calls her a good listener and describes sharing laughs with her and taking her to the ballet. O'Connor, who was a Renaissance Man, died in 2012, leaving a very interesting obituary.

In some sense Ayn Rand could be called, not a bad writer of adult fiction, as most literary types would call her, but as a very good writer of *young* adult fiction. And that is exactly what O'Connor says. And he is saying that as an old pro at the job of editing books for a big publishing company.

Why does O'Connor call Ayn Rand's novels "young adult fiction"? Because, he says, they are "epic; Wagnerian." He makes clear that he does not mean that as a fault. He loves her novels for what they are.

But what exactly does "epic; Wagnerian" mean? When I hear the word "epic," I think of movies with big battle scenes, or big action scenes of some sort, like the chariot race in "Ben-Hur" or the funeral scene in "Gandhi." I think of biopics, like *Les Miserables*, as novel or movie, covering as it does Jean Valjean's whole adult life. Mainly I think of *long* novels and movies, and ones that deal with war or political or societal issues involving large numbers of people and with historical consequences that will be felt for generations, and above all, that raise moral issues for the reader, eternally relevant to us even though we don't live in the France of the 1830s. Rand would say at this point "If this be young adult fiction, make the most of it!"

What else does "epic" imply? Webster says an epic is a long narrative poem in elevated style, recounting the deeds of a legendary or historical hero, or a novel or drama that suggests an epic.

Bingo! There's the rub – Rand would not want to see her novels as being *only* for young adults, or only for old adults, but for everyone. But if only young adults are receptive to inspiring tales of heroes, while those over 20 are already bitter and cynical, whose fault is that? Not Rand's.

A Rand reader has to be, not a rich, straight White male, as you may have heard, but a voracious reader. He has to be the kind of reader who is willing to tackle a thousand page book. Intellectually curious. In short, a nerd. But nerdy teens have no interest in reading "typical teen" stories. They want to read about characters who do things that neither typical teens nor typical anybody would ever dream of doing. And they read books beyond their years. Winston Churchill recalled that, as a boy, he was always in the lowest form in school, while reading books beyond his years. Sounded familiar to me! You could say, then, that it's just not about age per se at all. It's not that Rand wrote juvenile fiction, but that she wrote the kind of adult fiction read by juveniles.

When they first met, O'Connor says, Rand had already heard that he was telling others around the NAL office that Rand's books were "children's literature." She reminded him of this. He laughed. She laughed too. Apparently she did not mind him saying that. He does not make it clear in the interview, but perhaps she wanted her readers – however old – to become as little children and be inspired by heroic tales. It was Rand who said "To hold an unchanging youth is to reach at the end the vision with which one started."

Here's the other interesting thing about that interview. O'Connor claims that it was he – the Commie – who had to remind these businessmen at NAL that Rand's sales were a major contributor to their bottom line and they ought to be promoting her and taking her to lunch and entertaining her and introducing her to people in the publishing world. They were, he says, doing none of that. They were neglecting her. They had to be instructed in their capitalist self-interest by a Trot.

Surprising? Not a bit. Fabian socialist George Bernard Shaw was notorious among publishers as the most exacting horse trader of all the authors they knew. Being an author is a business, and so is editing. You haven't heard of socialist writers because they are socialists – you've heard of them because they were good at writing, and at marketing what they wrote, whether as fiction writers, professors or writers of other kinds. They had to be good businessmen to achieve fame. Their being socialists did not come from their being *bad* businessmen – it came from reading the socialist books they read in their youth. They do, however, often confess to feeling socialist guilt about any capitalist success they enjoy. O'Connor does not, in this interview, but Hiram Haydn does (Rand's editor at Random House in the 1950s) in his memoir *Words and Faces*. This is also not surprising. It's not surprising when they feel guilt and it's not surprising when they don't. On the one hand, they will feel guilty for editing a "right-wing" book like *Atlas Shrugged*. On the other hand, they won't feel guilty for doing whatever they have to do to get along in a capitalist world. They can always plead "I didn't make this world – I barely live in it!"

They don't expect to live moral lives in an immoral world. That expectation of harmony between the moral and the practical they leave to starry-eyed teenage idealists who lose themselves in the epic tales of the derring-do of heroes, from Siegfried and Tom Swift and Captain Kirk to Howard Roark and John Galt.

In Rand's time, the sure sign of "adult" fiction was "tearing the lid off the seamy side of life." If you wanted to be an adult reader, you read *Peyton Place* and saw "Who's Afraid of Virginia Woolf?" at the theater. Woo woo! We're going to watch drunken grownups yelling at each other, and see things that were hushed up in past fiction. That's adult fiction? – Rand asked, incredulous. No, that's just *Police Gazette* fiction, or let's be generous: those stories were sociology, not literature. After the initial morbid curiosity of a look down into the gutter, the reader might realize that true adult fiction bids us look up to heroes. Rand taught her readers that "there is nothing more boring than depravity."

Another reason we should not be surprised that O'Connor had to teach NAL how to treat their goldmine is precisely that he was a Communist rather than a liberal like his colleagues. If your views are shaped by a certain theory, you may sometimes be slavishly blindered by the assumptions of that theory, but you are also liberated from the assumptions of all the other theories.

He recalled in the interview, with indignation, that the president and other editors at NAL had never read Rand's books. They dismissed her as a "fascist," took her audience and sales for granted, and lived off her. He was different. He was coming into the company from another field – show business – and so came with a fresh pair of eyes. And he saw something in Rand's work that others did not see. The reason they did not read her books is that their liberal assumptions told them that there could not be anything there worth reading. O'Connor was more conscientious, and more curious – he wanted to know how Rand was selling so many books. Perhaps, as a Marxist, he understood that Rand was one of the means of production, and naturally he wanted to know what made her tick. "I'm a professional editor," he says. "I pride myself on that."

Of course they all knew, around the office, that Rand was keeping the lights on and the rent paid, but perhaps no one wanted to be the first one to say it – like in Rand's favorite children's story, "The Emperor's New Clothes." But O'Connor's left-wing credentials were secure. He was already far more left-wing than thou.

And then he left NAL to head up another publishing company. For this honest professional, reality won out over ideology. The entrepreneur won out over the armchair revolutionary. And then after that, at 60, he became a ski instructor. Fearless! Fearless at trying new professions, and doing many different things well, and in not being a slave to deduction – the classic mistake of the intellectual. Why, Patrick O'Connor was a regular Ayn Rand hero! But don't tell anyone that. We don't want to be thought juvenile.

2014

GREENLAND

Yesterday, in the atrium at 60 Wall Street, I heard someone smirk cynically as he asked his hapless breakfast companion, "Why do they call it Greenland? Anyone can see that it's white, cuz it's covered with snow and ice!" I've heard people say this before.

Fortunately for my mood, the companion refrained from answering that question with the Conventional Wisdom on this point, the story we all learned in school: Eric the Red was a greedy capitalist real estate developer, so he lied and fooled his fellow Icelanders into thinking that his newly-discovered land was green and fertile farmland, and so tricked them into settling on a big block of ice.

That story kept me fooled for years, after I first heard it in elementary school. Just look at a map of the world – Greenland is just one big expanse of white, right?

Wrong. This is just one example of how we believe what we want to believe, and what we all want to believe is what Church and State have always taught us about GREED! Most people will never question this story, and most people have never been to Greenland, or even looked up Eric the Red on Wikipedia. And so, as Ellsworth Toohey says in *The Fountainhead*, "…the racket is safe – for many, many centuries."

Greenland is the world's biggest island – about eight hundred thousand square miles. That is an Alaska and a half, and Alaska is two and a half Texi.

Out of that area, an area about the size of Colorado is unglaciated – one hundred thousand square miles. The unglaciated part is the coast. No trees grow on the island, but there is grass where there is soil along the coast, and even where the coast is bare rock, there is lichen, which is green. Eric the Red and his settlers were approaching Greenland from the sea. What did they see, from the sea? Green land. We look down on Greenland on a map and see white, as if we were approaching Earth from space. I'm pretty sure Eric did not descend on Greenland in a spacecraft. "Dat ban vun small step for a Viking ... vun yiant leap for mankind!"

Furthermore, Eric sailed up the west coast until he found a spot with enough grass to show that there was a settlement's-worth of tillable land there. He brought 25 shiploads of settlers from overcrowded Iceland. In fifteen years the settlement had grown to a population of five thousand. The Greenlanders ranged far and wide in their dragon boats, fishing, sealing, and trading with the Inuit. But mainly they farmed. Wherever grass was growing, crops could grow. If they had not found any grass they would not have tried to settle there. The settlement lasted for five hundred years. Did Eric lie?

These were, after all, settlers from ICELAND! No lush, tropical paradise either. No trees, just grass. Not that much different from coastal Greenland. Besides, since Eric never circumnavigated the island, he could not have known that it *was* an island, or how glaciated it was overall. So "Greenland" could not have been his name for the whole island. It must have been his name for just the settlement site and vicinity.

Richard Fletcher, in *The Barbarian Conversion*, 1997, buys into the "lying real estate hustler" story. Fletcher is writing a very learned tome on the spread of Christianity in the Middle Ages, and I was disappointed to find such an erudite scholar repeating the old joke. But that is what it is, and that is why people repeat it. Fletcher writes of Eric the Red: "On his return to Iceland he sought to recruit settlers for the land which, in one of the most inspired pieces of mendacity in the whole history of advertising, he temptingly called 'Greenland'." Funny, but false. Just as people continue to laugh at Sarah Palin for saying something that is perfectly true about Alaska and Russia, as people would know if they ever looked at a map. People repeat things, not because they are true, but because they sound witty, and drive home the usual altruist moral.

The 60 Wall Street atrium is one of many and fast-multiplying public spaces in New York and other cities. It is a pleasure to stroll through these spaces. At one table a tutor teaches a student English as a second language. At the next table an employer meets and interviews a prospective hiree. At another you would once have seen me being interviewed by Anne Heller for an article on Ayn Rand that Heller wrote while researching her Rand biography, and on another occasion you would have seen Jennifer Iannollo interviewing me for The Atlasphere website. At another table you would have seen the steering committee of Occupy Wall Street. I overheard one of the group's muckamucks present a proposal, after which the young man next to him shook his head and said "That is SO anarchist unfriendly!" At another table two businessmen are talking turkey in low tones. At another ten tables men in suits talk business on cellphones, and at the next twenty sit people working on their laptops and various other electronic devices. Other people are reading books – sometimes even the old-fashioned kind made of paper. Chess and Backgammon games go on every day. These atriums, and the hundreds of Starbucks and Starbucks clones, are the wave of the future. They are the office-away-from-the-office. They are the incubators of small businesses. The laboratories of innovation. The nurseries of entrepreneurs. They are where you go to watch the human mind at work, to watch humans be humans, in the best sense. It is like being a fly on the walls of thousands of the best and the brightest, the comers. Lots of women in smart business suits, changing from their flipflops into their office shoes on their way to work. Mr. Greenland is there every morning talking to the other fellow. Mr. G has a loud voice and it's not hard to eavesdrop on him. He seems to be conducting some kind of business from his table on his cellphone, and I think his companion works for him. This atrium really IS his office.

Man's temple can be found in things besides buildings and pipes and street grids and lighted windows after dark. It can be found in faces. If you want to tell who is working and who is just hanging around, look for the frowns. Rand said "A frown is the first touch of God on a man's forehead." Think of Michelangelo's Sistine Chapel. God reaches out and touches his finger to Adam's finger, giving him life. The finger, not the forehead, but same principle. This is another example of Rand, the atheist, using a religious image, because it is a familiar one and it works as a metaphor. She just gives the phrase a New and Deeper Meaning.

A frown can indicate displeasure, but it can also indicate the displeasure of finding a puzzle; a problem to be solved, after which that frown – watch that face in the atrium closely, now – turns into a look of concentration on solving that problem, and so becomes a look almost of ecstasy. "Rapt" means "captured." A raptor is a bird of prey. A person frowning with concentration has been captured. His time, his awareness, his everything in that moment, it seems, is captured, rapt and wrapped up in the task at hand, or rather, at mind. In *The Fountainhead*, Peter Keating says "Howard, you look natural only when you are one step from exploding." In other words, Roark loves to solve problems in his field of interest, architecture.

Rand is, as usual, improving on the Nietzsche she read in her teens. He wrote that the greatest experience a human can have is the Hour of the Great Contempt (*Verachtung*). When all the things you used to value don't matter to you anymore, and you feel dissatisfaction, and even disgust, at whatever used to satisfy you, that means you are growing. You sense that it is time to move on and find new mountains to climb. The Bible says "When I was a child, I thought like a child and acted like a child. But when I became a man, I put away childish things." Nathaniel Branden used to say "My definition of a hack is someone who is doing exactly the same thing next year that he did last year – no matter how good what he did last year was." Rand follows her "forehead" line with her claim that idiots smile all the time. Here she shows that she had limited experience with mental problems. Idiots do not smile all the time. This reminds us, too, that Rand was born in 1905.

But she bounces right back with another great insight: "All work is creative work if done by a creative mind." This is a good quote to mount on your cubicle wall, Dilbert, whenever you fall into doubt that you are not working up to your potential, or worse, that you are. No matter how lowly your line of work is, it involves problem solving. If you are Napoleon, deciding where to move whole armies around on a map of Europe, or whether you are a janitor, deciding how to move your cart around so as to get your mop and bucket to the boss's private privy without slopping water on his rug, and changing your routine because you find the boss *in* his privy just when you want to clean it – it's all problem solving, and not basically all that different in the mental operation you need to execute. More depends on the General's decisions than on the janitor's, but the mental operations are basically the same. This insight of Rand's has helped me over some bad moments, so I don't agree with the many "elitism" epithets hurled at her. And with it goes another hint of Branden's: When you suffer self-doubt, and berate yourself for making a mistake and doing something wrong, think about all the thousands of things you do right every day. Like tying your shoes. At some point in your past you had to learn how to do each and every one of those things for the first time. Good job you! Know what the hardest work that you will ever do is? Learning language – and you did most of that before you were ten.

Now look at all those furrowed brows in the atrium. Realize that there are plenty of times per day that those people might observe YOU frowning in rapt concentration. And then they will see your face relax into a satisfied smile, as your concentration pays off and the problem of the moment is solved. And they will hear you mutter to yourself, with Hank Rearden, that you feel ready for ten new problems to solve. And then you will turn and look around at all those other frowners in the atrium, and you will feel like their equal.

Funny – this is what New York, London, and other cities looked like two and three hundred years ago – all business then was done in taverns. All politics, too. You can see what that looked like in a movie from the 1930s called "Lloyd's of London." A boy walks into the vast, crowded, noisy, smoky interior of Lloyd's Inn, circa 1760, looking for a job running errands. He passes a man with long hair and square glasses introducing himself to two men sitting in a booth. "Dr. Johnson? I'm Dr. Benjamin Franklin."

"Ah, yes, Dr. Franklin! And this is Mr. Boswell."

So while the muckamucks are trying to manipulate us through guilt, and while we lap it up because it is so easy to put an anti-capitalist spin on every story – so easy to believe that Eric the Red was lying and that Greenland is white – Man is nevertheless meeting in atriums or in taverns, making deals, searching for arrangements that will be of benefit to both parties, and showing the way to a better future to those with eyes to see it. Go watch the very synapses of Man's creative mind at work. It's the best free show in town.

2015

AYN RAND AND THE INDIANS

In 1974, Ayn Rand was invited to address the graduating class at the US Military Academy at West Point, New York. In 2010, the Ayn Rand Institute published *100 Voices: An Oral History of Ayn Rand*, edited by Scott McConnell, and two of the interviewees in the book commented on Rand's answer to a question from a cadet about US mistreatment of the Indians.

You can listen to that Q & A for yourself by going to the ARI website and clicking on "Ayn Rand Multimedia Library: Philosophy – Who Needs It." If you do, you will understand why Rand always preferred to express herself through the written word and not the spoken. She was very careful in her choice of words, and if you answer questions off the cuff, you lose some of the control that you enjoy while writing. Off the cuff means you have no chance to polish your prose.

I, on the other hand, have had 30 or 40 years to polish my spontaneous, off-the-cuff answers to the questions put to Rand many winters ago. If she had been better prepared for the Indian question, then here is what she meant to say, and what she might have said further.

First of all, the question was open ended. The cadet (who was an Indian) just wanted Rand's thoughts on what he called the "cultural genocide" of the Indians, and the taking of their land. She should have focused on US government policy, because it was government that has sometimes been guilty of both taking land and making it hard for Indians to preserve their culture – mainly by putting Indian children in boarding schools where their own language and customs were forbidden. (And the Canadian government sometimes forcibly sterilized Indian children in their boarding schools. There is a documentary about that.) Since Rand was one of those being lumped together today as "libertarian," she and the cadet were in complete agreement and sympathy on these government violations of individual rights. On that head, Rand made the point that neither the US government nor anyone else is obliged to respect the sovereignty of tribal chiefs who do not respect the rights of their own subjects, and who commit aggression against their tribal neighbors. She was certainly right about American tribes constantly attacking each other. They did that. But they did also constantly try to set up alliances and peace treaties too. In other words, the American tribes were just like any other group of nations, big or small.

Rand's point was not as clear as polishing would have made it on the issue of Indian land rights. She would have, as a libertarian, agreed enthusiastically with President Washington's Indian policy. He recognized the Indian nations as nations, and even sent marshals to evict settlers from Cherokee land. If they wanted to settle there, they would have to treat with the sovereign Cherokee nation. If only his successors, especially Andy Jackson, had followed his policy! (Russell Means, founder of the American Indian Movement, told me that Washington was a hero of his.) Rand, though, believed that the Indians had no concept of property rights. Here she must have been fooled by

Comrade Professor. Our socialist intellectual Mandarins teach us all that the Indians lived in a communist paradise, innocent of any notions of money or property in land, before the evil capitalist White man came, and that is bunk. Every time I talk, on my walking tours, about the Dutch colony that became New York State, I have to listen as my brainwashed customers repeat to me the lecture they got in school to this effect. Ironically, the profs, in their zeal to paint the Indians as the good guys, insult them. The Indians were not stupid. They understood perfectly well that people living near each other have to reach, and respect, agreements about who gets to do what, when, with a defined piece of land. In short, they *did* have such a concept as property rights. Of course, with so few people spread over so much land, they did not invent surveyors' instruments, because they did not need them. "You may plant from this rock to the river during planting season, and I may hunt from this rock over yonder hill to the next river in hunting season" – that sort of treaty sufficed. Read *The Death and Rebirth of the Seneca*, by Anthony F. C. Wallace, for a fascinating look at the Seneca way of life.

Rand did not appear to know how much variety there was among Indian ways of life all over the Americas, or how much variety there was, and still is, among Federal Indian policies over the centuries, not to mention policies of other American nations, and state and local government policies and private dealings between White and Indian. And she did not know how much variety there was and is in an individual Indian's desired mix of traditional and modern work and pastimes. Some people like to hunt and beat drums when they are not busy programming a computer. Russell Means liked to emphasize that it is possible to be an Indian and still function in the modern world.

Rand said that White settlers had a right to "take over this country" insofar as they were bringing civilization. I would have asked her to expand on the phrase "take over this country." What that did end up meaning is that Indians, as American citizens, now benefit from the

American Bill of Rights and American courts. Indian citizenship was a long time coming, but it happened.

The most notorious removal of Indians by the government was the "Trail of Tears." This happened in 1838, and was only the latest phase in a series of removals that stretched back ten or more years. The nations affected were the Five Civilized Nations – the very peoples who *had* become settled, *had* built towns, *had* gotten their own written language (Sequoia's alphabet), and were developing representative government and the rule of law. In other words, these were exactly *not* the warlike savages of Rand's dim understanding. But in a sense her point is thus proved: It was not that White people had a right to rule the land, it was certain *principles* that were spreading from the Enlightenment thinkers to the Framers of the Constitution and Bill of Rights to the Five Civilized Nations. Rand did make clear that it was property rights and individual rights generally and the rule of law that she was concerned with.

Rand contradicted herself in her answer: She said that the Indians had no right to the land because they had no concept of property rights, and they made no use of the land, and were nomadic. But then she described them a moment later as *predominantly* nomadic. So some, then, were *not* nomadic. And they were the ones driven out and their homes burned by the US Army.

Rand railed angrily in her answer against the idea of group rights, and she explained her views on that in articles at some length.

Rand mentioned that the Indians sometimes came back to land they had already sold. This is where Comrade Professor claims that the innocent Indians just didn't understand property. More likely it was a different band of Indians, who did not consider themselves bound by a treaty made by some other chief, or it was the same band, but the hotheaded young braves were defying the old chiefs and reneging on the treaty. Or maybe they were starving. Again, they weren't stupid. The disagreement could have been worked out. But as long as the settlers voted and the Indians could not ...

Finally, Rand said that the Indians were fighting the Army and the settlers "for their wish to continue a primitive existence." No, they weren't. They were happy to buy from the settlers things that were useful to them, like iron and steel knives, pots and pans, horses, and guns. Today they are buying iPads. They were not Luddites. They were not *trying* to be primitive.

So they wanted to hunt, plant and fish. Didn't they have a right to do that on their own land? And those activities show that they *were* using the land. When Rand said that primitive people do not use the land, she is, I think, trying to apply the principle of Original Ownership written about by Hugo Grotius. Grotius was a Dutch legal theorist of about 1600. He explained the principle that no one has a right to land they don't use. I first learned of this principle in Rand's *Capitalism: The Unknown Ideal.* She was writing about the Homesteading program. The U.S. and state governments in the 19th Century sometimes applied the principle of Original Ownership by letting people occupy a piece of land for five years and clear and plow and raise crops on it, after which the government would recognize that settler as the original owner of the land because he had "mixed his labor with the land." That was John Locke's famous formula. But even though the Indians did not always grow crops, they often did, and in any case they were living off the land, by hunting, planting, fishing and gathering. Doesn't that fact make them the Original Owners?

Sometimes treaties were respected by both sides, and the Indians and the settlers got along. Sometimes not, and the Indians fought back as best they could. But they weren't as many and they weren't as well organized as Uncle Sam.

Colonel Herman Ivey, one of the interviewees who were there, recalls Rand saying at West Point "It is always going to transpire that when a superior technological culture meets up with an inferior one, the superior one will prevail." In the book there are quote marks around that sentence, but I don't hear it on the ARI website recording. But whoever said that, what does it mean? It means that Indians will trade beaver pelts for iron kettles, and so technology spreads. Rand was wrong if she thought the Indians were doing nothing with the land. They were living off it. There was other stuff besides the pelts and trees and game and corn and fish that they were not using, though, like the coal and uranium under the ground. Deals involving those things could be made, and finally they were. It's too bad Rand did not (as far as I know) know about the Native Claims Settlement Act of 1971.

In all the jokes about Nixon, and all the attention given to Watergate, how many Americans know that that Act, part of the Nixon program, was a great leap forward for Alaskan Natives? The Act constituted the Natives in each borough (county) of Alaska a corporation. Those corporations own the mineral rights of their land. They manage their own use of those rights, they invest the profits as they see fit, and they distribute the profits to members as dividends. In 1990 I met an older couple in Fairbanks with two grown adopted Doyon sons. The sons got monthly dividend checks from Doyon, Ltd., the most successful of the native corporations. Other native corporations have not managed their assets as well as Doyon has, and have sometimes lost money. But they are both free and responsible – the two things every group and every individual must be in a prosperous civilization.

Rand revealed the depths of her ignorance on this subject when she said that Indians to this day do not believe in individual rights "...if there ARE any Red Indians left." Then she added that the same goes for the Arabs – all nomadic, all ignorant of property rights, all motivated by envy of Israel's modern civilization.

Rand's friend Ruth Beebe Hill (remember the UFO story above?) wrote a novel called *Hanta Yo*. It's about the Dakota Indians. The novel has two forewords, one by Hill and one by her Dakota collaborator,

Chunksa Yuha. He explains that Hill wrote the book in English, Yuha translated it into Dakota, then they translated it back into English shorn of any concept that was not Dakota. One of the words that came out was "we." Total personal responsibility – that is the essence of Dakota ethics. Russell Means, seeking the 1988 Libertarian Party nomination for President, said that his American Indian Movement had tried to find political allies on the Left, then on the Right, then among the churches. In discovering libertarians, though, Means said "At last I've found a group of White people who think Indian."

If only Rand had done a little research.

2015

This is the talk I gave at Freedom Fest, Las Vegas, July, 2012.

AYN RAND: THE BOTTOM LINE

These are the ideas I have learned from a lifetime of reading Ayn Rand. Sometimes they were new to me, and sometimes they merely reinforced lessons I had learned from parents, teachers or others. If so, Rand usually said them better.

Regardless of any quirks, faults or mistakes of hers, and regardless of what things you may have heard about Rand, this is what I have taken away from the experience. This is the bottom line.

Take ideas seriously. Ideas have consequences.

Define your terms, and demand the same of the pusher of any theory.

Don't scorn theory. We need theory to explain and predict. But make sure yours do.

"Judge not, that ye be not judged" is a coward's code. Judge — and be prepared to be judged.

Every man can and should be his own philosopher (to some extent).

Adolescent boys, take heart: You can be both a nerd AND a jock — both an intellectual AND a man of action — you can both know AND do — you can read books AND get girls.

All of your actions should be consistent with each other. All your professed ideas should be consistent with each other. All your emotions should be consistent with each other. And all of your actions, ideas, and emotions should be consistent with each other. You must strive to be integrated.

Entrepreneurship — starting a company that will compete freely against others — is a civil liberty, to be guarded as jealously as freedom of speech, assembly, or religion.

Free enterprise is not for the rich, it is for the poor. The poor are not stupid. They know what they could be doing that would lift them out of poverty. Let them do it. The rich represent the world's past. The poor represent its future.

The honest and innocent man need not fear exposure. If the other guy acts furtive, secretive, petulant, and evasive, while yours is the face without pain or fear or guilt, everyone will flock to your banner.

Man lives by making choices. The object of every choice is to give yourself more, and not fewer, choices to make.

What is the meaning of life? Doing all that which makes it possible for you to ask that question.

Leave your money to those who would have made it anyway. Thus you make more possibilities possible.

Who saves lives — the legislator who makes seat belts mandatory, or the inventor and workers who make seat belts? Who made this possibility possible?

Freedom works AND freedom is right.

Evil is ultimately the result of evasion of reality, and is therefore self-defeating.

Scratch a Rand fan and you will find a Star Trek fan. Star Trek provides the young person with a goal for his world to strive toward: A Twenty-second Century in which Man thrives, war is behind him, poverty is a distant memory, group divisions are healed, and he is expanding into the galaxy. Why are John Galt and Mr. Spock both popular heroes? Efficacy.

A cult is a smaller religion as seen by a bigger one. A religion teaches you WHAT to think; philosophy teaches you HOW to think.

No one is born with any positive obligations. One negative one, yes— the obligation to respect and not violate the rights of others. And you will, and should, voluntarily take on positive obligations throughout your life, and you will gain honor from doing so. But the State, by getting you to believe that paying their taxes is a positive obligation you are born with, is merely robbing you through false guilt.

Deriving an *ought* from an *is* — a normative proposition from a factual one — is not impossible. It is easy. What you *are*, a human being, determines what you *ought* to do.

No one has a right to initiate force. An ethics of enlightened self-interest unites you and the other guy against any temptation on either part to cut corners by initiating force. If either does so, the two of you will thenceforth be tied to each other in mutual destruction, like two cats in a bag. In *The Fountainhead*, Gail Wynand says to himself "You were a ruler of men. You held a leash. A leash is only a rope with a noose at *both* ends."

Not all of Rand's ideas were original, nor should they be. If others have conceived some of her ideas in the past, or will again in the future, it is because we live in a universe of objective facts. The truth is out there, for anyone to independently discover. Only a religion would tell you that you cannot know certain things but through *their* teachings.

There are many moral principles on which Rand agrees with other moral thinkers, such as the Golden Rule.

Rand's one big, original moral teaching is her rejection of self-sacrifice. Sacrificing the self to others is as wrong as sacrificing others to self. Instead of arguing over who should sacrifice whom to whom, just make the pie bigger. Teach your kids that freedom to make bigger pies is itself a moral ideal.

When you fight a war, what end result are you fighting and hoping for, but a return to normalcy? Normalcy, not drama, is a moral ideal. You don't become more moral by wearing orange robes and shaving your head, to look different from others, or by dying as a self-sacrifice. Don't wish for a barricade to die on, but wish for the world to be what you hope to make it with your barricade. Then work to change it. Results, not drama. Osama bin Laden said "Our youth value death as yours do life." John Galt couldn't have put it any better.

Rand's heroes are not supermen, but men who survive as normal men in an abnormal world.

The ends do not justify the means. The means must be justified by not only the intended ends, but also by the unintended side effects. Everyone will rightly suspect the leader who promises peaceful ends after bloody war. Everyone will rightly trust a leader whose means match his promised ends. You take care of the means, and the ends will take care of themselves — and vice versa.

No one can blackmail a man who has made sure that he has done nothing he has to hide.

There is no "historical inevitability." Nothing is written until it is written. The fanatical Christian, waiting for Doomsday, and the fanatical Marxist, waiting for the Revolution, can justify any bloody atrocity by believing that history necessitates him killing you.

Just as the racist attributes to the group qualities that belong to the individual, like intelligence and moral character, the collectivist attributes to the group qualities that belong to the individual, like rights.

It was Rand who got me *out* of the Cold War mentality. Don't worry about Communist subversion – subvert them first. In free enterprise, do we or do we not have a better product to offer the world than Communism? There is nothing as subversive as free enterprise ... unless it is freedom of expression. Rand would have agreed with old Joe Kennedy and Gen. DeGaulle: they both advised President Kennedy that it was not necessary to wage a war – hot, cold, or counter-insurgent – to defeat the USSR. Just wait for socialism to collapse the Soviet economy. That is what eventually happened.

The rights of one man do not need to conflict with another's. If they do, you have defined them incorrectly. Define rights as: what our common *humanity* entitles us to, not as what the incumbent claims to entitle us to just before election day.

The interests of one man do not need to conflict with another's. In saying this, Rand was, as usual, reacting against Marxism. For Marx, the interest of Capital and the interest of Labor necessarily and irreconcilably conflict unto death. Rand disagreed. But she didn't stop there. She proposed a startling, outrageous claim, like Einstein's relativity of space-time: At the fundamental level (the only level Rand wrote about) you and the other guy applying for the same job do not have conflicting interests. You both have an interest in *a* job; not necessarily *that* job. It is not in your interest that the other guy go jobless. You both have an interest in a local economy with more jobs than applicants. Just because the other guy is your competitor at the moment, the "hard-hearted" Rand does not bid you see in him an enemy, still less a permanent one. Only the "compassionate" Altruists do that.

Only the power-seekers want you to believe that rights and interests necessarily conflict – because then they can be the ones dispensing jobs to you or the other guy, whoever will keep them in power.

Many speak of "balancing" rights or interests. You can't balance principles. There can be only one overarching principle in each case — because when you have two principles you want to apply, you need a third principle to tell you when to apply each of the first two.

The Altruist world said "Money can't buy happiness." Rand said "Money will take you where you want to go – but it won't replace you as the driver." What does a driver need? What do you need – to be happy? A sense of purpose.

If you want to enjoy a party more, take a moment to say a silent thank you to all those whose creative work made the party possible, like those who built the roof over your head and grew the food.

Before reading Rand, I played with toy soldiers until I found model cities more fascinating to play with than model battlefields. The game element was there, but the game was how to move people and freight around a city of the living, rather than bullets around a city of the dead. Reading Rand showed me the importance of my own youthful insight, and it showed me that I had found a kindred spirit.

In *Atlas Shrugged*, first we meet Ellis Wyatt, who bursts into Dagny's office uninvited, showing most people's idea of an "individualist," but later we see Dagny respecting Ken Danagger's right to the privacy of his office. Rand makes clear which kind of "individualism" she favors and why. Many readers have noted the respect for others that is part of the characterization of Rand's heroes. Thus Rand taught me a New and Deeper Meaning of individualism.

Are Rand's novels too talky? Look for the words "as if." In Dagny's morning-after scene with Hank, Rand shows us what Dagny says, but also what Dagny is thinking, and thirdly the *implications* that Dagny could write out in a treatise about her relationship to Hank if she wanted to. Rand's portrayal of, and her own, ability to see multitudes of implications in a glance at any given subject – the splendor in the grass, the world in a grain of sand – talky? How about exhilarating – breathtaking! This is how aware of what they are doing people *should* be.

Rand grew up on Hugo and the other 19ᵗʰ Century Romantic authors. From them she learned basic storytelling for a wide audience. She did not write for the critics or the professors, but for the general reading public. She was not trying to be the Next Big Thing in literature. She was trying to simply entertain and uplift, and Hugo seemed to show the way. Her literary motto might have been "If it ain't broke, don't fix it."

Rand will be remembered, not for her mistakes, but for these and other ideas she communicated that were both good and important. Like Victor Hugo, she entertained and uplifted through her fiction. She created heroes who give millions of readers a vision of the heroic — that is, the normal. The normal for self-actualizing Man.

That is the bottom line.

BIBLIOGRAPHY

Adams, Henry, *The Education of Henry Adams: An Autobiography*, Houghton-Mifflin, 1961.

Amar, Akhil Reed, *The Bill of Rights: Creation and Reconstruction*, Yale University Press, 1998.

Anderson, Poul, *War of Two Worlds*. New York: Ace Books, Inc. 1959.

Asimov, Isaac,
The Caves of Steel, Doubleday, 1953.
Nemesis, Bantam, 1989.

Atkinson, Brooks, *Broadway*, Limelight Editions, 1985.

Bacon, Sir Francis, *The New Atlantis*, 1626, public domain. Text on Constitution Society website.

Besinger, Curtis, *Working with Mr. Wright: What it was Like*, Cambridge University Press, 1995.

Bianco, Anthony, *Ghosts of 42nd Street: A History of America's Most Infamous Block,* Harper Collins, 2004.

Blake, William, *Europe: A Prophecy,* 1794 (see Wikipedia for illustrations and Bartleby.com for full text).

Bloom, Howard K., *The Lucifer Principle*, Grove/Atlantic, Inc., 1995.

Boylan, James, *The World and the 20s: The Golden Years of New York's Legendary Newspaper*, The Dial Press, 1973.

Branden, Barbara, *The Passion of Ayn Rand*, Doubleday, 1986.

Bryson, Bill and Ellen Titlebaum. *In a Sunburned Country*, Broadway Books, 2000.

Burns, Jennifer, *Goddess of the Market: Ayn Rand and the American Right*, Oxford Press, 2009.

Burrows, Edwin G., *Forgotten Patriots: The Untold Story of American Prisoners During the Revolutionary War*, Basic Books, 2008.

Caldwell, Mark. *New York Night: The Mystique and its History*, Scribners, 2005.

Capote, Truman, *In Cold Blood*, Random House, 1965.

Chase, William Parker, *New York: The Wonder City*, 1932, re-published 1984 with a forward by Paul Goldberger, by New York Bound, a New York-themed bookstore in Rockefeller Center (now gone).

Clarke, Arthur C.,
2001: A Space Odyssey, New American Library, 1968.
Voices From the Sky, Mayflower, 1965.

Collins, Kathleen, "The Girder and the Trellis," REASON magazine, November 1973.

Collins, Michael, *Carrying the Fire: An Astronaut's Journeys*, Rowman & Littlefield, 1974.

Cox, Stephen, *The Woman and the Dynamo: Isabel Paterson and the Idea of America,* Transaction Publishers, 2004.

Davis, Deborah. *Party of the Century: The Fabulous Story of Truman Capote and his Black and White Ball.* Hoboken: John Wiley & Sons, Inc., 2006.

De Borchgrave, Alexandra Villard and John Cullen, *Villard: The Life and Times of an American Titan*, Nan A. Talese/ Doubleday, 2001.

Durante, Dianne L.,
Forgotten Delights: The Producers: A Selection of Manhattan's Outdoor Sculpture, ForgottenDelights.com, 2003.
Outdoor Monuments of Manhattan: A Historical Guide, New York University Press, 2007.

Ellison, Harlan, *The Glass Teat*, Ace, 1970, E-Reads, 2013.

Fleming, Ian,
Live and Let Die, New York: The Macmillan Company, 1954.
You Only Live Twice, Jonathan Cape, 1964.

Fletcher, Richard. *The Barbarian Conversion: From Paganism to Christianity.* New York: Henry Holt and Company, 1997. On money and the spread of Christianity, see pages 425, 432, 457, 470, 484, 486, 492, 493, and 518.

Foote, Thelma Wills, *Black and White Manhattan: The History of Racial Formation in Colonial New York City*, Oxford University Press 2004.

Fowler, Gene, *Skyline: A Reporter's Reminiscence of the 1920s*, The Viking Press, 1961.

Fustel de Coulange, Numa Denis, *The Ancient City: A Study on the Religion, Laws and Institutions of Greece and Rome*, Doubleday, 1864.

Hamilton, Alexander, James Madison, John Jay, *The Federalist Papers*, serialized in *The Independent Journal* and *The New York Packet*, 1787-1788.

Haydn, Hiram C., *Words and Faces*, Harcourt Brace Jovanovich, 1974.

Heinlein, Robert A., *Stranger in a Strange Land*, G. P. Putnam's Sons, 1961.

Heller, Anne C., *Ayn Rand and the World She Made*, Nan A. Talese/ Doubleday, 2009.

Hessen, Robert, *Steel Titan: The Life of Charles M. Schwab*, U. of Pittsburgh Press, 1975.

Hill, Ruth Beebe, *Hanta Yo*, Doubleday, 1979.

Hugo, Victor, *Les Miserables*, A. Lecroix, Verboekhoven & Cie., 1862.

Irving, Washington, *A History of New York*, College and University Press, 1964.

Jacobs, Jane, *The Death and Life of Great American Cities*, Random House, 1961.

Kimmelman, Michael, "Sound Matters, Amply, Of Course," *New York Times*, Arts, Critic's Notebook, Wednesday, Dec. 30, 2015. Found this article just before press time, so not mentioned in this book. Opening a window changes the sound of a room. Part of the Grand Central experience is hearing the taps of shoes on marble, echoing in the vast concourse. We think of architecture as visual, and in a way tactile, but it is also aural.

Koolhaas, Rem, *Delirious New York: A Retroactive Manifesto for Manhattan*, The Monacelli Press, 1978.

Lee, Harper, *To Kill a Mockingbird*, J. B. Lippincott, 1960.

Lewis, Sinclair, *Babbitt*, Harcourt, Brace & Co., 1922.

Lorant, Stefan, *Sieg Heil!: An Illustrated History of Germany from Bismarck to Hitler*, Norton, 1974.

Mackesy, Piers, *The War for America, 1775-1783*, Harvard U. Press, 1964.

Maltin, Leonard, *Leonard Maltin's Movie Guide, 2012 Edition*, Plume/Penguin, 2011.

Mayhew, Robert, *Ayn Rand and Song of Russia: Communism and Anti-Communism in 1940s Hollywood*, The Scarecrow Press, Inc., 2005.

McConnell, Scott. *100 Voices: An Oral History of Ayn Rand*, New American Library, 2010.

Metalious, Grace, *Peyton Place*, Julian Messner, Inc., 1956.

Meyers, Jeffrey, *Bogart: A Life in Hollywood*, Houghton Mifflin, 1997.

Morris, John. *Londinium: London in the Roman Empire*, Weidenfeld & Nicolson, 1982.

Müller, Fritz, *The Living Arctic*, Methuen Publications, 1981.

Nietzsche, Friedrich, *Also Sprach Zarathustra*, in *The Portable Nietzsche*, ed. Walter Kaufmann, Viking Portable Library, 1954.

Paterson, Isabel, *The God of the Machine*, Transaction Publishers, 1943.

Rand, Ayn,
Anthem, Pamphleteers, Inc., 1946.
Atlas Shrugged, Random House, 1957.
Capitalism, The Unknown Ideal, New American Library, Inc., 1967.
The Fountainhead, Bobbs-Merrill, 1943.
Journals of Ayn Rand, ed. David Harriman, Dutton, 1997.
We The Living, Macmillan Publishers, 1936.

Rice, Kym S. *Early American Taverns: For the Entertainment of Friends and Strangers*, Regnery Gateway, 1983.

Richmond, I. A. *Roman Britain*, Penguin, 1955.

Riggenbach, Jeff. *Persuaded by Reason: Joan Kennedy Taylor and the Rebirth of American Individualism*, New York: Cook & Taylor Publishing, 2014.

Salinger, Sharon V., *Taverns and Drinking in Early America*, Johns Hopkins U. Press, 2004.

Sanders, James. *Celluloid Skyline: New York and the Movies*, Alfred A. Knopf, 2003.

Schoenberg, Dr. Philip Ernest, *Ghosts of Manhattan: Legendary Spirits and Notorious Haunts,* The History Press, 2012.

Scott, Sir Walter, *Ivanhoe*, A. Constable, 1820.

Shlaes, Amity, *Germany: The Empire Within*, Farrar, Straus, 1991.

Sienkiewicz, Henryk. *Quo Vadis?*, Little, Brown, 1895.

Smith, Hedrick, *The Russians*, Quadrangle/New York Times Book Co.

Starr, Tama, *Signs and Wonders: The Spectacular Marketing of America*, Doubleday Business, 1998.

Stern, Robert A., Gregory Gilmartin, Thomas Mellins, *New York 1930: Architecture and Urbanism Between the Two World Wars*, Rizzoli International Publications, 1987.

Sussman, Elisabeth with John G. Hanhardt, *City of Ambition: Artists & New York*, Whitney Museum of American Art, 1996. Reproductions of New York city-scape paintings.

Taylor, Alan, *The Divided Ground: Indians, Settlers, and the Northern Borderland of the American Revolution*, Alfred A. Knopf, 2006.

Toffler, Alvin, *Future Shock*, Random House, 1970.

Wallace, Anthony F. C. *The Death and Rebirth of the Seneca*, Vintage, 1972.

Werfel, Franz, *The Song of Bernadette*, Viking Press, 1942.

Willensky, Elliot and Norval White, *AIA Guide to New York City*, Third Edition, Harcourt Brace & Company, 1988.

Yunus, Muhammad, *Banker to the Poor: Micro-Lending and the Battle Against World Poverty*, PublicAffairs, 1999.

Zamyatin, Yevgeny, *We*, E.P. Dutton, 1924.

Printed in the United States
By Bookmasters